W9-ASM-089

FAIR OR FOUL

FAIR OR FOUL

Sports and Criminal Behavior in the United States

Christopher S. Kudlac

 PRAEGER

AN IMPRINT OF ABC-CLIO, LLC
Santa Barbara, California • Denver, Colorado • Oxford, England

Library of Congress Cataloging-in-Publication Data
Kudlac, Christopher S.
  Fair or foul : sports and criminal behavior in the United States / Christopher S. Kudlac.
    p. cm.
  Includes bibliographical references and index.
  ISBN 978-0-313-37825-6 (hard copy : alk. paper) — ISBN 978-0-313-37826-3 (ebook)
1. Sports—Corrupt practices—United States. 2. Criminal behavior—United States. I. Title.
  GV718.2.U6.K84 2010
  306.4'83—dc22   2009053023

ISBN: 978-0-313-37825-6
EISBN: 978-0-313-37826-3

14 13 12 11 10   1 2 3 4 5

This book is also available on the World Wide Web as an eBook.
Visit www.abc-clio.com for details.

Praeger
An Imprint of ABC-CLIO, LLC

ABC-CLIO, LLC
130 Cremona Drive, P.O. Box 1911
Santa Barbara, California 93116-1911

This book is printed on acid-free paper ∞

Manufactured in the United States of America

To Avery, Riley, and Holden

CONTENTS

ACKNOWLEDGMENTS

I would like to thank my wife Kate for everything she did to help me with this book. Not only did she take care of our kids and try to give me extra time to work on the book, but she edited and re-edited the entire manuscript. By the time the book was near completion, she knew the material better than I did. I would also like to thank my entire family for their support while I was writing the book. Additionally, I would like to thank my colleague Kim Tobin who took time to provide feedback on some of the early chapters. Finally, I would like to thank my editors Suzanne Staszak-Silva and Michael Wilt for making the experience as pleasant as possible.

INTRODUCTION

For generations, sports have dominated water cooler conversations across the country. During this same period, crime has been the most popular subject of the media, including the news, television, and movies. Over the last few years, we have seen an integration of these two worlds. More and more discussion and media coverage of the sports world focuses on crimes committed by athletes, steroid use, or disorderly fans. The sports page has looked more and more like the crime reports. One need only open the newspaper to read about the Barry Bonds steroids debate, Michael Vick's dog fighting conviction, or the fan and player fight during the Detroit Pistons and Indiana Pacers basketball game. This book is an examination of the increasingly connected worlds of sports and criminal behavior.

In the first part of the book, I examine criminal behavior among athletes. The influence of athletic membership on behavior begins in high school. Athletics hold a special place in many communities across the country. Towns support their athletic programs through pep rallies, fundraisers, and attendance at sporting events. Nothing is more American than the Friday night high school football game or the weekend afternoon soccer or baseball game. Parents encourage their children to participate in sports at earlier and earlier ages. But with all the talk of teamwork, fitness, and competition, is there a darker side to athletic participation? Are the stories in the paper an anomaly or is there something inherent in some sports or teams that encourages criminal behavior (for example, the Glen Ridge [NJ] High School football team rape case)? I discuss the issues of aggression, masculinity, and group mentality in relation to high school athletes' criminal behavior including a detailed examination of hazing.

Athletes continue to hold a special place in the community when they enter college. The sense of entitlement and privilege that began in high school continues into college. This is coupled with a greater sense of freedom, and in many cases, increased access to alcohol and drugs. The special treatment that colleges afford their athletes only heightens the student-athletes' sense that they are special and in some cases above the law. There are numerous examples of big-time college football and basketball programs (such as the University of Miami football team and University of Cincinnati basketball teams) that have looked the other way regarding their athletes' criminal behavior. I examine many explanations for the increased risk of criminal behavior among Division I athletes in basketball and football, including NCAA regulations which forbid student-athletes from working during the school year, cultural differences between athletes and other students present on campus, and a lack of accountability from the colleges.

The spotlight is greatest when the athletes enter the professional ranks. With increased money and fame, any criminal violations by professional athletes receive increased media attention. Recently, there has been an epidemic of professional athletes committing crimes, especially in the NFL and NBA. Along with violent and sexual offenses, the most widely discussed criminal activity has been drug use, specifically steroid use, among athletes. The criminal component to the steroid issue has been largely ignored in the press, with most of the discussion focusing on how it affects the athletes' performance. I will cover high-profile examples of professional athletes' criminal behavior including Barry Bonds, Michael Vick, and Adam "Pacman" Jones.

Other connections between sports and crime, such as spectator violence at sporting events, are also examined. Spectator violence can take many forms, from throwing bottles onto the field to attacking a player during a game to full-fledged riots after a game. Although the violence in the United States does not parallel the level in Europe and South America associated with soccer, there have been many unfortunate incidents. The brawl between the Detroit Pistons and Indiana Pacers that spilled into the crowd is one of the more high-profile examples of this issue. Spectator violence raises many issues including security at sporting events and excessive alcohol use surrounding sports. Additionally, I discuss the issue of whether the effects of watching sporting events extend beyond the fans at the game to those outside the arena or those watching at home.

Another link between crime and the sports world involves gambling. There are many different forms of gambling, some legal and some illegal, from casino gambling and lotteries to betting with bookies or online. Although more and more states are looking to gambling as a guaranteed revenue generator, there is also a dark side to gambling, with increasing crime rates and gambling addiction. Gambling has also impacted what takes place within the sports world; I address many high-profile examples of sports fixing including the 1918 Black Sox scandal, the Boston College basketball point shaving scandal, Pete Rose, and NBA referee Tim Donaghy.

Although the beginning of this book paints a negative (albeit realistic) picture of athletic participation in relation to criminal behavior, this is not the whole story. For many people athletics has served as a powerful positive force in their lives. Parents who encourage their children to participate in sports do so in the hope that sports will be beneficial for them. There are many benefits attributed to membership on sports teams including character building, exercise, friendship, learning how to win and lose, and the very basic benefit of giving kids a positive activity to keep them off the streets. A prime example of this is the Midnight Basketball program which operates in cities across the country and gives youths and young adults a safe environment and activity to keep them off the streets and away from crime during peak criminal hours.

Many correctional officials are well aware of the positives associated with athletic participation. I look at the key role that sport plays in the lives of prison inmates. For many inmates, playing sports provides a positive way to spend their time and an outlet for their aggression. Many prisons operate softball, basketball, and volleyball leagues. However, sports in prison have come under scrutiny from the public, especially weight lifting and boxing programs; many see sports as a way of breeding faster and stronger criminals and not an example of hard time or punishment. Corrections officials argue that sports are essential to maintaining a secure prison, serving as one of the few rewards that can be taken away from inmates, and helping to keep health care costs for inmates down. I explore the positive benefits of sports participation in prison and out.

CRIMINOLOGICAL THEORY AND ATHLETES

The first three chapters of the book examine the relationship between athletic participation at various levels (Chapter 1, High School; Chapter 2, College; and Chapter 3, Professional). Each chapter presents specific issues related to crimes committed by the athletes and the research surrounding the major issues. It is nearly impossible to talk about athletes in general because of the many differences that can encompass them, from a swimmer to a wrestler to a football player. Even within the same sport, it is hard to make comparisons; for example, there are vast differences between a high school football player who rarely makes it into the game and a starting quarterback in the NFL. Although some criminological theories fit more closely with high school athletics compared to professional athletes, there are some generalizations that can be made and some theories that apply to athletes in general. It is possible to draw some general conclusions about athletic participation and its relationship to criminal behavior. While all sports are included in some of the discussions and research, there is a bias toward the more popular, revenue-generating team sports like football, baseball, and basketball. Additionally, this book focuses almost exclusively on male sports. While some discussions of athletics include comparisons between male and female athletes, most of the examples and research focus on male athletes.

With this being said, criminological theory can offer us some guidance in comparisons between someone we would consider an athlete versus a non-athlete in terms of criminal behavior. Momentarily putting aside social factors, which undoubtedly influence a person's criminality and will be examined specifically in relation to high school (Chapter 1), college (Chapter 2), and professional athletes (Chapter 3), there are some basic core differences between athletes and non-athletes that are important in explaining crime. Take this typical description: *An aggressive male, with an athletic build who is between the ages of 16 and 25.* Is this describing the typical athlete or criminal? According to research, this description would fit both. The majority of high school, college, and professional athletes discussed in the book have the same characteristics as much of the criminal population. So an underlying question of the first half of the book is: does being an athlete make an individual more likely to commit crime?

In *Crime and Human Nature,* Wilson and Hernstein argue that there are certain constitutional factors that contribute to criminal behavior. Constitutional factors are characteristics that are usually present at or soon after birth whose behavioral consequences appear during the child's development. This is not to suggest that there is a crime gene or that some people are born criminals. However, some characteristics that are inheritable affect, to some extent, the likelihood that individuals will engage in criminal activities.[1] Individuals differ at birth in the degree to which they are at risk for committing crime. Biological factors correlate with crime; however, they are generally not recognized as causing crime. Biological factors set in motion a series of psychological and social events in a person's life that lead to crime. They are distal, indirect causes at best. While reading the following discussion of Wilson and Hernstein's arguments, keep in mind your stereotypical idea of an "athlete."

Early theories of criminology focused on biology as a possible explanation for criminal behavior. Although many of these theories have been discredited, some theories are still worthwhile in looking at criminal behavior among athletes. One of the earliest (and most controversial) criminological theories focused on body type (somatype) and the idea that body type influenced the risk of criminality. While many shake off the notion today that there is a "criminal" body type, there is research that demonstrates a correlation between body type and criminal behavior.[2] There are three general body types: endomorphs, mesomorphs, and ectomorphs. Endomorphs tend toward rounder bodies, a mesomorph toward heavy-boned muscularity, and ectomorphs toward linearity. There have been many studies that have examined the impact of body type on criminal behavior; the general finding is that criminals' body types differ on average from the general population. Criminals tend to be more mesomorphs than ectomorphs. Obviously, there are differences even among criminals with this depending on what type of criminal behavior you are discussing, for example, violent crimes versus tax fraud. This does not mean that body type causes crime; however, there is a correlation between mesomorphs and criminal behavior. Additionally, studies have looked at andromorphy, which assesses the relative maleness of a person's overall physique. The research demonstrates the more "masculine" body type characterizes the average criminal.[3] Some studies suggest that body types also have correlations with personality types, for example, mesomorphs have been found to be more expressive, domineering, and given to higher levels of activity.[4] Additionally, criminal theorist William H. Sheldon argued that mesomorphs are more unrestrained and have an impulsive self-gratification. These personality characteristics have also been found to correlate with criminal behavior.[5] Athletes are more likely to be mesomorphs and many of the personality traits associated with mesomorphs can be found in athletes (especially boxers, and football and hockey players).

Besides body type, gender is another constitutional factor that impacts criminal behavior. There is no more consistent pattern, historical and cross-cultural, than males commit more crime than women. This is surprising given the changing place of women in society. Even as there have been many social and cultural changes between men and women, especially greater equality for women, this has not affected the fact that males commit many more crimes than women. Males in 1960 were responsible for 82.5% of arrests for homicide; in 2000, males were responsible for 87.5%. Although women comprise 51% of the population, they are arrested for only 18% of all violent crimes and 32% of property crimes, relatively consistent with the numbers from decades earlier.[6] These ideas are supported by examining athletes and criminal behavior, with more male athletes committing crimes than female athletes.

Additionally, age is a constitutional factor that impacts crime. Crime increases during early adolescence and doesn't begin to decline until the mid-twenties. This also would correspond with much of the discussion of athletes, as there seems to be a spike in the later stages of high school, into college, and the beginning of the professional career with a general decline in athletes who play past their mid-twenties. The other constitutional factor that Wilson and Herrnstein examined is intelligence, which they argue shows a clear and consistent pattern between criminality and low intelligence. This is something that has not been thoroughly investigated in relation to athletics.

Another interesting factor that impacts criminal behavior is personality, which is also to some degree inheritable. Research has shown that criminals are typically aggressive, impulsive, and cruel.[7] Aggression is a trait that is rewarded in athletics and is sometimes hard for athletes to leave on the field. Personality and behavioral problems are related to the environment in which a person is raised; however, each characteristic comes with some genetic inheritance. Societal reactions to such predispositions may determine, to a large degree, the form of continued behavior. For example, someone who is 6-feet 8-inches tall and 300 pounds with an aggressive personality is going to elicit different reactions from people (for example, schools, the community, and sports teams) than someone who is 5-feet 8-inches tall, 175 pounds, and introverted.

Now what do being young, athletically built, and male all have in common? It seems that young male mesomorphs have higher testosterone than their counterparts (and many athletes as well). This may explain greater levels of aggressive behavior among this group. High blood testosterone levels have been linked with increased aggressiveness. Male sex-hormone testosterone levels have been linked with aggression in teenagers[8] while other studies show that adolescent problem behavior and teenage violence rise in proportion to the amount of testosterone in the blood of young males.[9] Research has concluded that there is a "moderately strong relationship between testosterone and adult deviance." The relationship is "largely mediated by the influence of testosterone on social integration and prior involvement in juvenile delinquency."[10] This means that high levels of testosterone have some effect on behavior but the effect is also going to be determined by the social environment (for example, whether the behavior, possibly violent behavior, is encouraged, rewarded, etc.).

Interestingly, steroid use, which is discussed in greater detail in Chapter 3, raises the level of testosterone and has been linked with aggressive behavior and destructive urges.[11] Testosterone alone would not explain aggressive or criminal behavior, as most young males have high levels of testosterone and most do not commit crimes. However, others have found that high levels of testosterone combined with low levels of serotonin are responsible for aggressive behavior. Testosterone in one respect produces dominance-seeking behavior, but not necessarily aggression because the body produces serotonin which induces calmer responses. If the person has low levels of serotonin, the person will experience greater frustrations and be more likely to act out aggressively, especially if he also has higher levels of testosterone.[12] It is interesting to take note of this type of brain activity and chemicals when looking for explanations for criminal behavior, but they cannot be examined in isolation from the social environment in which a child, teen, and adult live. Starting a discussion of theory with biological factors may seem to place them as more important than others, but they are just some of the many explanations for the connection between athletics and criminal behavior. Not every young, athletically built male commits crimes, thus it is important to analyze the social atmosphere in which the athletes play. In the first half of the book, I explore what it means to be an "athlete" in every sense of the word, not just biologically but sociologically, psychologically, and culturally. How an athlete is treated by his peers, coaches, and teachers in high school, how he is recruited and viewed on a college campus, and how much money and freedom he has as a professional will all be examined in the chapters ahead.

Although some of the criminal issues and theories in the book cut across every level of participation, there are specific topics for high school athletics that do not apply to professional athletes. The chapters are set up to focus on each level specifically, but there is much that is universal to all athletes within each chapter. For instance, the chapter on high school contains a section on hazing, which is something that begins in high school and presents many problems for high school athletes and administrators. However, hazing takes place in college and the professional ranks as well. The discussion focuses on high school athletes in Chapter 1, but college and professional athletes are also detailed. In Chapter 2, sexual assaults among athletes are detailed; this is an issue that has received substantial attention among college athletes. However, it is also an issue that affects high school and professional athletes. Then in Chapter 3, steroid use is discussed. While most of the attention and debate surrounding steroid use by athletes has focused on professional athletes, this is an issue that is also pertinent to high school and college athletes.

Chapter 1

HIGH SCHOOL ATHLETES
AND CRIME

"**F**ive students have been charged with more than 50 counts relating to a northern Utah crime spree."[1] "Six students accused of holding down and sodomizing six younger students with a broomstick."[2] "Police break up a steroid ring involving high school students."[3] What do all these stories have in common? All involve male high school athletes. In this chapter I examine criminal behavior among high school athletes and whether or not it is increasing. I evaluate research on whether participating in high school athletics increases, decreases, or makes no difference in participating in criminal behavior. Are some sports more likely to affect criminal behavior? Does it matter if you play football, which is more aggressive and team oriented, or run track, which has less status in most schools and is more individualistic? Then I look at the age-old practice of hazing, which has become increasingly more violent and sexual in recent years, with a discussion of many high profile examples.

According to the National Federation of State High School Associations, the number of student participants in high school athletics increased for the 19th consecutive year during the 2007−2008 academic year, setting an all-time high of 7,429,381. Both boys' and girls' participation figures reached all-time highs, with 3,057,266 girls and 4,372,115 boys participating in 2007 to 2008, meaning that more than half (54.8%) of students enrolled in high schools participate in athletics.[4] High school athletes encompass a wide range of sports and personalities, so one cannot generalize about the effects of athletic participation on behavior. For many athletes, participation in their chosen sport is a positive experience, but there are many factors that can affect that. Some students participate in many sports, identifying only with other athletes, while others see sports as only part of their high school experience. Sports may have a different effect on the student who plays football, basketball, and baseball than the student who only plays golf or runs track. Additionally, the meaning of participating on the football team might take on a different context for the student in a small town, where high school players achieve semi-celebrity status, versus a larger city, where they may play in relative anonymity. The high school sports experience is also very different for those who are members of many different academic and social clubs versus the student who only participates in sports. All of these conditions may also influence how student-athletes view themselves, which is an important factor in whether or not they will engage in criminal behavior.

"JOCK" STEREOTYPE

The stereotype of the "jock" is one that is well-known to all who have attended high school or watched a Hollywood teen film. They are big, muscular, dim-witted bullies who take a few too many liberties with female students, but that is where the stereotype stops. The traditional stereotype does not involve serious criminal behavior. It involves the occasional late night party, some underage drinking, and the occasional fight. All of this is typically chalked up to "boys will be boys."

Hollywood has made the jock stereotype into a staple of most high school movies. In *The Breakfast Club*, the self-described jock is serving detention for assaulting another student in the locker room. In the dark teen movie *Heathers*, the two jock characters, Kurt and Ram, are shown as over-sexed, bullying dimwits. When the two main characters, J.D. and Veronica, discuss the jocks' deaths, J.D. states, "Football season's over, Veronica. Kurt and Ram had nothing to offer the school but date-rapes and AIDS jokes." The stereotype continues in football movies like *Varsity Blues* and *Friday Night Lights*, and was depicted as one the clichéd high school movie characters in *Not Another Teen Movie*.

But with all of this negative stereotyping also comes positive generalizations. The jocks are typically the most popular students in school. They date the best-looking girls, attend the best parties, and get away with everything. In many towns across the country, athletics is an important part of the school and town pride. Like the turning of the seasons and holidays, many people mark the calendar with the changing from football season to basketball to baseball season. Sports can be seen as an important ritual for American society. The star athletes are given praise, admiration, and a little leeway in terms of academic and criminal infractions. There are countless stories of the police looking the other way for underage drinking, drunk driving, or other petty offenses when the perpetrator is the town's star athlete. This is one of the taken-for-granted benefits of being a jock.

But if you watch the news or read the newspaper today, it seems like the traditional notions of jocks and high school athletes have changed.

Today, it seems the stereotype of the jock has become more negative, with increased attention on criminal behavior committed by athletes. One issue of interest is whether high school athletes are more likely to be involved in criminal activity than high school students not on sports teams. If so, is it only certain sports and certain types of criminal behavior?

CRIMINOLOGICAL THEORY: HIGH SCHOOL ATHLETIC PARTICIPATION AND JUVENILE DELINQUENCY

We build athletes up as the symbolic protectors of school and community pride, treat them like demigods, sometimes place them above the laws of the school and the community, and then shake our heads in confusion and disbelief when they occasionally call our bluff.

Andrew W. Miracle, Jr. and C. Roger Rees[5]

With the increasing problem of juvenile delinquency, sports are often mentioned as a positive activity for kids to be involved in. Sports proponents typically justify participation in athletics with the notion that sports are a deterrent against crime and delinquency. The claim has been made throughout the past century and has taken on a common sense status. However, the claim has not been backed up by any strong empirical research. Research is mixed at best and when looking at certain crimes tends to support the opposite notion that sports participation may actually contribute to criminal or deviant behavior.

Still, many believe that participation in extracurricular activities acts as a protector from delinquent behavior because of the positive peer support, adult role models, and the fact that it is a positive activity during free time. Additionally, youths have the opportunity to build a stronger social network and system of support. Participation in these programs is valued by adults for the potential positive or pro-social benefits.[6] These ideas would be supported by criminological theory.

Social Control theory would point to a deterrent value for sports participation in terms of juvenile delinquency. The theory asserts that certain personality and environmental influences inhibit delinquent behavior. For example, a person's integration with positive social institutions and with significant others would increase their resistance to criminal temptations. Social Control theory asserts that the more controls (outer and inner) a person has in his or her life the less likely he or she will be to commit crime. The theory states, and it seems that many parents subscribe to its basic notion, that the more involvement youths have in traditional activities (such as sports teams), the less likely they will be to get into trouble.

Within this idea of social control, Social Bonding theory contends that the stronger the social bonds an individual has with the social group or community, the less likely he or she is to act deviantly. The four components that bond a youth to society are identified by Hirschi in his 1969 book *Causes of Delinquency*: attachment, commitment, involvement, and belief. Attachments are seen as a person's shared interests with others. Commitment is the amount of energy and effort put into activities with others. Involvement is the amount of time spent with others in shared activities. Belief is a shared value and moral system.[7] It would seem that sports, depending on level of participation, would act as a bonding agent for youths to society.

The more attachments youths have to peers, teachers, and coaches the less likely they will behave in a delinquent manner. Most sports involve other members and teammates for the youths to bond with along with at least one coach. Sports involve commitment as well. Hirschi would argue that:

> The idea, then, is that the person invests time, energy, himself, in a certain line of activity—say, getting an education, building up a business, acquiring a reputation for virtue. Whenever he considers deviant behavior, he must consider the costs of this deviant behavior, the risk he runs of losing the investment he has made in conventional behavior.[8]

Hirschi reinforces the idealistic view of sports in his writings about involvement by stating "idle hands are the devil's workshop." If a person is busy playing sports they will have little time to be involved with crime. The more attachments, commitments, and involvements youths have to the school, sports team, and community the more likely they will be to conform to the norms of society. This is one of the basic tenets behind support for athletic participation. It is a positive activity in which the youth will make friends, become part of a group, and learn about commitment, responsibility, and teamwork. For most youths, this is true; however, what if the team culture and attitude is not a positive one? Can these positive aspects of athletic participation turn negative or even criminal? Additionally, the theory of participation on sports teams as a form of social control is inadequate to explain any long-term effects because for most youths sports are seasonal and their involvement only lasts for a few years during high school.

Additional theories on juvenile delinquency would also suggest a deterrent effect for sports participation. Some theories point to boredom or a need by juveniles to assert their masculinity as a reason for delinquency; sports would seem to help ease both of these problems by providing a positive arena to demonstrate their "manhood." Sports participation would reduce the strain some juveniles feel over their status compared to adults, which is often an impetus for criminal behavior. Additionally, peer pressure is a popular explanation for juvenile delinquency. According to criminologist Ronald Akers "the single best predictor of adolescent behavior, conforming or deviant, is the behavior of close friends. Both drugs and delinquency are primarily group behaviors."[9] Sports team members would seem to have more socially acceptable values and norms (discussed in more detail later in the chapter) than students involved with non-organized activities or juveniles who participated in no activities.

Other theories suggest that participation on some sports teams might increase delinquency among its members. There may be a subculture of deviance (or violence) that exists with some teams. Subcultures are groups of people with shared values that may be in opposition to, or outside of, mainstream society. Violent subcultures are decidedly violent and are built around violent themes and around values supporting violent activities. Groups expect violence and legitimize it when it occurs. "The use of violence. . . . is not necessarily viewed as illicit conduct, and the users do not have to deal with feelings of guilt about their aggression."[10] Violence can become a way of life for the group and result in members' greater willingness to use it. Violent team sports, with their sense of teamwork, "us against the world" attitude, and complete focus on their aggressive sport may be comparable to a violent subculture.

Building on subculture theories, the idea of positive deviance (a strict adherence by athletes to a code of ethics that sometimes runs counter to societal norms) asserts that much of the deviance committed by athletes:

> Does not involve disregarding or rejecting commonly accepted cultural goals or means to those goals, nor does it result from alienation from society. Instead, it is grounded in athletes' uncritical acceptance of and commitment to what they have been told by important people in their lives ever since they began participating in competitive programs; in a real sense, it is the result of being too committed to the goals and norms of sport.[11]

The idea of positive deviance can explain how athletes "do harmful things to themselves and perhaps others while motivated by a sense of duty and honor."[12] The strong bonds that athletes make can form the basis of the criminal behavior. Sport sociologists Robert Hughes and Jay Coakley argue in their article, "Positive Deviance among Athletes":

> In the case of athletes in highly visible sports, this process of developing fraternity, superiority, and disdain for outsiders might also lead some of them to naively assume they are somehow beyond the law, and the people outside

the athletic fraternity do not deserve their respect. This could lead to serious cases of negative deviance including, for example, assault, sexual assault, and rape (including gang rape), the destruction of property, reckless driving, and alcohol abuse.[13]

The theory of positive deviance is especially helpful in understanding crime among high school athletes who are very impressionable and group minded (see Glen Ridge Case).

Additionally, labeling theory is useful in understanding delinquency committed by athletes. The theory explains how the behavior of an individual may be influenced by the labels or names used to describe or classify him (such as ex-convict or "jock"). The theory points to the possible effects of stereotyping a person which might lead to a self-fulfilling prophecy where the individual tries to live up the label assigned to him.

> Despite their all-American outward appearance, some male athletes did see drinking, drugs and sexual promiscuity as part of what it meant to be a man. The ethics of playing with pain and doing what it takes to win can lead to abuses that could be labeled delinquent if they were not in sport.[14]

In many cases, a high school athlete may be trying to live up to an image of a "star" athlete or "jock" that has been portrayed to him by his older teammates, ex-players, friends, and the media. Additionally, the social status given to athletes may create a sense of entitlement and belief that they are above the law.

RESEARCH ON HIGH SCHOOL ATHLETIC PARTICIPATION AND DELINQUENCY

In the United States, sports are often seen as a cure-all. Participation in athletics is seen as a great way to build character in the nation's youth. Generations of this way of thinking have resulted in sports as a family tradition. We have even turned to sports in times of national tragedy to help buoy our nation's spirits and foster pride in our country, as seen with Major League Baseball and the National Football League after the events of 9/11. Although it is commonly believed that sports are always a positive influence, the research simply does not support this claim.

Sports are supposed to pay off in many different ways. There are the pro-social messages of striving to do your best, dedication, practice, respect for authority, sportsmanship, and fair play. Additionally, there is a socialization value in which kids learn to deal with other kids, including those of different backgrounds. Supposedly, the thrill of sports will take the place of the thrill of crime and drug use. The skills learned on the sports field are assumed to be transferable to the classroom, business world, and life in general.[15] The sports myth also holds that athletics is a vehicle to obtain a college education. All of these pro-social messages are why sports are the most popular extracurricular activity in high schools.

This positive view of athletic participation has taken some hits recently, with the many criminal incidents facing college and professional athletes and the proliferation of performance-enhancing drugs among athletes. The wholesome family image of the sporting world has been shattered in recent years by athletes like Barry Bonds, Michael Vick, and Mike Tyson. The cracks in the image of the sports world have led people to question just how valuable and positive the effects of athletic participation are among our youth.[16]

Other recent social issues have added to the questioning of the benefits of sports participation. First, feminist scholars have argued that sports, particularly team sports, reflect male dominance, objectify women, and encourage physical and aggressive behavior toward women. These attitudes toward women could very well originate in the culture of many high school athletic teams. This was coupled with society's growing awareness of date rape and domestic violence toward women across society. These helped lead to a growing concern with the connection between sports and violence against women. Additionally, the media became more willing to cover incidents involving domestic violence and date rape, particularly when committed by professional athletes.[17] The increased attention by scholars and the popular media has led to a complete turn around, to a point now where it is assumed by many that professional athletes are more likely to be violent toward women. Although the relationship between high school athletes and violence toward women has not been clearly demonstrated, there has been research examining this relationship among college and professional athletes that will be addressed in Chapters 2 and 3.

Additionally, most studies find little difference in character between students who participate in high school athletics and those who do not. One study found that athletes had a slight increase in self-esteem and attention to academics. However, they also found a significant increase in aggression, reduced belief in the importance of being honest, and reduced self-control.[18] The finding regarding self-control is noteworthy because recent criminological theories have pointed to self-control as a key concept in the explanation of all forms of crime as well as other types of behavior. In *A General Theory of Crime* Gottfredson and Hirschi argue that the management of self-control is the key to explaining criminal behavior.[19]

Although the notion of the many benefits of sports has a long history in this country, there is little scientific evidence to support this ideal. The research on high school athletes and crime has focused on a variety of different crimes. Most of the studies focus on drinking, drug use, and aggressive behavior. Not surprisingly, participation in sports has been found to be positively related to involvement with aggressive behavior, suggesting that sports act as a risk factor rather than a protective factor from violence.[20] This is not surprising; for some, sports aggression and violence are inherent in the sport and may attract a more aggressive person to sports to begin with (selection bias). Conversely, the aggression and violence that are praised on the playing field may spill over to other aspects of the athlete's life.

Research on the values associated with aggressive sports such as football and hockey have consistently been linked with violence against women. Homophobia and sexual locker room conversations have also become associated with this type of sport. Researchers have found that the culture of these sports is similar to rape-prone societies. In anthropologist Peggy Sanday's study of sexual assaults among college athletes, she discussed how sexual assault rates vary considerably from country to country around the world. She found that countries with high sexual assault rates shared three characteristics: male-dominated, highly tolerant of violence, and sex-segregated. These cultures are described as "rape cultures."[21] These characteristics could also describe your typical high school or college sports team's locker room. Although much of the focus on sexual assaults committed by athletes is directed toward college and professional athletes (see Chapters 2 and 3), the idea that these attitudes and behaviors do not begin until an athlete reaches a Division I school is unfounded. The same aggressive, misogynistic, and homophobic attitudes discussed with college athletes exist among high school teams as well and may take on even more importance with younger and more impressionable youth.

This is supported by another study that found that college men who participated in aggressive high school sports scored higher on measures of sexism, were more accepting of violence as a way to solve problems, were more accepting of rape myths, and generally showed more hostility toward women. They also reported higher levels of aggression toward dating partners, including hitting, kicking, pushing, and psychological abuse as well as more sexually coercive behavior such as using threats or physical force to obtain sexual activity.[22]

This being said, the research is still somewhat mixed. For example, one study found that youths whose parents were substance abusers showed decreased delinquency after participation in a three-month sports program. But another study found that Canadian secondary school students who participated in organized sports had higher levels of delinquent activity.[23] Other studies found that youths (10-, 12- and 14-year-olds) involved with physical activity had lower levels of substance abuse.[24] Another study found that participation in sports was related to higher levels of drinking alcohol.[25] One reason why the research has been somewhat mixed is that it depends on the context and structure of the sports program and experience that the youth encounters.[26] "It is the consensus among social scientists studying sports that whereas athletic participation per se is not good or bad, the environment of participation, or what has been called the social content of competition, is important."[27] Whereas well-organized and supervised sports programs might benefit student-athletes, less structured programs could lead to a negative learning experience. Even beyond the supervision or structure of the sports team, the message and values that are being fostered by the coach and other players are extremely important. A coach who stresses "win at all costs" or uses derogatory terms toward women and homosexuals would have a different impact on his or her players than one who stresses the spirit of healthy competition and sportsmanship.

To understand the relationship between athletic participation and crime, one needs to look at more than just whether the youth played on a sports team or not. We need to look at the context and culture of the team, school, and town and also look at how the individual views his or her participation (for example, do they identify themselves as jocks or athletes or is it just one activity that they participate in among many others). The study by Miller and colleagues ("Jocks, Gender, Binge Drinking, and Adolescent Violence") is helpful in understanding the relationship, comparing those students who identified themselves as jocks with those who simply participated in athletics.[28] They found a positive correlation with those who fit the "jock identity" and binge drinking. They also discovered that those white male teens who identified themselves as jocks were more likely to engage in non-family violence. However, the results did not hold true for black athletes. Additionally, the athletes who were more likely to support aggression on the field were more likely to be aggressive off the field as well. This is referred to as Cultural Spillover theory; the more aggressive and violent behavior becomes sanctioned on the field, the greater the likelihood for illegitimate violence in a non-sport context. The findings from this study support this theory but only in a non-family setting, not among family members (issues of domestic violence among athletes will be discussed in Chapter 3). This study suggests that the relationship between athletic participation and violence may vary by race or location (city versus suburbs). Their study also helps us understand why female athletic participation has not been connected to crime; female athletes are less likely to have a "jock identity."

As mentioned in the introduction, the fact that some research shows a negative relationship between athletic participation and criminal behavior

while other research shows higher levels of delinquency like fighting, drinking, and drug use among athletes might be explained by the theory of "positive deviance." Positive deviance theory asserts that an over-conformity to
the athletic norms of physical strength, machismo, competitiveness, and
winning may be responsible for some athletes behaving in socially unacceptable ways.[29] Some athletes might not buy into all of these aspects or their
team culture might not push these values as much as other more positive
values. In addition, the schools, communities, and law enforcement might
exacerbate the problem by not punishing the athletes' negative behavior.
High school athletes are at an important point in their lives where they
begin to think for themselves and stray from their parents' authority.
If schools do not properly discipline athletes who misbehave or do not
achieve satisfactory grades, the athletes are more likely to push for more
freedom. If law enforcement lets athletes pass on minor offenses, they may
be more likely to continue with their delinquency and push the envelope to
see how much they can get away with. Giving high school athletes too
much status or "power" can contribute to their sense of entitlement and
superiority.

To illustrate how the treatment of high school athletes in some towns
may contribute to criminal behavior, we can examine an incident involving
football players from a small town in Ohio. In Kenton, Ohio, a city of
8,000, which draws 4,000 to their high school football games, a judge demonstrated the preferential treatment that athletes receive. Two high school
football players played a prank where they stole a decoy deer and placed it
in the center of the road to make motorists swerve to avoid it. When two
other teenagers swerved to avoid the deer, their car rolled off the road into
a ditch. One of the boys suffered brain damage, the other broke bones in
his neck, arm, and leg, wore a neck brace for three months, and had 10 sur-
geries. The boys who played the prank were sentenced to 60 days at a juvenile detention center. However, when issuing the sentence, the judge said
that the boys could complete the football season before serving their sentence. The judge said "I shouldn't be doing this, but I'm going to. I see
positive things about participating in football."[30] This case brings to light
the continued notion that participating on a team is a positive use of the
boys' time. The judge believed that being part of the football team would
help the boys stay out of trouble and serve as a strong support system. The
idea that being part of the football team may have helped contribute to the
criminal behavior was not raised by the judge. The judge's decision also
shows the type of preferential treatment to which athletes become accus-
tomed. This case begs the question: would the judge have ruled the same
way for a member of the debate team or even a member of the soccer team?

Although drawing on solid or consistent conclusions from academic research is always challenging, several trends can be seen in the studies done on the effects of sports participation on high school students' behavior. Many findings have disputed the previously assumed positive effects of sports participation. What we are left with is the acknowledgment that there may be some negative implications to participation on a sports team.

High Profile Example: Glen Ridge High School Rape Case

Sexual and drinking exploits are common parts of the athlete image. Players are straight and conformist in public, but, they learn how to use this public conformity to hide private nonconformity. Stories about athletes' rule-breaking behavior abound, especially in regard to drinking, sex, and drug use. Such exploits are used by athletes to support their macho image.[31]

One of the more high profile cases that raised questions about criminal behavior and culture among high school athletes took place in Glen Ridge, New Jersey. The 1989 case has been well documented in the press, most notably by Leftkowitz in *Our Guys*. It involved members of Glen Ridge's football team sexually assaulting a mentally retarded female student in the basement of two of the athletes. The story exploded in the New Jersey and New York media in part because of the setting. Glen Ridge is an affluent, mostly white town with very little crime. These were "good" kids from solid families. To many in the media, this did not fit the stereotype for a group sexual assault. The incident began with 13 males in the basement; six left after they began to feel uncomfortable with the actions of their team-mates. The victim was forced to perform oral sex and was penetrated with various objects, most notably a baseball bat and broomstick. After the sexual assault was over, they told the victim to keep their actions a secret because she would be kicked out of school if she told anyone. All of the participants then put their hands in together, like a sports team cheer.

An interesting aspect of the case, which came under intense scrutiny, is that all of the perpetrators were athletes. For many, the fact that the perpetrators were part of a sports team became an important factor as details of the case started to come out. The victim, like many in town, looked up to the boys, because of their membership on the town's football team. The gang, or team, nature of the assault also became an important aspect of the case. In Leftkowitz's research on the case, he looked at the town and all of the participants' histories to try and understand how this event could take place in such a "nice" community. Was this an isolated event by the athletes? Was it a half hour of bad judgment by the perpetrators or was this event just one in a pattern of immoral and illegal behavior? When he looked at the academic, sports, and even home life of the boys it was discovered that the boys lacked proper female role models. They had never had a female in a position of authority (outside of classroom teachers) and only one of the perpetrators even had a sister. This was compounded by their complete focus on the sports world, which is sex-segregated by team and by sport in most cases. The boys did not know how to interact with females in a healthy and normal way. This is coupled with the fact that aggression was something that was prized in the sports world; this aggression in many cases was hard to leave on the field. The boys had previous run-ins with the law including underage drinking, fights, and thefts. This does not even come close to describing the behavior that they got away with at school, with one of the perpetrators often exposing himself during class. Sex-segregation, lack of female authority figures or even equals, constant praise for aggression, and lack of any consequences for negative and anti-social behavior came together in Glen Ridge to cause this event. The problem is that this is the exact environment that exists in many towns across the country where athletes are placed on a pedestal. Three of the boys were eventually found guilty of aggravated sexual assault charges and served more than three years in an institution for young adult offenders.

HAZING

College campuses and Hollywood have traditionally held the monopoly on images of hazing. There is no shortage of comedies that poke fun at fraternity hazing, most notably in *Animal House* and more recently in the movie *Old School*. For anyone who attended a college or university with fraternities and sororities, the image of pledges wearing pins or doing silly antics across the campus was a common sight. Hazing has traditionally been associated with college fraternities and sororities, and even to some extent the military. But increasingly it has become the domain of sports teams, and not just college sports teams but high school (and to a lesser extent professional teams) as well.

In 2000, Alfred University in conjunction with the National Collegiate Athletic Association (NCAA) surveyed about 10,000 athletes at 224 colleges about their high school experiences. The survey showed that hazing is more common than previously thought. The Alfred University study found that nearly half (48%) of high school students had participated in some form of hazing, with 1.5 million high school students being hazed each year. The hazing was not limited to sports teams, but athletes faced the greatest risk of enduring these often-dangerous initiations, with about half of the victims being athletes.[32]

Hazing can take many forms but is typically associated with rituals or activities required for initiation into an organization. Hazing can be criminal or non-criminal. It involves established members of the group or team intimidating rookies or new members. The Alfred University study defined hazing as "any activity expected of someone joining the group that humiliates, degrades, abuses or endangers, regardless of the person's willingness to participate. This does not include "team building" activities such as rookies carrying the balls, team parties with community games, or going out with your teammates, unless an atmosphere of humiliation, abuse or danger arises."

Criminal hazing activities are generally considered to be physically abusive, hazardous, and/or sexually violating. The specific behaviors or activities within these categories vary widely among participants, groups, and settings. Although alcohol use is common in many types of hazing, other examples of hazing practices include personal servitude; sleep deprivation, and restrictions on personal hygiene; yelling, swearing, and insulting new members/rookies; being forced to wear embarrassing or humiliating attire in public; consumption of vile substances or smearing of such on one's skin; brandings; physical beatings; binge drinking and drinking games; sexual simulation and sexual assault.[33]

Sports hazing differs from the traditional fraternity style hazing in two major ways. First, sports teams typically have one big night of hazing activities whereas fraternity hazing can stretch out over months. Additionally, fraternity hazing typically is used to determine if new pledges have what it takes to become full members of the organization; with sports hazing, the participants have typically already become members of the team. The hazing is perpetrated by older members of the team as a rite of passage; the rookies go along with the initiation in many cases simply to gain peer acceptance from their teammates.[34]

High school athletes are less mentally and physically able to handle hazing. In the Alfred University study only 12% of respondents indicated that they had been hazed, yet when asked about specific activities that they participated in, 79% of the respondents had been subjected to what was considered questionable or unacceptable hazing. Half of the students were required to participate in drinking contests or alcohol related initiations while two thirds involved humiliating hazing such as having male students dress up in female clothes and wear them in public. Many of the sports-related hazing takes place during pre-season workouts or camps. Hazing occurred in both male and female sports teams; 68% of male athletes and 63% of female athletes took part in criminal, dangerous, and/or alcohol-related hazing, but the more violent and sexual hazing seems to take place on the male teams.

Hazing at the high school level is particularly troubling because during the developmental stage of adolescence, students are more vulnerable to peer pressure. This is due to the tremendous need for belonging, making friends, and finding approval in one's peer group. Further, the danger of hazing at the high school level is heightened by the lack of awareness and policy development/enforcement around this issue. Hazing in high school will also lead to the greater likelihood of hazing in college and the professional ranks, as the practice is seen as a tradition that new members must inevitably go through. Although many colleges and universities in the United States have instituted anti-hazing policies and educational awareness programs related to hazing, very few secondary schools have done the same.[35]

According to the Alfred University study, hazing varies among sports teams with football players, swimmers, divers, lacrosse players, and water polo players reporting more than athletes in other sports in the survey. Students involved in tennis, fencing, and track reported the least amount of hazing. They also found that 42% of those who endured hazing in college said they were also hazed in high school.

Hazing rituals inevitably vary from team to team but a common process has been observed. First, new members are invited to an event and typically are aware that an initiation is to occur. Second, new members are welcomed to the event and often encouraged to drink alcohol. This is typically followed by joking and taunting at the rookies' expense. Then, a list of activities is presented for the new members to complete. If they complete the activities they will be welcomed as full members of the team. After the rituals, new members are welcomed onto the team by the veterans and both groups express their enthusiasm for the team. The veterans talk about the necessity of secrecy about the events and promote a team mentality over all that happened.[36]

Hazing rituals are typically kept secret from those outside of the team and organization. The hazing process is rationalized by those involved as necessary to build team unity and weed out any members not worthy of full status on the team. The term "being rookied" is well known to those in the sports world. The idea that rookies or new members of the team need to earn their way to become fully accepted on the team may take the form of having to carry the water or equipment bag or having to prove oneself on the field. The rituals can take place before formal initiation ceremonies, immediately after, or even weeks after the season begins.

The hazing may occur secretly away from the school or team activities without any knowledge or approval from the coaches or may happen out in the open and be a sort of "open secret" among the coaches (or a combination of both). The events are typically well known to the new members, which only heighten their anxiety about the rituals, as the sense of tradition that accompanies the practice serves to legitimize the activities. The rituals are seen as the only path to acceptance among the other team members. Some rituals take place in public, these are typically more lighthearted and meant to mildly embarrass, but the intensity increases with the private activities. Veteran members typically try to replicate or "improve" on the hazing that was done to them.[37]

In the past, most people brushed off the dangers of high school hazing. To earlier generations, hazing rituals typically consisted of scavenger hunts, clearing the lunch trays for upperclassmen, or dressing in silly outfits. Starting in the 1980s, hazing rites have typically increased in the amount of humiliation and physical and sexual abuse involved. There are more cases of extreme violence and sexual behavior including penetration that qualifies much more as criminal behavior than hazing rituals of the past. Along with some high profile hazing incidents, the media attention of high school shootings has caused parents and school officials to look differently at bullying and hazing in schools. Parents looking to protect their children and school officials looking to protect the school from lawsuits have taken a more proactive approach to hazing.[38]

The findings of the Alfred University study and some recent high profile hazing cases have led states to pass anti-hazing laws. There are anti-hazing laws in 44 states, with some making it a felony and others a misdemeanor.[39] In most states that have anti-hazing laws, consent of the victim cannot be used as a defense. Even if someone agrees to a potentially hazardous action, it is not viewed as true consent when considering peer pressure and the desire to belong to the group. Some states have also made it a crime to fail to report hazing. In Massachusetts, "whoever knows that another person is the victim of hazing . . . and is at the scene of the crime shall, to the extent that such a person can do without danger or peril to himself or others, report such crime to an appropriate law enforcement official as soon as reasonably practicable." These laws have been the result of the growing dangers associated with hazing across the country, including some high profile deaths.

In 1990, Nick Haben, who was a rookie member of the lacrosse club team at Western Illinois University, died during a hazing incident.[40] Although Nick was a non-drinker, he participated in the day-long hazing ritual that contained many alcohol-drinking activities. After continued drinking, Nick fell into a coma. None of the upperclassmen running the initiation thought to call 911 or take Nick to the hospital; they continued on with the hazing with Nick passed out on the ground. Nick was found dead on the floor of one of the lacrosse team's upperclassmen the next morning at 8 o'clock after the two lacrosse players noticed that his face was purple from lack of oxygen. Marc Anderson, one of the lacrosse team leaders, said "before we heard Nick was dead it was one of the best times I ever had. The night was fun. I'm glad I had the experience, the brotherhood, the bonding." Illinois did not have a strict anti-hazing law, so the defendants were tried for serving alcohol to a minor and received community service for their role in the hazing death. In 1996, Nick's mom successfully lobbied for an anti-hazing law in Illinois that included felony hazing for the type of behavior her son was subjected to.

Some recent examples of high school hazing incidents demonstrate the continued severity of the issue.

- A new member to the Kirtland Central High School (New Mexico) football program suffered a concussion when he was repeatedly hit on the head during an apparent initiation rite. The varsity team apparently had an initiation for new teammates in which boys were held down, thumped on the head, and asked to name ten types of fruit. One player did not want to participate, and several players used more force than usual.[41]
- Eight members of the Trumbull High School (Connecticut) wrestling team were arrested and charged in connection with the brutal hazing of a 15-year-old sophomore. Police officials said the sophomore, who had joined the team that school year, had been hogtied, slammed into a wall, imprisoned several times in a gymnasium locker, and held down once while teammates forced a plastic knife into his rectum.[42]

Another case that received national attention and was the subject of an episode of ESPN's *Outside the Lines* involved the Wilson High School (New York) baseball team. There was an alleged incident on the bus ride home from an away game when three varsity ballplayers allegedly sexually abused two junior varsity team members. The three boys were charged with multiple counts of sexual assault. The hazing took place in the back of the bus while the coaches sat in the front of the bus. What makes matters more interesting is that this case led to the discovery of prior hazing incidents on the team. In addition, one of the alleged perpetrators of the most recent incident was a victim of prior hazing. "The victim-turned-attacker said in a statement that he participated because it was done to him. In fact, he was the one who allegedly inserted a cell phone into the rectum of one of the restrained junior varsity victims."[43] This pattern of victim turned attacker is typical of the cycle of hazing and what makes matters worse is that the intensity typically increases as victims turn into perpetrators.

The world of sports is often depicted as a "man's" world and as a place for men to display their manhood. This raises the question about many of the recent examples of hazing that involve charges of sexual assault and often homosexual/homoerotic behavior. Hazing rituals often include simulated sex acts, touching or being touched by teammates' genitals, being verbally abused by homophobic or sexist names, dressing as women, and in some cases being sodomized with various objects. Some theorists argue that both latent homosexuality and homophobia are playing a huge role in recent cases of hazing, and that our societal standards that dictate what a "real man" is are partially to blame. These sexually-oriented activities are meant to humiliate initiates and test their team loyalty by submitting them to "forbidden" or "unmanly" activities.[44] The activities demonstrate a level of dominance by the perpetrators and an attempt to demonstrate their own masculinity by making the participants submissive (and what better way to demonstrate this than to have them submit to homosexual behavior, a taboo in the sports world). It should be noted that hazing victims are rarely forced to undergo heterosexual activities.

College campuses have also seen an increase in hazing incidents, from sports teams as well as fraternities. Northwestern University has seen hazing incidents in a few of their teams over the past couple of years. The women's soccer team got in trouble when pictures of a hazing incident appeared on a Web site. The pictures displayed Northwestern soccer players clad only in T-shirts and underwear, some with blindfolds on and others with their hands tied behind their backs. Other women had words or pictures scrawled on their bodies and clothes, and it appeared that alcohol was involved. This was followed by news that the swim team was also involved in hazing involving underage drinking, swimming in Lake Michigan when the beaches were closed, and "additional inappropriate behavior." News of the swim team was followed by a hazing incident by the students who perform as "Willie the Wildcat," the school's mascot, who staged a fake kidnapping of new students who were candidates to fill the position.[45] In researching college sports hazing incidents, I discovered quite a few incidents of women's sports teams. For example:

- Frostburg State University field hockey players were urged to drink so much beer and liquor that one was hospitalized with a 0.365% blood-alcohol level. The freshmen players also were pelted with flour, ice, and eggs, and made to sit in their own vomit and urine.[46]

- The Maine softball team was placed on probation for three years and three players were suspended for up to 10 games by the school for hazing violations. The university began an investigation one summer after photos appeared online showing members of the softball team apparently drinking alcohol and making lewd gestures at a party in 2006.[47]

One of the more widely covered college hazing incidents involved the hockey team at the University of Vermont in 2000. The freshmen on the hockey team were, among other things, forced to wear women's panties, dip their genitals in beer, and parade without clothing through a house in an "elephant walk" in which they moved in a line while gripping each other's private parts. After the allegations surfaced, the university decided to cancel the remainder of the season. One of the older players on the hockey team summarized the mindset of many athletes that go along with hazing incidents, "It's a team sport and a team game. You go along with your team and what the team decides to do and you support that no matter what. You don't want to upset the team chemistry."[48]

Hazing is not limited to high school and college teams; it also has been a tradition in many professional teams as well. The newspapers often report on the treatment rookie players are subjected to by the veterans. The tone and description of the hazing on professional sports team is markedly different than on the high school sports teams:

> Lorenzen Wright engineered a prank on some Hawk rookies—the old car full of popcorn—and tells the *Atlanta Journal Constitution*'s Sekou Smith about rookie hazing: "Jermaine O'Neal and I came into the league together," Wright said. "JO told me that when he was in Portland that Gary Trent, Rasheed Wallace and all them jumped him, took all his clothes, locked him out of his room and then trashed his whole room. And I'm talking about flushing sheets down the toilets, soaked all his clothes and everything."[49]

Many teams have an annual rookie dinner where the rookies have to pay the tab while the veterans eat and drink their way through meals that cost thousands of dollars. In one case, four rookies from the National Hockey League's Tampa Bay Lightning had to pitch in $6,000 each to cover a bill of $24,000 to feed their teammates and team trainers. "It's safe to say," a local writer suggested, "when the waiter brought the wine list, the players went straight for the good stuff." The ramifications, however, go beyond dollars spent and expensive food consumed to influence the very culture of professional hockey: "Lightning rookies were somewhat mum about the whole thing, unsure if they were allowed to talk about the meal, but it's really no secret. It has been going on in the NHL for years."[50]

Major League Baseball also has it own set of hazing rituals: forcing rookies to dress up, Halloween style, in public. Typically carried out at the start of a road trip, rookies must appear costumed as they load equipment onto the team bus and make their way through airports and flights. The New York Yankees, one writer observes, seem to have "set the highest standard in recent years. In 2005, the rookies wore cheerleader outfits, and last year the players had to dress up as George Steinbrenner. This year, they went for a "Wizard of Oz" theme."[51]

The professional athletes' hazing rituals do not enter into dangerous or criminal hazing but rather fall on the embarrassing side and more traditional ideas of hazing rituals. Hazing will continue with sports teams. The only question is where the line will be drawn between the harmless team building traditions of rookies carrying the equipment bags versus sexually violent attacks on new members in high school.

HIGH PROFILE EXAMPLE: MEPHAM HIGH SCHOOL FOOTBALL TEAM

In August 2003, the Mepham High School football team (Bellmore-Merick, Long Island, New York) went to a five-day football camp in Wayne County, Pennsylvania. The students slept in cabins, with the coaches sleeping in separate ones. After the coaches went to sleep, at least three upperclassmen (aged 15, 16, and 17) sexually assaulted three members of the team. They allegedly rubbed heat-producing mineral ice on broomsticks, pinecones, and golf balls and used those items to penetrate at least three freshman players while the rest of the boys in the cabin watched.[52] The incidents happened over several nights. One of the students was injured so badly that he required surgery.[53] When rumors of the incident began to spread around town and school, players who witnessed the attacks refused to talk, even though the coach of the team, Kevin McElroy, told them to and warned them that the season would end if they didn't come forward. Still no players came forward and the victims were laughed at in the halls, called "faggot" and "broomstick boy." The superintendent of the school, Thomas Caramore, initially tried to keep the incident quiet and would not cooperate with Pennsylvania authorities who contacted him looking for information about the students involved in the incident. The students involved in the incident received no punishment for the first two weeks of school.[54] As the story began to come out and pressure built, the three football players were suspended from the football team. Then on September 17, 2003, they were suspended from school and the school board decided to cancel the football season. The school superintendent said that the season was cancelled not because of "hazing" but because the team-mates never reported the incident.[55]

The story continued to make news as the father of the purported ring-leader, a lineman on the football team, died on October 5. The father was allegedly devastated by the charges his son was facing. The following day it was announced that the lineman along with the two other students would be charged with 10 criminal charges including deviant sexual intercourse, aggravated assault, kidnapping, unlawful restraint and false imprisonment.[56] Each of the students faced up to 20 years in prison (this fact changed after a Pennsylvania judge decided the players would be tried as juveniles).

The victims continued to be harassed and received threats from other students and members of the community who were angry over the foot-ball season's cancellation. The incident caused debates throughout the town regarding whether hazing was widespread in the town and how re-sponsible the coaches are for what happens with the team. An interesting aspect of the case is that the school superintendent continued to maintain that the incident was not hazing:

> Caramore told parents in a speech, adding that whatever happened *wasn't* hazing: "None of us in Bellmore-Merrick has used that term to define what is, in fact, a brutal crime." The hazing-or-not debate is a key factor in the legal battles to come. Because if these attacks are accepted as hazing, then the school is responsible.[57]

The investigation of the case also centered on the school's slow response to the incident. The position of the school and coaches worsened when news broke that one of the perpetrators had made threats to one of the freshman players in July before the sleep-away camp. A freshman who was not happy with being called derogatory names by the junior lineman went to Coach McElroy and told him what was happening. The name-calling stopped but the upperclass-man reportedly told the freshman "Don't even think about sleeping at camp." The freshman involved in that incident went unharmed at the camp.[58]

The 2003 assault raised questions about whether this was part of the culture at Mepham or just an isolated incident. Although some in the town, including school officials and the football coach, said that hazing did not happen in Mepham, people in the town knew differently. Back in 1994, Wesley Berger was a Mepham freshman football player when, dur-ing the beginning of the season, another player tried to flush his head in a urinal. After he resisted, he remembers a junior varsity coach telling him to roll with it. Once the season started, eight players tackled him in the locker room and lowered him into the toilet; this time, he said, it contained urine. They hit his head on the porcelain and he got a concussion. Berger won a civil suit against the school.[59]

The Pennsylvania grand jury that investigated the attacks determined that the coaches should not be held criminally responsible for the assaults. The grand jury report said the incident was a result of "old traditions of violent hazing that coaches and school officials could not curb." The report detailed the history of hazing that took place in Mepham including beating new members of the team and "dunking their heads into toilets. Additionally, once each school year, older Mepham students would beat up younger ones on school grounds in a ritual called 'Freshman Friday.'"[60] The grand jury report also provided details regarding the attacks:

> During the first day of camp, the hazing was minor, such as one player smearing gel and powder into another's hair. On the second day, the incidents became brutal. Two of the attackers held down one of the freshmen while the third sodomized the freshman with a broomstick coated with Mineral Ice, a pain-relieving ointment. Other players laughed. Over the next few days, the broomstick assaults were repeated. Duct tape was yanked from the victims' bottoms and pubic areas, and two of the victims were forced to smear Mineral Ice on their testicles, and then kick each other there.[61]

On January 13, 2004, the three football players admitted their guilt in a Pennsylvania courtroom. One of the three players was sentenced to boot camp, another one was sentenced to a residential treatment facility for juveniles, and the third player returned home on probation but could not attend Mepham High School. Additionally, all three of the defendants had to pay court costs and medical bills to the three victims. [62]

All five of the coaches were fired from their positions and removed from their teaching positions at the high school. Four of the former coaches filed a lawsuit against the parents of three players involved in the attacks. The lawsuit contends that the boys' parents should have known their sons were "prone to acts of violence and demonstrated a vicious and dangerous propensity to commit assault and battery upon others."[63] The victims of the attack are suing their attackers, the school district, and the former coaches. Their lawsuit contends that officials negligently failed to supervise players at the Pennsylvania training camp and to curb a culture of hazing at Mepham High School. In 2004, football returned to Mepham and two of the victims returned to the team. The school district has stopped overnight training-camp trips, reinforced an anti-hazing policy, and emphasized a program of character education that stresses integrity, responsibility, and compassion.[64]

CONCLUSION

High school athletics is the most popular and closely followed activity in high school. It is the highest athletic level in which many of us have participated, as there are fewer who participate in college athletics and a rare few who make it to the professional ranks. With this being said, it is the most familiar to us and for most of us it was probably a wonderful experience, something on which we look back fondly. This makes it more difficult to look at critically. However, as time goes by the idea that high school athletic participation is the way to build character and avoid criminal behavior is coming under attack both by the growing number of incidents in the media and also by academic research. Another difficulty in summarizing the role of high school athletic participation is that it is also the hardest level (compared to college and professional) to draw conclusions about because it varies the most. It is hard to make conclusions about a high school athlete because that title could include a person who only participated in high school track or it could include the student whose whole life revolved around playing football, basketball, and baseball.

The high school student-athletes who are most at risk for criminal behavior are those who identify themselves as "jocks." For athletes whose biggest peer influence is their teammates, team culture can have a huge impact on their behavior, both on and off the field. If the team values aggression and deviance, it will produce individual athletes who are violent and prone to criminal behavior. If locker room conversation revolves around sexist ideas and homophobic beliefs, the athletes who walk out of that locker room will be more likely to devalue others and be more prone to sexual assault.

When a team's culture is deviant, those who have internalized the "jock identity" may be the most likely to go on to commit crimes; however, all members of the team are affected. Some members of the team may go along with the deviant behavior simply to be part of the group, such as in the Glen Ridge rape case. This is also the case with hazing, beginning in high school and continuing at higher levels. Often hazing is an accepted part of joining a team, and coaches may look the other way when it occurs. Hazing includes physical and mental abuse, sexual violations, and embarrassment. Although not all hazing is criminal, many athletes go along with the criminal acts simply to be an accepted part of the team.

The issues raised with high school athletics may be the most important because the athletes are still at their most impressionable period. The experiences they have with or have because of their participation with sports will have a great impact on their behavior in the future, especially if their future includes college athletics.

Chapter 2

COLLEGE ATHLETES AND CRIME

Athletes continue to hold a special place in the community when they enter college. The sense of entitlement and privilege that began in high school carries over into college. This is coupled with a greater sense of freedom, and in many cases increased access to alcohol and drugs. The special treatment that colleges afford their athletes only heightens the student-athletes' sense that they are special and in some cases above the law. There are numerous examples of big time college football and basketball programs (for example, the Penn State University football team and University of Cincinnati basketball teams) that have looked the other way from their athletes' criminal behavior. Many explanations will be examined to account for an increased risk of criminal behavior among Division I athletes in basketball and football including cultural differences between athletes and other students on campus and a lack of accountability from the colleges.

Preferential treatment of athletes starts at a very young age. By the time child athletes hit their teen years, they are already showing that they are bigger and faster than the average student. They are already receiving more attention from other students, particularly female students. The athletes' accomplishments are praised by the schools that they attend more so than academic or social clubs. They are excused early for away games and their schools host pep rallies and bonfires before a big game. Teachers offer them encouragement and many become a little lax with grading. Some get through high school with help from other students or teachers. Others are just passed along because of their athletic ability, especially when a college scholarship becomes likely. All of this special treatment is only intensified as the athlete enters college. In college, courses are picked for them by the athletic department to revolve around their sports schedule and they are assigned tutors to help them with their classes. This opens the door for athletes to take the easy way out when it comes to course work. For example, Florida State University was investigated for cheating during the 2007–2008 season. The university found that an athletic department employee typed papers for players and filled in answers on quizzes, sometimes without the player being present for the quiz. As a result, 25 FSU players were suspended from their 2008 Music City bowl game.[1]

Along with special treatment by the administration, the admiration of fellow students also increases. As athletes move through college, sports agents approach them waving all sorts of money. Coaches tolerate and support them when they run into problems with academics or the law. They are treated differently than other students and after a while it is no surprise that they start to believe that they are better and more deserving. From the time they first show athletic prowess they are held less accountable for their actions and some start to believe that they can get away with anything.

There are more than 380,000 student-athletes at more than 1,000 National Collegiate Athletic Association (NCAA) colleges and universities. College athletes become an even more "special" class than high school athletes, as only the best athletes make the jump into college athletics. College athletes are higher up on the "performance pyramid" of the sports world.[2] For example, in 2007, 156,096 men played high school basketball as seniors yet there were only 4,735 freshman roster spots on college teams. Only 3% of high school basketball players play in the NCAA. Other sports have similar numbers, 3.3% of high school athletes who play women's basketball play in college, with 5.7% of high school football players, 6.1% of high school baseball players, 11% of men's high school ice hockey and 5.5% of high school men's soccer playing in the NCAA. For many sports, college athletics serves as the "minor leagues" or stepping stone to professional athletics. Colleges and universities spend a large amount of money on facilities, coaches, and equipment hoping to produce revenue from their athletic programs. More and more though, colleges have to balance the benefits of the athletic programs with the negative attention of crimes committed by their athletes on campus.

CRIMINOLOGICAL THEORY: COLLEGE ATHLETES AND CRIMINAL BEHAVIOR

Most of the theories discussed in relation to high school athletes and criminal behavior apply to college athletes as well. The importance of peer groups and formation of subcultures (sometimes violent) would all be important in understanding crimes committed by college athletes. Additionally, the idea of social control and bonding would apply to college student-athletes. Sports provide a positive activity that would involve a huge time commitment on the student's part. This could reduce the chance of law-breaking because students would have less idle time and increased motivation to avoid trouble to maintain their athletic eligibility.

Yet, there are some important differences between the experiences of high school athletes and college athletes that might affect their propensity to commit crime. One of the biggest differences between high school and college, for all students, is the greater freedom that students are afforded. For most students, this is the first time that they are not living under the watchful eyes of their parents. The increased freedom leads to greater experimentation with drugs, most notably alcohol, among college students. Alcohol abuse is almost synonymous with college campuses. Studies consistently find that college athletes drink more than non-athletes (for most athletes this is a crime as most college students are underage). Not only does the research show that athletes drink more than non-athletes, but that they binge drink more and engage in riskier behaviors, including sexual behaviors.[3] Alcohol use has consistently been linked to aggression and criminal behavior. Increased alcohol use by athletes, some who are prone to aggression already, may provide the added spark toward crime.

The research also shows that high school athletes drink more than non-athletes and this difference continues into college. Studies that compared self-identified 'jocks" in high school found they were more likely to engage in problem drinking than their non-jock peers.[4] Colleges and universities compound the problem by sending students mixed messages concerning alcohol use by endorsing the alcohol industry through advertising at collegiate sporting events and allowing tailgating before games.

It is also important to look at the backgrounds of many of the athletes who are brought onto college campuses. Since colleges have special (more lenient) admissions criteria for athletes, some student-athletes do not fit in as well academically as many of the other students on campus. Student-athletes are also often from a different socioeconomic group than their classmates. Many of the athletes, especially those in the higher profile, revenue-generating sports like football and basketball, come from disadvantaged backgrounds. This is compounded by the fact that student-athletes are under much tighter restrictions in terms of time (but also NCAA regulations) in their ability to have a job during the school year. Thus, it is not surprising when student-athletes are involved in crimes like petty theft on campus or taking money or clothes from team boosters. For example, in 2005 University of Connecticut basketball players Marcus Williams and A. J. Price were arrested and charged with trying to sell at pawn shops four stolen laptops valued at $11,000. The laptops were stolen from other students on campus. Both faced multiple felony counts, were placed in a special probation program for first-time offenders, and received university penalties.[5]

A.J. Price, who was not a starter on the basketball team at the time of the incident, was suspended by the university for the 2005–2006 academic year due to violations of the University Student Code of Conduct. He was not permitted to take classes during the Fall 2005 semester, but returned to classes in the Spring 2006 semester. He resumed his basketball career the following year (2007) and went on to be drafted in the second round of the 2009 NBA draft by the Indiana Pacers. Marcus Williams, who was the starting point guard at the time, was suspended for only four months from the basketball team activities but, unlike Price, was allowed to attend classes during the Fall 2005 semester and resume basketball activities during the Spring 2006 semester (he missed the first 11 games of the season).[6] Marcus Williams was drafted in the first round of the 2006 National Basketball Association (NBA) draft by the New Jersey Nets. A few months after the University of Connecticut incident, a similar story arose at nearby Central Connecticut State University, where three university football players were arrested in the theft of laptop computers and other electronic equipment from campus dorm rooms.[7]

However, one study in which college athletes who were convicted of burglaries were interviewed about why they committed their crimes found that they did not do it for material gain but rather because of "defective character traits, the use of alcohol, peer pressure, and the quest for excitement."[8]

College administrators acknowledge that it is expecting a lot to place students from different cultural and economic backgrounds onto a college campus and assume everything will be okay. Tom Osbourne, the former coach of the University of Nebraska, said in 1997 that the biggest change in recruiting over the past decades had nothing to do with size and skill but: "We have a tremendous breakdown in our families. When I first started recruiting 34 years ago, we seldom saw a player from a single-parent family." Now many coaches say it's the norm, and athletes from "such homes often carry heavy baggage that can impact their socialization."[9]

Studies have also shown that being the victim of prior abuse is associated with later abusive behaviors. One study demonstrated that athletes who reported a history of prior abuse were more likely to later display abusive behavior. The results of the study support the theory that modeling may be an important determinant of these behaviors.[10] Athletes may simply be imitating or patterning their behaviors from prior experiences in the home, or possibly the aggression on the playing field.

Although some maintain that athletes appear to commit more crimes than non-athletes because of the heightened media attention given to crimes committed by athletes because of their status, there are also the crimes that we do not hear about. Preferential treatment is given to athletes by all involved in the college community. This treatment some-times results in criminal charges "going away" before they reach the pub-lic to protect the athlete, coach, and college. The athlete, coach, and college all benefit if charges can stay out of the newspaper. This treatment does not benefit the victims. However, money and community pressure can sometimes make victims think twice about going public with accusa-tions against an athlete. A Des Moines attorney who has represented ath-letes at the University of Iowa says: "My real successes are the ones you never hear about. In my view, I've already lost once something gets into the newspaper." The University of Iowa was in the news when in 2002, an Iowa City couple with ties to the men's basketball team tried to per-suade a victim in an alleged sexual assault involving basketball star Pierre Pierce to resolve the matter quietly outside of the legal system. Pierce was eventually kicked off the team and served 11 months in prison for an unrelated third-degree burglary, assault with intent to commit sexual abuse, false imprisonment, and fourth-degree criminal mischief in 2005. Expert legal assistance, often provided pro bono to star athletes and some-thing typically not available to the average student/victim, also tilts the power to the athlete.[11]

Many college athletes are privileged with scholarships, make-work jobs, tutoring, and plenty of attention from alumni and the media; this status often distorts or prevents realistic daily relationships with other people, most notably women. Added to this special status and privileged life, many sports have become increasingly aggressive, so much so that violence may be seen as an occupational hazard for many college athletes (and high school and professional as well).[12] Athletes can develop unrealistic views of themselves that are encouraged and reinforced when everyone around them from friends to fans and the media treat them as special. For many players, this sense of being special is central to their identity and strongly influences their expectations from people and their treatment of others. Although they may be special as athletes, many athletes have trouble relin-quishing this image in their daily life. Their personal interactions are of-ten colored by this inflated view of themselves. It requires great emotional maturity to maintain relationships based on equality and reciprocity when you are surrounded by people eager to participate in your every need.[13] In *Sports Heroes Fallen Idols: How Star Athletes Pursue Self-Destructive Paths and Jeopardize Their Careers,* Teitelbaum states:

> When you are among the high-flying adored, your view of the world becomes blurred. Off the field, some act as if they are above the rules of society; hubris and an attitude of entitlement ("I can do whatever I want") become central

to the psyche of many athletes. They may deny that they are vulnerable to reprisals and feel omnipotent and grandiose as well as entitled.[14]

And these feelings will only increase as a college athlete moves into the professional ranks.

CRIME ON CAMPUS—THE RESEARCH

The title of an article in *Sports Illustrated* reads, "An American Disgrace: A Violent and Unprecedented Lawlessness Has Arisen among College Athletes in All Parts of the Country." The article begins, "As the stories about Oklahoma and Colorado on the following pages suggest, today's university kids—the athletes among them, anyway—are more likely to stand accused of rape, assault, break-ins and drug trafficking than they are of Joe College pranks."[15] The amazing thing about this story is that it is from 1989. Crime among college athletes became a major issue for college administrators, coaches, and the media two decades ago as stories of violent crimes committed by athletes on college campuses began to fill the sports pages. It is increasingly common for big time college football or basketball programs to feature players who have been convicted of violent crimes. Even more disheartening is the leniency that colleges show toward their top athletes' crimes or backgrounds but do not afford to the average student. This is not surprising since top athletes are given special treatment by the school throughout their collegiate athletic career, beginning most notably in the admissions process where athletes are held to different standards both academically and criminally.

Crime by student athletes is becoming an increasing concern as evidenced by California's passage of a bill (in 2006) that prohibits athletes in California public colleges and community colleges from participating as members of any intercollegiate team, or in any intercollegiate athletic event, if the athlete is convicted of certain specified crimes, until after completing the entire term of his or her probationary period or successfully completing his or her entire assigned prison term and parole period.[16] Some universities automatically suspend from competition an athlete charged with a serious crime. Others wait for court rulings. The idea that this bill is even necessary shows the depth of the problem in college athletics.

Chapter 1 examined the research on how high school athletic participation affects criminal behavior. Now we will consider if the effects are different for college athletic participation. There have been no studies (according to my research) that have looked at criminal behavior in general for college athletes versus non-athletes. There are studies that compare college student-athletes and non-athletes with specific crimes like sexual assault, assault, drug use, and drunk driving. There are also indications that antisocial and maladaptive behavior patterns (gambling, drinking, and drug use) among athletes emerge by the time the player reaches the college level. In a study comparing college student athletes with non-student athletes, psychologist Stephen Weis found that athletes scored significantly higher on a maladaptive behavior scale than the non-athletes.[17]

Anecdotally, the news media is filled with crimes perpetrated by college athletes. However, the question remains whether we are more likely to hear about an athlete's crime than crimes by the average college student. For example, a yearlong study of online newspaper stories about intercollegiate athletics in the Big Ten Conference found a small number of stories about negative off-field incidents were often repeated among news organizations, creating a negative perception of student-athletes and their actions that was incorrect.[18] This is certainly a problem in this media world, where a single story can dominate the headlines for weeks on end (for example, the Duke lacrosse team case). But can this media saturation of certain stories explain away the numerous stories of college athletes' transgressions?

Although not a scientific study, ESPN did an analysis of Pennsylvania court records and reports from 2002 to 2008 and found that 46 Penn State football players faced 163 criminal charges. Twenty-seven players were convicted of, or have pled guilty to, a combined 45 counts. In 2007 alone, there were 17 players involved with 72 different crime charges, with nine convictions.[19] For example, beginning with an April 2007 fight which led to several arrests—but resulted in just two pleaded-down assault convictions—Penn State players have been connected to a series of run-ins with the law. In addition to numerous underage drinking citations and a driving under the influence (DUI) charge, there was another fight involving several players, a rape charge against a player that was later dropped, and an assault charge after a player pulled a knife on a teammate.[20]

Additionally, these statistics do not include those of LaVon Chisley, a former Penn State defensive end, who was kicked out of school in 2005 for poor grades, and was convicted of first degree murder in 2007. Chisley stabbed 26-year-old Penn State senior Langston Carraway 93 times in June 2006.[21] Unfortunately, Penn State's football program is not alone (or unusual) with its criminal problems.

In 2003, the Baylor University basketball team was thrust into the national spotlight for all the wrong reasons. Basketball player Carlton Dotson murdered his former teammate and roommate Patrick Dennehy. Dotson and Dennehy went to a deserted gravel pit to shoot their guns when Dotson shot Dennehy twice. Dennehy was not found for six weeks as Dotson fled to his home in Maryland. A few days before the body was found, Dotson was arrested in his home state of Maryland after calling authorities saying he was hearing voices and needed help. Dotson confessed to killing Dennehy but claimed he acted in self-defense. In 2004, Dotson was ruled incompetent to stand trial and was sent to a state mental hospital. However, a psychiatrist there said Dotson appeared to be faking some of his symptoms and a trial date was set.[22] The murder was just the beginning of the ugliness at Baylor as investigations into the crime led to the discovery that the coach of the basketball team, Dave Bliss, had used money from boosters to pay the tuitions of Dennehy and another player (demonstrating the type of preferential treatment star athletes receive in college). Bliss then encouraged his coaches and the team to lie to investigators about Patrick Dennehy, telling them to tell investigators that he acquired the money for school by dealing drugs. Bliss was recorded secretly on tape by one of his assistants encouraging them to lie. Dotson, after fighting extradition from Maryland, was eventually returned to Texas to stand trial. However, before the trial began, Dotson pled guilty to the murder and was sentenced to 35 years in prison. Bliss and the athletic director were forced to resign and the NCAA placed the team on probation for five years.

Baylor University was just one of many colleges facing increasing media attention and scrutiny regarding their athletes' criminal behavior. Each incident that hits the news is followed by the question of whether athletes are more likely to be involved in crime than non-athletes. Some research has looked at specific types of criminal behavior and college athletes. The research on drug use shows that male student athletes are at higher risk for heavy drinking, drunk driving, and performance-enhancing drug use.[23] However, athletes' increased drug use doesn't seem to be universal, as research shows that marijuana use is greater in non-athletes than athletes (lifetime use seems to be equivalent).[24] Studies also find that athletes binge drink and get drunk more often than non-athletes. These behaviors might be explained in part by the athletes' riskier personalities and greater sensation seeking.[25] Additionally, the dual role of athlete and student, which brings with it greater time demands, responsibilities, and expectations, may increase stress levels, which has been associated with drinking.

Other studies have demonstrated a higher rate of violence against those of the same sex and sexual assaults on those of the opposite sex.[26] One study found that while athletes comprised only 2% of the campus population, they were implicated in 20% of reported cases of sexual assaults or attempted sexual assaults, 14% of cases of sexual abuse, and 11% of battery cases including coercion and intimidation.[27] This increased risk of criminal behavior by Division I athletes may be the result, in part, of their background. Many athletes come from environments that are much different than the rest of their classmates. This is illustrated by looking at the most cited reasons for high school athletes skipping college and entering the NBA: financial hardship and desire to remove their single mothers from unsafe neighborhoods.[28] These players under NBA regulations now have to attend college for at least one year. Many of the top athletes come from backgrounds in which they are exposed to violence or abuse, either in their own homes or neighborhoods.[29] In addition, many athletes do not have the same financial backing and academic skills as their classmates, which only creates more problems for athletes trying to fit in on campus. The financial problems are magnified by NCAA regulations, which prohibit student-athletes from working during the school year.

Student-athletes' graduation rate is something that has been examined quite extensively over the last decade with increased attention on the distinction between student-athletes and the student body at Division I schools. The federal graduation rate, which is calculated by looking at the percentage of students who graduate within six years of enrolling at the school, for Division I student-athletes who started college in 2001 was 64%. This was the highest rate ever for student-athletes and was two points higher than the non-student athletes. However, the rate varies depending on the sport with men's basketball graduating at 49% and football at 56%, while women's gymnastics graduated 85%. The federal graduation rate for Division II athletes was 55%.[30] In 2005, the NCAA created its own measure called the Graduation Success Rate (GSR), which does not penalize student-athletes who transfer to another college, to assess a school's success with student-athletes' academics. The NCAA has become increasingly aggressive with mandatory graduation rates for schools with the threat of lost scholarships for failing to meet graduation requirements. These requirements by the NCAA are an attempt to reinforce the idea that the athletes are there not just to play sports, but also to receive an education. Additionally, the colleges are giving something back to the players, a degree, instead of just using them as money-makers for the school.

HIGH PROFILE EXAMPLE: MAURICE CLARETT

Maurice Clarett scored the winning touchdown for Ohio State in the national championship game in 2002. He was a freshman sensation for scoring touchdowns but everything else that happened to him is all too common for big time college football. Clarett was involved in a scandal involving academics, boosters, and crime that culminated in his imprisonment in 2006.

Clarett was raised in Youngstown, Ohio, where he was an All-American high school football player. In his freshman year at Ohio State University he set the freshman rushing record and scored 18 touchdowns, leading the Buckeyes to a 14-0 record and a national title. In July 2003, *The New York Times* reported the claims of a former Ohio State teaching assistant, who said that Clarett received preferential treatment in a class when he was allowed to take an oral final exam. The investigation into these claims did not find sufficient evidence of academic misconduct.[31] However, Clarett was suspended before the 2003 season for lying on a police report about the theft of cash, clothing, and stereo equipment from a car. He claimed that more than $10,000 in items and cash were stolen from a vehicle he borrowed from a Columbus, Ohio car dealership. He later pled guilty to a lesser charge.[32]

After his sophomore season Clarett dropped out of Ohio State to pursue a career in the National Football League (NFL). The only problem was that the NFL requires players to be at least three years out of high school before they are eligible for the draft. Clarett (along with University of Southern California's Mike Williams) challenged the NFL's age policy. They initially won a federal ruling that the NFL could not bar them from participating in the 2004 NFL Draft. This decision was later overturned by the United States Court of Appeals, and Clarett's appeal was refused by the Supreme Court. The NCAA refused to reinstate Clarett's and Williams' college eligibility. After not playing in the 2004 season, he was then eligible for the 2005 draft. He was selected by the Denver Broncos in the third round. However, after not playing for two full seasons and being noticeably out of shape, he was cut during training camp.

On January 1, 2006, Clarett was arrested for brandishing a gun outside a Columbus bar and demanding money and cell phones from two people. Clarett turned himself into police on January 2 and faced two counts of aggravated robbery. While out on bail awaiting his trial, Clarett was pulled over for driving erratically. When police approached the car they found him sitting on a 9-millimeter handgun, with an assault rifle lying across the front passenger seat, a handgun in front of that seat, and another handgun in a backpack.[33] When Clarett resisted arrest, the police used a taser on him but it was ineffective due to the bulletproof vest he was wearing. The police were forced to use Mace® to subdue him. Clarett was driving near the house of one of the witnesses set to testify against him in his upcoming robbery trial. Clarett pled guilty to aggravated robbery and carrying a concealed weapon (the gun he was sitting on during his second arrest) and was sentenced to seven and a half years in prison. He is eligible for parole after three and a half years.[34]

Clarett's case illustrates many of the problems with big time college athletics. Clarett grew up in rough Youngstown neighborhoods where drug dealing and shootings were frequent. Clarett has said that he has attended funerals of almost a dozen close friends.[35] When asked about Clarett after his second arrest, Andy Geiger, the Ohio State University Athletic Director during Clarett's freshman year, said, "Do we bear responsibility? Maybe, because we took him in the first place. If we're guilty of something that is borderline corrupt, it's sometimes bringing people into the community that don't really fit. I would plead guilty to that." Geiger was forced to resign after NCAA investigations into the university's football and basketball programs.

Additionally, those who knew Clarett said that he had a strong sense of entitlement. According to the teaching assistant who accused Clarett and his professor of academic misconduct, when Clarett was informed that he was doing poorly in class and needed to work harder, Clarett responded: "Why don't you take care of me?" His former high school football coach, Thom McDaniels, believes that part of Clarett's problem is that he experienced too much fame, too quickly. McDaniel said: "When you're young, and you're famous, and you reach a certain level of celebrity status, if you're not careful, you might believe you're more important than you actually are."[36] This sense of privilege and entitlement can be seen in his receiving free gifts from boosters, most notably the car he was driving which was broken into. Freshmen at Ohio State are required to live in dormitories; Clarett enrolled a semester early at Ohio State after finishing high school early. After living a short time in the dorms, he demanded to live off-campus, which Ohio State allowed. This was the beginning of Clarett seeing that the rules did not apply to him because of what a great athlete he was. Clarett's father saw this as the beginning of the end for Clarett:

> They made a major mistake by letting him enroll early. When the season started and he exploded, he was on every talk show. He was treated like a rock star. That really distorts a person's personality because everywhere you go people want to do favors for you.[37]

Clarett was not shy about accepting the favors. Part of the reason for his suspension before his sophomore year was because the NCAA started to investigate him for accepting gifts from a hometown associate. Clarett had received $500 in cash and allowed thousands of dollars in cell phone bills to be paid for by Bobby Dellimuti, a caterer who also gambled regularly on football.[38] A rough background, celebrity-like status, a sense of entitlement, and a lack of accountability for his behavior lead to the downfall of this talented football player.

SEXUAL ASSAULTS AND ATHLETES

> If one combines this early reinforcement of physical dominance with the ongoing contempt for girls and women, one can see how the end product for some of the more angry or disturbed players is rape.[39]

College campuses are one of the most dangerous places in terms of sexual assault. Research shows that as many as a quarter of college women have been sexually assaulted during the course of their college career.[40] Athletes have received their fair share of the blame for the number of sexual assaults on campuses across the country. There are two schools of thought on athletes and sexual assaults: one suggests that athletes are no more likely than non-athletes to commit sexual assaults (or any crime for that matter). Rather they are more likely to receive media attention, creating a distorted perception of their criminal behavior. Others contend that athletes, in part because of their backgrounds, aggressive nature, and a sense of entitlement are more likely to commit sexual assaults.

Many athletic teams have faced rape allegations. Some, like the Duke University lacrosse team, turn out to be false, while other schools have not been so fortunate. The University of Colorado football team came under scrutiny with multiple allegations of sexual assault: between 1997 and 2008 at least ten women came forward with charges. In December 2001, three women said they were raped during a football recruiting weekend. Formal criminal charges were not filed because of lack of evidence. However, four players pled guilty to charges of giving alcohol to minors. In February 2003 it was revealed that a member of the athletic department used an escort service during high school recruiting trips. These stories demonstrate the lack of accountability that players are shown by coaches and the athletic department. Additionally, the players' behavior can be expected when the people in charge are not setting a good example.

Then in 2004, Kate Hnida, a former place kicker for the team, revealed that she was sexually harassed and raped by a teammate in 2000. The football coach, Gary Barnett, responded that, "Well, Katie was a girl. And not only was she a girl but she is terrible." The following day, the police released a report in which another woman, who worked for the athletic department, claimed she was raped by members of the football team in 2001. After the woman told Coach Barnett about the rape, the coach has been quoted as saying he "would back his player 100 percent if she took this forward in the criminal process." This quote once again demonstrates the lack of accountability and preferential treatment athletes are given in revenue-producing sports. In 2005, two of the alleged rape victims sued the University of Colorado, claiming the university was "deliberately indifferent" to the risk that players and recruits posed to the student body. U.S. District Judge Blackburn dismissed the case, but his ruling was overturned, sending the case to trial.[41] The Colorado case demonstrates how ingrained sexist attitudes are in many sports teams and also the lengths that coaches will go to back their players.

Although there have not been many studies on college athletes and crime in general, there has been much research on sexual assaults on college campuses. Research has consistently shown that members of athletic teams are more likely to engage in group sexual assaults than non-student athletes (this is also true of members of fraternities and the military).[42] Other research has looked at whether individual college athletes are more likely to commit sexual assaults. Two studies are of particular note.

The Crosset, Benedict, and McDonald study examined college athletic participation at Division I institutions and reported sexual assaults. They evaluated judicial affair data for perennial Top 20 basketball or football teams. For the three years of judicial affairs data that they examined, male student-athletes represented 3.3% of the total male population at the colleges yet represented 19% of the reported perpetrators of sexual assaults. Furthermore, male basketball and football players made up 30% of the student-athlete population but were responsible for 67% of the reported sexual assaults.[43]

This disparity between sports teams is particularly important and addressed in the Humphrey and Kahn study. They examined both athletic and fraternity memberships' connection with rape. What is important about their study is that they did not simply look at whether someone was an athlete or not, rather they looked to identify the culture of each team. For example, one sports team may have a culture that fosters attitudes or behaviors that lead to violence against women while other teams' cultures may not. The members of teams identified by students as high-risk were more likely to report committing sexual aggression, having hostility toward women, and having peer support for sexual assaults than athletes on teams identified as low-risk (and the non-student athletes). There was no difference in any of the measures of sexual aggression between the members of the low-risk sports teams and the non-student athletes.[44] Not all sports teams are the same; they may have different cultures and effects on behavior. Research that looks at sports participation versus non-sports participation is not adequate; it is necessary to look at not only what sports team (football versus golf), but the culture of that particular team.

The research has also demonstrated that any effects from athletic participation vary widely by sport, with football and basketball demonstrating the strongest connections. The relationship between sports and violence against women doesn't seem to extend to sports like golf and tennis. Additionally, different teams or schools have different cultures surrounding their sporting teams. For example among colleges, the relationship between sports and violence seems to be stronger at large Division I schools and less at smaller Division II or III schools where athletes are more commonly integrated into the student body. And even within the Division I ranks, not all basketball or football teams are the same. Some schools consistently see criminal problems with their athletes while other schools rarely, if ever, have to deal with crimes committed by their players. This can be explained in part by the types of athletes that schools recruit, with some schools being more forgiving in terms of a player's criminal history and academic background. In addition, the culture of the team is also affected by the coach's leadership and discipline, oversight by the school administration, the involvement of college boosters, and the presence of campus police and local law enforcement. All of this can either make an environment where athletes see themselves as separate from other students and having free reign of the campus or an environment where athletes see themselves as part of the campus community with respect for other students and the law. For example, colleges and universities have found that when male athletes are segregated into special dorms away from women and non-athletes, violence, damage to buildings, and disciplinary action can follow. The NCAA outlawed team dormitories beginning in 1996.[45] This regulation points to the importance of peer groups on the athletes' behavior. Separate dorms for athletes would only reinforce the "special" status of athletes and reinforce the culture (positive or negative) of the team.

Other explanations for the higher rate of sexual assaults by athletes typically center on the aggressive nature of sports, excessive focus on masculinity or degradation of anything feminine, sexist attitudes among athletes typified by the stereotypical "locker room" conversations, many athletes coming from abusive/neglected backgrounds, and alcohol/drug (steroid) use. Although the actual participation in sports does not cause men to assault women, it can help to incite such behaviors in those athletes who are predisposed toward such acts. And certainly the culture of male athletics (using sexist locker room dialogue, rewarding aggressiveness, legitimizing violence) helps to sustain negative attitudes toward women.[46]

Just as important is what takes place away from the field, where athletes are treated like celebrities by the school, fans, classmates, alumni, and law enforcement. This opens athletes to opportunities with women that are not available to the average student. Additionally, alcohol is often a key component in many sexual assaults and as previously noted, athletes have been found to drink alcohol more frequently than non-athletes. Their increased sexual opportunities can become abusive when the athlete generalizes access to all women but then the privilege is denied by an unwilling participant. These opportunities off the field and their status as celebrities are more important in trying to explain the impact of athletic participation on criminal behavior than anything that takes place in the context of the sports team.

Some still contend that athletes do not commit sexual assaults at higher rates but rather are targeted (for example, Duke University lacrosse team) because of their high profile status. However, studies do not support this contention since even studies that use self-report data show athletes with higher levels of physical and sexual abuse. For example, one study found that athletes had higher levels of self-reported physical and sexual abuse yet none of the athletes in the sample had been publicly accused of abuse.[47]

Victims of sexual abuse by athletes and criminal prosecutors have further asserted that athletes' status on campus and with the public makes it exceptionally difficult to convict them of crime.[48] According to a 2003 *USA Today* investigation of 168 sexual-assault allegations involving professional or NCAA Division I athletes, only 22 cases even went to trial, with six resulting in a conviction. In 46 of the cases, a plea agreement was reached, which brings the total conviction rate in resolved cases to 32%, well below the national average in rape cases of 52%.[49] Therefore, athletes are getting off at a much greater rate than non-athletes, even though studies demonstrate they are committing more sexual assaults.

Athletes, because of their status and the fact that they generate money for college and pro teams, have a better chance of acquittal or lighter sentences than other men accused of violent crimes against women. For many, the more popular and powerful you are, the less likely the victim will be believed. Although the media may make the problem look worse than it is, there is evidence to suggest that due to the aggressive nature of some sports, there should be concern regarding athletes. Some athletes are not able to "turn off" the aggression off the field. This theory is supported by studies of police and military personnel, who also have a high incidence of committing violence toward women. This is compounded by the fact that because of athletes' social status they, in many cases, have more opportunities with women, which only increases the chance for problems.[50]

High Profile Example: Chris Collins
(Oklahoma State University Football Player)

Chris Collins, a 17-year-old junior football player at Texas High School in Texarkana was arrested and charged with sexually assaulting an intoxicated 12-year-old girl at an after-prom party in a hotel in May 2004. Two other men also were charged in the assault. Collins pled not guilty in March 2005 after being indicted in December 2004. He admitted to having sex with the girl at a hotel and also to having sex with her a week earlier (which the girl denied) but said that she told him that she was 16 years old (which the girl denied). With the charges still pending, Collins was suspended from the football team for his senior year and a scholarship offer from the University of Texas was rescinded. However, Oklahoma State University offered Collins a scholarship where, during his freshman year, he was the Cowboys' second leading tackler before a knee injury ended his season in the sixth game.

As a sophomore, Collins had 31 tackles through the first four games. Then one day before his trial was to begin, Collins pled guilty to a felony charge of aggravated sexual assault. After the jury initially recommended that his sentence be served through probation, the judge sentenced him to five years in prison.[51] Initially, Oklahoma State's athletic director said the school was uncertain whether Collins would play in their upcoming game, but the next day they announced that they decided to suspend him for the rest of the season. Finally, six days after the sentence, Oklahoma State permanently dismissed Collins from the football team (he was allowed to keep his scholarship). Gary Shutt, Oklahoma State University director of communications, was asked whether the school was aware of the charges when they recruited Collins, he said: "Well there's some things we were aware of but some things we weren't. There's sealed documents for lack of a better term, information that we didn't get. But we had a lot of information and we were willing to take a second chance on a young man."[52] Collins' sentence was later reduced to 10 months probation.

The Collins story demonstrates a number of problems with big time college sports today. The most basic one is the "win at any cost" motto, in which winning is now tied to millions of dollars in revenue. The amount of money involved in college athletics has pushed some colleges to look past criminal behavior and character issues among their recruits and players. In the past, it was common for schools to look the other way in regard to academic issues. The increased money has also led to more pressure on college coaches to win now. That is why it is also common for coaches to stand behind their players when they run into trouble, not to mention the "all for one, one for all" mantra that many coaches teach their players. Additionally, the coaches typically justify their support of their athletes by stating that they are trying to help the players build a better life. They argue that turning their back on the players when they get in trouble would not help anyone, particularly the athlete's future. However, by continually overlooking their players' misdeeds (either committed before they came to college or while at college), they help perpetuate repeat offending by not holding the player accountable for their actions. Athletes, in many cases, never face any consequences for their "bad" behavior whether it is in class, where many times they are passed along without doing the work, or off the field where their criminal behavior is downplayed, ignored, and made to go away by coaches and administrators.

Collins was given a second chance by Oklahoma State with the offer of a full scholarship, something that a student who could not play football like he could would have never received. Regarding the decision to recruit Collins, Oklahoma State University football coach Mike Gundy acknowledged the possibility that Collins would go to trial, but had confidence in the background check they had undertaken.

> The people that had dealt with him throughout his life said he made a terrible mistake, but he was not a bad person. Because of that, I made the decision to bring him in here. And since he's been here, he's been very good.[53]

Giving a young man a second chance is an honorable intention; however, the reality is that these opportunities only come because of Collins' size, speed, and ability to tackle another football player. More and more colleges are wrestling with the issue of whether to afford second and even third and fourth chances to talented student-athletes when they can help the school win on the playing field and at the bank.

CONCLUSION

College campuses become communities unto themselves, a bigger version of the high school world from which athletes already began to reap the benefits of being a star athlete. The college campus also brings greater freedom as students move toward being adults. With this freedom typically comes increased experimentation with alcohol, drugs, and sex. This combination is one of the reasons why college campuses have one of the highest rates of sexual assaults. Athletes on many campuses are treated like celebrities, separate from other students. This status often results in preferential treatment and increased sexual opportunities. This alone would not necessarily lead to problems. However, add in the continuing lack of accountability toward the athletes' behavior, the continued reinforcement of aggression on the playing field, and the expectation that everyone wants to be with you and the result is that college athletes, not surprisingly, engage in sexual assaults more often than other students.

The professionalization of certain college sports (football and basketball most notably) only exacerbates many of the problems with college athletes. The pedestal on which college athletes are placed continues to be raised higher and higher as the amount of attention and money involved in these sports grows. This raises the stakes for the college to make sure that the students avoid trouble academically and criminally. In *Out of Bounds: Inside the NBA's Culture of Rape, Violence and Crime,* Benedict argues that:

> Institutions of higher learning are not bottom line driven business enterprises whose mission is merely to entertain (at least they are not supposed to be). And they do have a responsibility to train and educate young minds to address and improve the world's social ills and problems. They certainly should not be in league with a system that shepherds gifted yet criminally troubled and academically inept athletes through schools, only so they can remain eligible long enough to make their way into the NBA draft. Of course, not all players coming out of college and entering NBA are criminals or academically deficient. But the ones who end up in handcuffs as pros often are.[54]

Unfortunately, the amount of pressure on the schools to succeed has led them to lower their admission requirements (regarding character and academics) of those they bring on campus and increasingly protect and provide for the athletes once they are there. This does the athletes a great disservice—one that follows them even if they become a professional.

Chapter 3

PROFESSIONAL ATHLETES AND CRIME

Sports kept me off the streets. . . . It kept me from getting into what was going on, the bad stuff. Lots of guys I knew have had bad problems.

Michael Vick, 2001[1]

The first week of December 2008, New York Giants wide receiver Plaxico Burress was arrested for accidentally shooting himself in a night club in New York City. He did not have a permit to carry the weapon in New York. The same week, O.J. Simpson made national headlines when he was sentenced for kidnapping charges stemming from a botched robbery of sports memorabilia in Las Vegas. As if these incidents were not bad enough for the sports world, Carolina Panthers Jeremey Bridges was arrested and charged with two counts of simple assault and battery and one count of communicating threats. This was Bridges' second arrest in 16 months. The first came when he was charged with pointing a gun at a woman outside a strip club; he was later convicted of a misdemeanor assault charge.[2] Additionally, six NFL players were suspended that week for testing positive for a diuretic that can be used as a masking agent for steroids. Unfortunately for sports fans, these weeks have become all too common.

The professional sports world has been hit hard by criminal stories over the last few years. The sports page has looked more like the crime blotter with Kobe Bryant (2004), Barry Bonds (2006), and Michael Vick (2007) dominating the sports headlines. Unfortunately for all three, the stories had to deal with their criminal behavior. Michael Vick's dog fighting charges, Barry Bonds' association with steroids and subsequent federal charges for perjury, and Kobe Bryant's rape charge became the focus of the sports world. This chapter will examine the world of professional athletics and its growing connection with crime. The sense of superiority (elite deviance) that comes with the money and fame of being a professional athlete will be examined. Specific attention will be given to steroid use and crimes against women. Examples from Major League Baseball, the NBA, and the NFL will be presented.

The problem of criminal behavior among professional athletes is in many ways simply an extension of the problem of college athletes. Take for example running back Laurence Phillips. Phillips was living in a foster home in California when he was recruited by the University of Nebraska. He played running back for the Cornhuskers, where during his junior year, he was arrested for assaulting his ex-girlfriend. He dragged her down a flight of stairs by her hair and shirt and repeatedly banged her head into a mailbox. She had to be taken to the hospital where she received stitches on her head. Despite the severity of the attack, Coach Tom Osbourne did not kick him off the team but suspended him for six games. Phillips played in the final three games of the season. He finished the season by leading Nebraska to a win in the 1996 Fiesta Bowl and national title, where he ran for 165 yards and three touchdowns.

When he decided to leave college a year early, his past did not discourage an NFL team from paying him millions of dollars. The St. Louis Rams picked him sixth overall in the 1996 NFL draft. While with the Rams for less than two seasons, he was arrested three times, served a jail sentence for domestic violence and was sued by two different women, one for domestic violence and the other for sexual assault.[3] He was finally cut by the St. Louis Rams after he was reportedly fined 56 times for violating team rules. However, within a week the Miami Dolphins signed Phillips to a contract. He played just two games for the Dolphins before they cut him. Even though he was only with the Dolphins briefly, he was charged with assaulting a woman at a night club, to which he eventually pled no contest. After the Dolphins, Phillips played for NFL Europe then had short stints with the San Francisco 49ers, the Canadian football league, and the arena football league. If you are a talented player, there will always be a team willing to look past criminal behavior. This does nothing to discourage the player from breaking the law.

Professional athletes are the cream of the crop of athletic ability and are some of society's most recognizable people. The fact that many of them are involved in criminal behavior should not be surprising given the nature of their profession and the privileged lives they live. Many professional sports rely on aggression and players who display a level of violence that is not welcome in most job fields, so it is not surprising that many athletes have a propensity for aggression and violence off the field as well, especially when their behavior is rarely punished. Their fame and wealth also insulates them from adherence to social norms, luring athletes to indulge in illicit behavior and enabling popular athletes to routinely escape accountability. The public has been more than willing to overlook the criminal behavior of athletes. Fans, in general, have not walked away from their team or sport because of the increasing criminal behavior perpetuated by the players. The public looks to sports as an escape and it is not willing to surrender this escape because of the behavior of the players.

CRIMINOLOGY THEORY: PROFESSIONAL ATHLETES AND CRIMINAL BEHAVIOR

I think our society's worship of elite athletes, because we coddle and fawn over them, in some ways we've created antisocial beings who believe their needs come first.

> Merrill J. Melnick, a sports sociologist at the State
> University of New York at Brockport[4]

Many criminal theories would not be applicable to professional athletes because of their class status. The problem with many criminal theories is the underlying assumption that crime is more likely to occur in the lower classes. In 2007, the minimum salary was $285,000 for NFL players; in 2009, the NBA minimum salary was $457,588.[5] The average salary in the NFL in 2009 was roughly $770,000.[6] During the 2007–2008 year, the average NBA salary was $5.356 million. Professional athletes present a contradiction in that they have a high income yet many came from lower class backgrounds.

Theories that focus on crimes committed by members of the upper class or the wealthy typically focus on white-collar crimes like embezzlement or fraud. Criminologist Edwin H. Sutherland defined white-collar crime as violations of the law "committed by a person of respectability and high social status in the course of his occupation."[7] He claimed that many people fail to recognize that people in high standing in society often commit crimes but are not recognized as much by members of society or the courts. Sutherland said that:

> My thesis is that the traditional/conception(s) and explanations of crime (are) misleading and incorrect; that crime is in fact not closely correlated with poverty or with the psychopathic and sociopathic conditions associated with poverty, and that an adequate explanation of criminal behavior must proceed along quite different lines. The conventional explanations are invalid principally because they are derived from biased samples. The samples are biased in that they have not included vast areas of criminal behavior of persons not in the lower class.[8]

Now Sutherland, who was writing in the 1930s and 1940s, was referring to members of the upper class working, for example, in the oil industry, stock exchange, and politics. But Sutherland did note, as would apply to professional athletes, white-collar criminals are far less likely to be investigated, arrested, or prosecuted than are other types of offenders. When they are, on rare occasions, convicted, white-collar criminals are far less likely to receive active prison terms than are "common criminals." The sentences they receive are likely to be shorter as well because of their social standing. In many cases, white-collar criminals are well respected in their communities. More and more in criminology, white-collar crime has focused on the type of offense being committed rather than the occupation or social standing of the offender. There is very little research on violent or street crimes committed by the wealthy.[9] Typically, the focus on class structure and crimes leads to the conclusion that class structure gives rise to different types of criminality. This is where professional athletes do not fit in, they are wealthy and yet, in many cases, commit violent and gun-related crimes. I use the term *wealthy* deliberately, rather than upper class. The notion of class includes more than simply income.

Additionally, theories involving elite deviance have traditionally been restricted to the activities of persons and organizations of the highest social status, involved in the systematic exploitation of the powerless by economic domination, denial of human rights, and crimes of governmental control. It causes vast amounts of injury, has incalculable monetary costs, and undermines public trust in political and economic institutions. The notion of "elite deviance" typically centers on crimes committed by companies or chief executive officers (CEOs)[10] rather than simply people with high incomes like professional athletes.

Criminologists Hirschi and Gottfredson, who attempted to come up with a "general theory of crime," wrote that: "we outline a general theory of crime capable of organizing the facts about white-collar crime at the same time it is capable of organizing the facts about all forms of crime."[11] They state that white-collar criminals are motivated by the same forces that drive other criminals: self-interest, the pursuit of pleasure, and the avoidance of pain. Part of their theory asserts that a single mechanism: low self-control, accounts for all crimes. Self-control is the degree to which a person is vulnerable to temptations of the moment. They argue that it is acquired early in life and is the number one factor of individual level criminal behavior. Self-control develops by the end of childhood and is fostered through parental emotional investment in the child, which includes monitoring the child's behavior, recognizing deviance when it occurs, and punishing the child. They suggest that some people have a lasting tendency to ignore the long-term consequences of their behavior, that such people tend to be impulsive, reckless, and self-centered, and that crime is often the end result of such tendencies.[12] While self-control is an important condition, this denies that structural or situational factors also affect a person's propensity to commit crime.

Building on their work, future studies have identified characteristics of people with low self-control. Some of the findings are that risk-seeking is an important determinant of self-control and that people with little self-control are drawn to activities that are adventurous and exciting. These people prefer physical activity over contemplation or conversation and tend to be indifferent or insensitive to the needs of others. Although they may not necessarily be antisocial or malicious, they are predisposed to being self-centered, have low frustration tolerance, and are inclined to handle conflict through confrontation.[13] This corresponds with the situation for many professional athletes. The term "terminal adolescence" has been used to describe the emotional state of many professional athletes. Because so many have been coddled since childhood, their emotional growth may be stunted. Self-centeredness, insensitivity to the needs of others, and a sense of invincibility which is typical of adolescence, are prominent in many professional athletes. When they are young, their peer group and teachers allow them to do what they want. Their status as jocks prevents them from normal social development. The athletes have rarely been held accountable for their behavior, which makes them unable to handle any problems, personal or professional, that may arise.[14] In many cases the athletes never grow up because they never have to. They have been treated as objects and thus treat others as objects. Because they have never been held accountable, they have a more difficult time identifying society's boundaries.[15] Adding to their lack of self-control, many professional athletes display a narcissistic personality. They are self-absorbed, have an exaggerated sense of self-importance and entitlement, and show insensitivity to the needs and feelings of others.[16]

Many professional athletes are in the position of being well-known rich celebrities. However, this does not completely cover up the fact that many came from rough backgrounds. Many athletes were raised in crime-ridden inner cities, so while they may receive large pay checks, their roots, and in many cases friends, still have connections to their old neighborhoods. Many of the professional athletes discussed in the book (i.e., Michael Vick, who is discussed in the next section) have a hard time escaping the bad influences of their friends from the old neighborhood. This situation has been termed "ghetto loyalty,"[17] which is felt primarily among black athletes from poor backgrounds who feel an obligation to help their friends from home. As simple as it sounds, many professional athletes' problems stem from their reluctance or inability to escape the influence of their old friends. It is a difficult situation for many athletes who are suddenly multi-millionaires. They need people around them who they can trust, as most of us would, so they turn to their old friends. Yet, for many athletes their oldest friends still have ties to the old neighborhoods and the criminal element that comes with it. The problem with "ghetto loyalty" is that often the "friends" do not have the player's best interest in mind and may take advantage of the player's new-found wealth and celebrity status. Many of their neighborhood friends have not left their criminal behavior behind. However, these friends may be the only people that the player feels comfortable with and feels that he can trust. According to a *Sports Illustrated* article on Michael Vick,[18] there are four rea-sons why this loyalty is felt so strongly by the athlete. First, many of the play-ers from crime- and gang-ridden neighborhoods are given a "pass" when they are growing up; they are left alone because the community recognizes that they have a shot to be a star. However, this "pass" leads to a sense of indebt-edness for the player when they make it big. Also, for many of these athletes, these friends may have been the only people there for them since they were a child which creates strong bonds. There is also pressure to give back to the community and for the player not to forget where he came from. And finally, many of the players are fearful and may only feel safe when they surround themselves with people they have known for a long time.

At a professional level, athletes have away games and travel to other cities to play their matches, leaving their families at home. This is nothing earth-shattering; however, when you plug this into crime patterns you find that it has a significant effect. Spending periods of time apart may cause problems in the home environment which can have an effect on family cohesion and is a major issue with athletes' arrests. Breakups of marriage and instances of domestic violence can be the result of intense training and team obligations. This weakening of family ties and lack of a stable home where the entire family is together puts an elite athlete into a cohort that has some of the key characteristics indicative of a fatherless family. Of course the money and fame help with some issues, but it can also be a double-edged sword in terms of exposure and accessibility to the formal legal structure.[19]

Cultural spillover theory is very helpful in understanding the connec-tion between professional athletes and criminal behavior. The main idea behind cultural spillover theory is that the more any given culture (includ-ing a subculture) tends to endorse the use of violence to attain socially approved ends, the greater the likelihood that this "legitimate violence" will be generalized to other aspects of life where the use of violence is less socially approved.[20] Put differently, cultural support for the use of vio-lence in one area of life may "spill over" into other areas of life where its use may be inappropriate. An example of this theory in effect is previous research that has demonstrated that rates of domestic violence are higher among couples where at least one person is on active duty. The finding suggests that the violence that is taught and used in the military spills over into a soldier's other areas of life, with his or her spouse, where the violence is not appropriate.

The theory draws many of its ideas from subculture theory which states that the norms and values of the group that you belong to may differ from the wider society. In some violent subcultures there are support, rewards, and encouragement of violence, which makes violent behavior more likely. Some occupations, like police officers, can be viewed as subcultures where workers adhere to a set of norms and values that may be unique to the job. If you think of professional athletes and their occupation, the term "violent occupational subculture" could apply. Within their occupation, violence is seen as legitimate and rewarded. This legitimate use of violence in one aspect of the athlete's life may spill over into other aspects of their lives as well. As Bloom and Smith argue in their article about hockey players and violence:

> The legitimization-of-violence thesis suggests that hockey players who approve of violence that is generally considered acceptable within the context of the game, may also approve of more illegitimate violence in other social settings and behave accordingly.[21]

Cultural spillover theory builds on these ideas and suggests that the more a culture supports legitimate violence to attain its goals, the more illegitimate violence will occur in that society. So sports in which violence is encouraged and rewarded may see an increase of illegal violence among its participants. This theory holds promise for looking at criminal behavior among boxers, hockey players, football players, Ultimate Fighting Championship fighters, and other sports in which violence is an integral part of the game. A study by Bloom and Smith found that players from the more competitive Canadian hockey leagues were more likely to approve of violence and to act violently in non-sport settings than players in less competitive leagues and non-hockey players.[22] An article in *The Indiana Law Journal* suggests that:

> The most commonly asserted arguments to explain the possible higher incidence of criminal activity among athletes are that athletes' disregard for rules, violence against women, and drug related activities result from a combination of factors: athletes are conditioned to believe that they are entitled to behave that way; athletic competition and their subculture of sports perpetuate drug use; and the subculture of men's sports devalues women and encourages violence.[23]

Even on the professional level, when dealing with men in their twenties, many of the explanations of criminal behavior among athletes deal with their peer group and subcultures that they belong to. These ideas are demonstrated most clearly with the case of former Atlanta Falcons quarterback Michael Vick.

HIGH PROFILE EXAMPLE: MICHAEL VICK

Michael Vick was an electrifying player from his first year as a quarterback at Virginia Tech University. In 1999, Vick, after being red-shirted his freshman year, lead Virginia Tech to an 11-1 record and became an instant sensation across the country. Vick continued to excel as a sophomore and following the end of the season decided to enter the NFL draft. Vick, whose family was still living in the housing project where he grew up, was taken with the number one overall pick by the Atlanta Falcons. As a rookie with the Falcons, Vick became one of the most talked about players in the league. His ability to run as a quarterback made him a unique talent. Vick became a Pro-Bowler in his second year, leading the Falcons to the playoffs. However, off-field problems started to surface for the young player. In November 2006, he was fined $10,000 by the league for making obscene gestures to the home fans while leaving the field. Then in January, Vick's water bottle was confiscated going through airport security when they found a "marijuana-like" substance in a hidden compartment in the bottle. Laboratory tests would later conclude that the substance was not marijuana and no charges were filed. These were minor events compared to the discovery of a dog fighting operation at one of Vick's Virginia homes in April 2007. A small complex of sheds used for training and fighting the dogs was discovered behind the main house where the police removed 54 dogs (when the police searched the house again in June, they discovered the remains of seven more dogs) along with a so-called rape stand used to hold dogs in place for mating, an electronic treadmill modified for dogs, and bloody carpeting.[24]

The operation, named "Bad Newz Kennels," was run by Vick along with Purnell Peace, Quanis Phillips, and Tony Taylor. Police discovered a series of dogfights in which the operation participated, including several fights in the fall of 2003 when Vick was sidelined with a broken leg. Vick was charged in July 2007. The indictment revealed that in April 2007 Vick, along with Peace and Phillips, "executed approximately eight dogs that did not perform well in 'testing' sessions by various methods, including hanging, drowning and/or slamming at least one dog's body to the ground."[25] They were charged with felony charges of conspiring to travel in interstate commerce in aid of unlawful activities and conspiring to sponsor a dog in an animal-fighting venture. After Vick's associates all reached plea agreements and agreed to testify against him, he reached his own agreement on August 24, 2007. He pled guilty to one felony count of conspiracy to operate an interstate dog fighting operation. Vick admitted to providing most of the financing for the operation, as well as participating directly in several dog fights in Virginia, Maryland, North Carolina, and South Carolina. He also admitted to sharing in the proceeds from these dog fights. Additionally, he acknowledged that he knew his associates killed several dogs that didn't perform well. However, he denied actually killing any dogs himself. While awaiting sentencing, Vick failed a drug test in September 2007 and was placed under house arrest until sentencing. He entered prison early to begin serving his time in order to be released earlier and hopefully resume his football career. In December 2007, he was sentenced to 23 months in prison, more than Peace, Phillips, and Taylor and also more than the 12 to 18 months prosecutors originally suggested as part of Vick's plea agreement. The lengthier sentence was handed down because the judge said Vick lied about the extent of his involvement with the operation.[26] On July 20, 2009, Vick was released after serving 18 months in prison and an additional two months in home confinement. A week after being released, he was conditionally reinstated by NFL commissioner Roger Godell. After being reinstated, he was signed by the Philadelphia Eagles on August 13, 2009, to a two-year contract (he was fully reinstated and played in Week 3 of the season).[27] Eagles coach Andy Reid, after saying "This is America—we do make mistakes," continued with, "I'm a believer that as long as people go through the right process, they deserve a second chance."[28] Eagles team president Joe Banner had similar sentiments on Vick: "It was very tough initially, but everybody we talked to said the same thing, that he was remorseful and that he had gone through an incredible transformation, that he was basically good at heart. We heard this over and over again from people who felt he deserved a second chance."

Michael Vick suffered from bad judgment throughout his career. He was never able to remove himself from his hometown. As soon as the football season was over, he would return to Newport News, Virginia, and hung out almost exclusively with his friends from childhood. Vick suffered from "ghetto loyalty" in that he was not able to escape the world and friends from where he grew up. Vick was interviewed on *60 Minutes* by James Brown days after signing with the Philadelphia Eagles. He was asked why he didn't stop the dog fighting operation:

"When I was in prison. I was disgusted, you know, because of what I let happen to those animals," Vick said. "I could've put a stop to it. I could've walked away from it. I could've shut the whole operation down."

"But you didn't. Why not?" Brown asked.

"But I didn't," Vick acknowledged.

Asked what kept him going, Vick told Brown, "Not being able to say, or tell certain people around me that, 'Look, we can't do this anymore. I'm concerned about my career. I'm concerned about my family'."

For many athletes, who have never really grown up, peer pressure and not wanting to look like they have "sold out" can still have a powerful effect on their behavior.

Vick grew up in Newport News, Virginia, with two sisters and a younger brother. His brother, also a football player, has had his own share of criminal problems. Marcus Vick followed his brother to Virginia Tech University to play quarterback. He was redshirted and did not play his freshman year in 2002; the following year he served as the back-up quarterback. Then as he was entering his third year at Virginia Tech he was suspended for the 2004 season after two off-field incidents. In May 2004, he was convicted of three counts of contributing to the delinquency of a minor. Vick, along with two teammates, had provided alcohol to 14- and 15-year-old girls. He was sentenced to 30 days in jail and fined. The second incident involved a July 3, 2004, traffic stop in which Vick eventually pled guilty to reckless driving and no contest to marijuana possession. He was fined $300, had his license suspended for 60 days, and was ordered to complete 24 hours of community service.[29] He was readmitted to the football program in January 2005. During the 2005 season, Vick was the quarterback who led Virginia Tech to an 11-2 record and a Gator Bowl victory. However, the Bowl victory did not go by without incident as Vick stomped on the leg of Elvis Dumervil, a Louisville defensive end. Vick was subsequently kicked out of Virginia Tech after school officials learned about another off-field incident for driving with a suspended or revoked driver's license and speeding; these were Vick's eighth and ninth traffic offenses since he enrolled at Virginia Tech in 2002. The president of the university stated that Vick was kicked off the team "due to a cumulative effect of legal infractions and unsportsmanlike play."[30]

After being dismissed from Virginia Tech, Marcus Vick declared himself eligible for the NFL draft. Days after his declaration, he was arrested in his hometown for waving a firearm at three teenagers during an altercation in the parking lot of a McDonalds. Police said the parents of a 17-year-old boy reported that Vick pointed a handgun at their son and two others.

He was not drafted in the NFL draft but was signed to a one-year contract with the Miami Dolphins, where he spent most of the season on their practice squad, only playing in one game. After the season ended he was cut from the Dolphins. He continued to have problems with the law after his release. In September 2008, he settled a lawsuit with a teenage girl who claimed she suffered psychological trauma from their nearly two-year sexual relationship. In October 2008, Vick was convicted of eluding police, driving under the influence (DUI), and driving on the wrong side of the road after an incident in June 2008 where he fled a bicycle patrol officer who observed him and a woman in a dispute. When the officer approached the car, Vick sped away. He was pulled over by another officer and failed a sobriety test. He received a 12-month suspended jail sentence on the DUI charge, had to pay $530 in fines, and lost his license for a year. Currently, Marcus Vick is unsigned.[31]

RESEARCH ON PROFESSIONAL ATHLETES AND CRIME

While there has been a limited amount of research examining professional athletes and criminal behavior, there has been no shortage of media coverage of the subject. Although media coverage alone is not enough to suggest there is a problem, the fact that in 1997 the NFL introduced its own anti-crime policy should provide some evidence that criminal behavior is a concern among professional athletes. The policy initially led to fines and/or mandated counseling for players who had pled guilty to violent crimes or accepted plea bargains. Paul Tagliabue, the commissioner of the league stated, "as an organization whose continued success depends on integrity and public confidence, the NFL simply cannot tolerate conduct that victimizes other individuals and results in a loss of respect for NFL players." In 1998, the league began fining employees for violations. Crimes that fall under the league's programs include the use or threat of physical violence, the use of a deadly weapon, illegal possession of a weapon, hate crimes, the destruction of property, and domestic violence. Any NFL employee or player charged with one of these crimes must undergo counseling. A conviction or guilty plea will subject the player to a fine or the possibility of suspension without pay as determined by the commissioner. Under the policy, a longer suspension, and possibly banishment, can follow a second conviction.[32]

Jeff Benedict and Don Yaeger did a study on NFL players' criminal behavior which revealed that 21% of them had been formally charged with a serious crime (the findings vary by race with 28% of black players and 9% of white players having an arrest). The authors note that the percentage of players with a criminal record is conservative and is likely higher (especially because juvenile offenses were not included). They examined players during the 1996–1997 season and concluded:

> NFL teams are recruiting a new breed of criminal players, the likes of which should disturb all NFL fans. Gone are the good old days of NFL recruits having rap sheets detailing merely drunken brawls and vandalism. In are the days of lethal violence, rape, armed robbery, home invasion, kidnapping, and drug dealing.[33]

The players who had criminal records had on average 2.42 arrests per player. Of the players with criminal records, 29% had been arrested before entering the NFL, 56% were arrested after entering the NFL, and 15% were arrested both before entering the NFL and after. After researching the crimes committed by NFL players, the authors note that the athletes are treated differently than other criminals. They are rarely held accountable for their crimes or stigmatized for their actions due to their athleticism. Simply put, the NFL's criminal players are treated differently than virtually every other criminal who commits similar crimes.[34]

However, Jeff Benedict then did a study with Alfred Blumstein comparing the criminal violence of NFL players with the general population.[35] They found that the chance that a male living in a U.S. city with a population of more than 250,000 (reasonably representative of NFL cities) would be arrested for one of the offenses examined in the NFL study at one time in their lives was 23% (varying greatly by race: 51% for blacks and 14% for whites).[36] While recognizing some limitation in their study, they conclude that the NFL players seem to have a lower rate of violence than the general population. Their study is interesting and points out the surprisingly high percentage of the general population that has been arrested. However, there is one issue that I have with their study. They used the arrest rate of 20-year-old males for the calculations of the general population or comparison group. Although this may be a reasonable representation of the basic breakdown of NFL players, most NFL players are millionaires (the league minimum when their study was conducted was $200,000). I am not sure if the general population is an accurate comparison group for NFL players given their income. Blumstein and Benedict recognize this issue and point out part of the image problem the NFL has:

> Arrest data on these other comparison groups (those making more than $200,000 per year) is not available. But those people would tend to be corporate executives or professionals, undoubtedly of a very different socioeconomic status, and much more likely to be exemplars of traditional anti-violence middle-class norms. Thus, even if data were available for such a group, comparison with them seems less than appropriate.[37]

Many people believe that professional players should, because of money and celebrity, adopt a more mainstream attitude and behavior. Many fans see professional athletes as extremely blessed and lucky and think that their behavior should correspond with their now high-profile and high-paying position. While these expectations may be too high, I believe that these higher expectations of behavior are part of the problem for professional athletes and sports leagues and may lead to the increased media attention on athletes' transgressions.

In 1983, Isaiah Thomas of the Detroit Pistons stated the following regarding the image of professional athletes as criminals:

> If there are 276 players in the NBA and 276 other people, of those 276 ordinary people, you're going to have 10 or 15 who don't conform to the norms of society, that do drugs. Well, that's what we have in the NBA: 10 or 15 of our 276—maybe not even that many. I think that's damned good.[38]

However, after studying NFL players, Jeff Benedict did a similar study of NBA players and their criminal backgrounds. He used the names of the NBA's players in the 2001–2002 season (he excluded foreign-born players) and found that 40% have had formal criminal complaints for a serious crime filed against them. Benedict notes:

> It should not be surprising that so many NBA players are being arrested these days. We should be surprised that players aren't being arrested even more. After all, they are, by and large, adolescents who are excessively paid and over-hyped to play a boy's game while living in a cocoon where they are pampered, protected, and never told no. When they are accused of breaking the law, handlers and the best lawyers money can buy rush to their side. Excuses are made, exceptions to the rules are demanded, and quick and dirty forgiveness is expected through lawyerly denials, public apologies, and an occasional hand-slapping in the form of a one or two-game suspension and a small fine.[39]

In his research, he found that females were the most frequent victims of the players' criminal behavior and that police officers were second. He argues that many of these players have never been told no or held accountable for their behavior and start to believe they are above the law. Women are in a position to tell the athletes no, which can result in sexual assaults or abuse. Police officers also have the ability to tell the players no and this often results in either verbal or physical confrontations. He also found that about a third of the NBA players with an arrest record had already been in trouble with the law before leaving college (one out of every three players with an arrest record in the NBA was arrested while on college scholarship).[40]

Benedict argues that the culture of NBA players encourages many of their criminal encounters. The players are on the road for long stretches of time away from the stability of their family (possibly wife and kids), they make frequent visits to strip clubs and night clubs which can increase the chances of "getting into trouble," and additionally he finds that many NBA players have a penchant for guns. The fact that many NBA players (and professional athletes in general) find it necessary to carry a firearm suggests many things. First, players because of their wealth and fame are at a greater risk to be criminally victimized. But part of the fear that drives gun ownership may have to do with the type of people they associate with and the places where they hang out. Professional athletes and guns will be discussed in greater detail later in the chapter.

HIGH PROFILE EXAMPLE: ADAM "PACMAN" JONES

Football player Adam "Pacman" Jones' name has become familiar to sports fans, not because of his accomplishments on the field (although he is a very good cornerback), but because of his repeated transgressions off the field. Jones went to college at the University of West Virginia where he left after his junior year. At West Virginia, he allegedly beat another student with a pool cue during a bar altercation. He was charged with malicious assault, a felony that eventually was reduced to a misdemeanor.[41] In 2005, Jones was drafted sixth overall by the Tennessee Titans. In his two years in Tennessee he had 10 incidents requiring police attention, five arrests, no convictions, and two cases still pending.[42] His most famous run-in with police happened in Las Vegas on February 19, 2007, during the NBA's All-Star weekend. Jones was at a strip club when he threw thousands of dollars on the stage (known as "making it rain"). When the dancers started to collect the money, Jones allegedly grabbed one of the dancers by the hair, hitting her head against the stage. This lead to an altercation between his group and the bouncers of the club which left one of the bouncers paralyzed after being shot by one of Jones' associates. Under the NFL's new player code of conduct policy (implemented in April 2007), Jones was suspended for a year. Commissioner Roger Goodell ushered in the policy, which takes a strong stand toward criminal behavior:

> While criminal activity is clearly outside the scope of permissible conduct, and persons who engage in criminal activity will be subject to discipline, the

standard of conduct for persons employed in the NFL is considerably higher. It is not enough simply to avoid being found guilty of a crime. Instead, as an employee of the NFL or a member club, you are held to a higher standard and expected to conduct yourself in a way that is responsible, promotes the values upon which the league is based, and is lawful. Persons who fail to live up to this standard of conduct are guilty of conduct detrimental and subject to discipline, even where the conduct itself does not result in conviction of a crime.[43]

The other football player suspended by the commissioner was Cincinnati Bengals wide receiver Chris Henry, who was arrested four times in just over a year (he also played at West Virginia University with Jones).[44] Henry was suspended for eight games. He was one of nine Bengals arrested in the past nine months.[45]

Adam Jones was traded to the Dallas Cowboys in 2008 and after serving a 17-month suspension was allowed to start the season. Jones joined Tank Johnson on the Cowboys, who was arrested for illegal firearm possession in December 2006 (he had three arrests in 18 months with the Chicago Bears) and was famously allowed to travel with the Chicago Bears to the Super Bowl in February 2007 while under house arrest, during which he was allowed to leave the house for work.

Jones did not last long in Dallas before he ran into trouble again in October 2008, getting into a fight with one of his bodyguards. He was suspended for four games. Jones was released by the Cowboys at the end of the season when allegations of another incident surfaced. Jones was accused of arranging to have someone shoot at three men outside of an Atlanta area strip club in June 2007 (while he was under NFL suspension). One of the alleged victims said that they were shot at as they left the club after having a dispute with Jones inside the club. Jones denied the charges and the police have not made any arrests.[46] In August 2009, Jones allegedly signed a one-year contract with the Winnipeg Blue Bombers of the Canadian Football League in hopes of making it back to the NFL. Days after the story broke, the Winnipeg Blue Bombers made an announcement that they would not be signing Jones to a contract.

The following is a chronology of Adam Jones' legal trouble:

- *April 2005.* Named on an incident report after a fight in a Georgia strip club. Case was dismissed.
- *June 2005.* Police found marijuana in a Nashville hotel room occupied by two of Jones' friends. Jones was present, but one of the friends took responsibility.

- *July 2005.* Arrested and charged with two counts of misdemeanor assault and one felony count of vandalism after a fight at a Nashville nightclub. Charges were dismissed.
- *February 2006.* Charged with felony and misdemeanor obstruction of justice after an incident outside a house in Fayetteville, Georgia.
- *March 2006.* Arrested and charged with marijuana possession in Fayetteville. Charge was dismissed.
- *April 2006.* Police said a vehicle registered to Jones was involved in a drug trafficking ring in Nashville. The car was confiscated from an acquaintance of Jones, and 1,653 pounds of marijuana, 128 pounds of cocaine, and $608,000 were seized. Jones was not charged.
- *April 2006.* Jones was at a gas station at 1:50 A.M. when gunshots were fired after an altercation. Police questioned Jones, who was labeled as a witness.
- *August 2006.* Arrested and charged with public drunkenness and disorderly conduct after an incident at a nightclub in Murfreesboro, Tennessee. In January, a judge ruled charges would be dropped if Jones had six months of good behavior.
- *October 2006.* Issued a citation for misdemeanor assault after being accused of spitting in the face of a 21-year-old woman at a Nashville nightclub. Charge was dismissed.
- *February 2007.* Questioned by Las Vegas police after a triple shooting at a strip club left a security guard paralyzed. On March 26, police recommended prosecutors file a felony charge of coercion and misdemeanor charges of battery and threat to life against Jones.[47]

Jones, like other potential draft picks coming out of college, was put through rigorous evaluations and background checks.

> Prior to the 2005 draft, Jones had one issue in his past. While enrolled at West Virginia University, Jones was involved in a fight. He was arrested and put on probation for the incident. Still, coaches' evaluations, support group evaluations, educational evaluations and personality profiling of Jones were all excellent. You would be hard-pressed to find anyone inside West Virginia University who would say anything negative about him.[48]

These evaluations must not have examined his past too thoroughly. Looking at Jones' upbringing offers some clues to explain his downward spiral of criminal behavior. Jones was raised by his mother, Deborah Jones, and his grandmother, Christine Jones (she died when he was a freshman in college). His father was murdered when Jones was four years old. Deborah Jones had her own share of criminal problems, serving three years in prison. She has been quoted as saying "I have probably been to every jail in Georgia. I've sold dope. Disorderly conduct. I've done everything."[49] Pacman sounded similar in a 2005 interview he gave when he was on the Tennessee Titans: "Anything you can name, I have done it. When I walked around, everybody in the neighborhood would tell their children to stay away from me. I have been in the worst situation that there could be."[50] He flunked out of two junior high schools before attending Westlake High School and becoming a star on the football team. The head coach of the football team, Dallas Allen, remembers meeting Jones for the first time. He said that Jones walked into his office as a freshman and told him that he was going to start. Then, on the first day of school, Jones got into a fight and was suspended for the first three games.[51]

Like Michael Vick, Jones seemed unable to leave his past behind him when he made the NFL. Jones maintained a home in a nice suburb of Atlanta, only a few minutes from the housing project where he grew up, and spent all of his down-time there. One of Jones' former Titan teammates says that Jones' posse sometimes numbered a half dozen or more and that Jones stresses the loyalty that he feels toward his friends from the Washington Road (Atlanta) days. Jones' continuing behavior suggests a systematic disregard for authority and a potentially fatal attraction to danger,[52] possibly some of the same characteristics that made him a star on the football field (and will probably lead another NFL team to take a chance on him).

STEROID USE AMONG ATHLETES

Steroids were not illegal until the Anabolic Steroid Control Act of 1990 which placed steroids into Schedule III of the Controlled Substances Act as of February 27, 1991. The law defines steroids as any drug or hormonal substance chemically and pharmacologically related to testosterone (other than estrogens, progestins, and corticosteroids) that promote muscle growth. The possession or sale of anabolic steroids without a valid prescription is illegal. Steroids are prescribed by doctors to deal with issues related to low levels of testosterone produced by the body or issues with body wasting (for example, patients with AIDS). Federal law mandates simple possession of illicitly obtained anabolic steroids carries a maximum penalty of one year in prison and a minimum $1,000 fine for the first offence (individual states have their own laws and penalties).

Athletes take steroids to enhance their performance and physical appearance. They are taken orally or injected in "cycles" of weeks or months. Cycling involves taking multiple doses of steroids over a specific period of time, stopping for a period, and starting again. In addition, users often combine several different types of steroids to maximize their effectiveness while minimizing negative effects (referred to as "stacking").[53]

The side effects for steroid abuse are a common theme among news reports, with most reports focusing on the negative effects that steroids can have on teenagers. The negative effects of steroid use on teenagers have become an increasing concern as use among high school athletes becomes more widely known. Steroids can have a devastating impact on high school athletes and was one of the biggest motivations for the Congressional committee that was formed to look at the issue. There have been a number of high school students who committed suicide after using steroids. The most well known is Taylor Hooton, whose father started the Taylor Hooton Foundation after his son committed suicide in 2003 because of the depression he suffered as a side-effect of steroid use.

The major side effects from abusing anabolic steroids can include liver tumors and cancer, jaundice, fluid retention, and high blood pressure. Other side effects include kidney tumors, severe acne, and trembling. In addition, there are some gender-specific side effects. Men often see a shrinking of the testicles, reduced sperm count, infertility, baldness, development of breast tissue, and increased risk for prostate cancer. Women sometimes start to grow facial hair and exhibit male-pattern baldness, experience changes in or cessation of the menstrual cycle, and a deepened voice. The damage to teens can be the most striking with their growth halted through premature skeletal maturation and accelerated puberty changes. This means that adolescents risk remaining short for the remainder of their lives if they take anabolic steroids before the typical adolescent growth spurt.

One of the more widely discussed side effects of steroid use is "roid rage." Research has shown that aggression and other psychiatric side effects may result from steroid abuse. Many users report feeling good about themselves while on anabolic steroids, but researchers report that extreme mood swings also can occur, including manic-like symptoms leading to violence. Depression often is seen when the drugs are stopped and may contribute to dependence on anabolic steroids. Researchers also report that users may suffer from paranoid jealousy, extreme irritability, delusions, and impaired judgment stemming from feelings of invincibility.[54] These effects can prove especially dangerous for athletes who may already be prone to aggressive behavior.

One of the more interesting aspects of the steroid issue is that the criminal implications are rarely discussed. Most of the discussion focuses on the integrity of the game or cheating in the sport but rarely is it mentioned that steroid use is illegal without a prescription. Even the athletes who have faced criminal charges related to steroids (i.e., Barry Bonds, Roger Clemens, Marion Jones) have done so because of perjury charges related to their testimony denying steroid use. The criminal element of steroids is almost never discussed as would be the case with a drug like cocaine or marijuana.

Steroids have been used by athletes since the 1970s (or earlier) but it has only been over the last decade that their use has come into the mainstream. The 1998 home run chase by Mark McGwire and Sammy Sosa, which made a mockery of Roger Maris' long-standing single season home run record, was praised at the time as saving national interest in baseball, but is now looked back on as a direct result of steroid use by athletes. The use of steroids by baseball players became so widespread that the mid-1990s through 2005 is now referred to by many as "the steroid era" because of the astronomical number of home runs that were seen as, at least in part, due to the use of performance-enhancing drugs by the players. There have been assertions that many officials and owners in baseball were aware of the widespread use of steroids but didn't comment on it because of the positive effects it was having on the financial aspects of the game. The silence on steroid use quickly changed as public opinion and media scrutiny of the issue intensified. The issue was placed squarely in the national spotlight when President Bush gave his State of the Union address in January 2004:

> To help children make right choices, they need good examples. Athletics play such an important role in our society, but, unfortunately, some in professional sports are not setting much of an example. The use of performance-enhancing drugs like steroids in baseball, football, and other sports is dangerous, and it sends the wrong message, that there are shortcuts to accomplishment, and that performance is more important than character.

This culminated in a hearing before the House Government Reform committee on March 17, 2005, in which many of the stars of baseball were called to testify. Mark McGwire, Jose Canseco, Curt Schilling, Sammy Sosa, Rafael Palmeiro, and Frank Thomas testified while Barry Bonds and Jason Giambi were not required to attend due to their involvement in the ongoing BALCO investigation. During the hearing, Rafael Palmeiro famously waved his finger at the committee members and said:

"Let me start by telling you this: I have never used steroids, period. I don't know how to say it any more clearly than that. Never." Palmeiro tested positive for steroids the following August and was suspended for 10 games by Major League Baseball.

The result of the hearing was increased drug testing and penalties for steroid use. Additionally, Major League Baseball recruited former senator George Mitchell to conduct an investigation of the steroid era, which resulted in the "Mitchell Report." The Mitchell Report examined the use of steroids in baseball and named 86 players linked to steroids (including seven Most Valuable Players [MVPs] and 31 All-Stars). The report concluded that Major League Baseball was slow to react to steroid use and laid out a testing plan for the league to move forward.

For a first positive steroid test, a player is suspended for 50 games by Major League Baseball. A second positive test carries a 100-game suspension and a third positive test carries a lifetime ban. This policy was implemented in November 2005 after Congress chastised MLB for its lenient policy that was put in place in January 2005, before the Congressional hearing (first offense, 10 games; second, 20 games; third, 60 games; fourth, one year; and fifth, commissioner's decision). However, this was a sharp increase over the policy that had been in place since 2002, where a first offense carried counseling as its penalty.

The NFL began testing players for steroids in 1989, with a first positive test resulting in a minimum four-game suspension, a second positive test carrying a six-game minimum, and a third positive test resulting in a one-year minimum suspension. According to a health survey of 2,552 retired NFL players from the 1940s to the 1990s, 20.3% of the players from the 1980s answered yes when asked "During the time in which it was acceptable to use performance-enhancing steroids, did you use steroids?" The study found that use was the most frequent in the years just prior to the NFL testing policy. Of all of the retired players, 9.1% answered yes to the question. Offensive linemen (16.3%) and defensive linemen (14.8%) reported the highest proportion of steroid use. The study also found that those who used steroids had significantly higher rates of herniated disks, knee ligament injuries, and meniscus injuries. In addition they indicated more elbow, foot, ankle, and toe problems than those who said they played steroid-free. It also found a link between steroids and depression, attention deficit disorder, and increased alcohol consumption.[55]

The NBA began testing for steroids in 1999, with a first positive test resulting in a five-game suspension, a second positive resulting in a 10-game suspension, and third offense coming with a 25-game suspension. After being scolded by members of Congress during their hearing on performance-enhancing drugs in sports, the NBA increased their penalties. The NBA's current policy is a 10-game penalty for the first offense, the second infraction is 25 games, and the third a full season. It's not until the fourth strike that a player is banned from the league. The National Hockey League began testing for steroids during the 2004–2005 season. For a first violation, a player is suspended for 20 games, 60 games for a second violation, and a permanent ban for a third violation.[56] The Olympics has the strictest testing system with a two-year ban for one positive test followed by a lifetime ban for a second positive test.

The NCAA tests Division I and II athletes randomly for steroids throughout the year and during championship or playoff rounds. Following a first positive test, an athlete cannot compete in any intercollegiate sport for one year and loses one of four years of eligibility. After the second positive test, the athlete loses all remaining eligibility and is permanently banned from intercollegiate competition.[57]

Steroid use has become an important topic for high school athletes as well. In 2006, New Jersey became the first state to institute a statewide steroid-testing policy for high school athletes, followed by Florida in 2007. In 2008, Texas began a massive testing program, testing between 40,000 and 50,000 students a year (only two people tested positive out of the first 10,000 students).[58] Penalties vary greatly by state: Texas suspends athletes for 30 days for the first positive test, 90 days for Florida, and one year in New Jersey.[59]

Studies show that between 2.7% to 3.5% percent of high school seniors have used steroids at some time in their lives with 1.8% having used in the past year.[60] Males consistently report higher rates of use than females; for example, in 2008, 2.5% of 12th-grade males versus 0.6% of 12th-grade females reported past-year use. The NCAA on average finds between 1% and 2% positive tests for steroids with its testing program.

HIGH PROFILE EXAMPLE: BARRY BONDS AND BALCO (BAY AREA LAB COOPERATIVE)

Barry Bonds has become the face of the steroid issue. Bonds was an all-star player for the Pittsburgh Pirates beginning in 1986 and winning two Most Valuable Player awards with the Pirates. In 1993, he signed with the San Francisco Giants and his appearance and level of play changed. Bonds began hitting home runs at a record rate, first beating the single season home run record in 2001 and then topping the career home run record in 2007. Bonds was not signed by a team in 2008. All of this happened under increasing speculation about his steroid use.

In 1998, Bonds reconnected with a boyhood friend and personal trainer Greg Anderson. Bonds hired Anderson as his trainer and started to receive supplements from him after undergoing blood and urine analysis at the Bay Area Lab Cooperative (BALCO). Bonds did a photo shoot promoting BALCO's nutritional supplements.[61] On September 5, 2003, BALCO was raided by federal investigators and its owner Victor Conte was arrested.[62] The BALCO grand jury heard many athletes testify about their association with BALCO. Bonds, along with baseball players Jason Giambi, Gary Sheffield, Benito Santiago, football players Bill Romanowski and Barrett Robbins, track and field stars Marion Jones and Tim Montgomery, and boxer Shane Mosley were among the athletes who testified. The BALCO scandal became the focal point of the steroid discussion as players' testimony, which was supposed to be confidential, was leaked to the media. Bonds denied ever knowingly using steroids. On December 3, 2004, the *San Francisco Chronicle* reported on Bond's grand jury testimony that he admitted to unknowingly using steroids known as "the clear" and "the cream" during the 2003 season. Bonds said his personal trainer, Greg Anderson, provided the steroids. His denials would lead to subsequent federal charges of perjury and obstruction of justice in November 2007.

Victor Conte and Greg Anderson, Bond's personal trainer, were indicted in February 2004 for various charges related to steroid distribution. On July 15, 2005, Conte pled guilty to steroid distribution and money laundering in a deal with federal prosecutors and spent four months in prison and four months under house arrest. Anderson pled guilty to the same charges in exchange for a six-month prison sentence of which he served three months in prison and three months under house arrest. Adding more intrigue to the case, in 2006 Anderson was subpoenaed to testify in a grand jury investigating Bond's perjury during the grand jury investigating BALCO. Anderson refused to testify and was imprisoned on contempt of court charges. Additionally, *San Francisco Chronicle* reporters Lance Williams and Mark Fainaru-Wada, who reported on the leaked BALCO grand jury testimony and subsequently wrote the book *Game of Shadows* about the case, were called to testify about their sources. The reporters refused to reveal their source and were threatened with jail time for contempt of court. Before the reporters were sentenced to prison, one of Victor Conte's attorneys, Troy Ellerman, admitted that he allowed *San Francisco Chronicle* reporters Lance Williams and Mark Fainaru-Wada to view transcripts of the grand jury testimony of baseball stars Barry Bonds, Jason Giambi, and Gary Sheffield, and sprinter Tim Montgomery. On July 12, 2007, Ellerman was sentenced to 30 months in prison, of which he served 16 months. Barry Bonds' trial is scheduled to begin in 2010.

Just as it looked like Bonds would be the biggest star linked to steroids, in February 2009, *Sports Illustrated* revealed that New York Yankees' third baseman Alex Rodriguez, widely considered the best player in baseball, had failed a steroid test in 2003. Two days later, Rodriguez admitted to using steroids from 2001 to 2003. His connection to steroids was a big blow to the sport as many saw him as the future home run king who could restore some legitimacy to the record that had been tarnished by Bonds. One of the interesting aspects of the Rodriguez story is the test itself. The Major League Baseball Player's Association (MLBPA) agreed to confidential survey testing for steroids in 2003. There were to be no penalties associated with the tests and the names of those who failed were to remain sealed. The intent of the test was to see if more than 5% of players were using steroids. If the 5% threshold was reached, then mandatory testing would begin the following year with penalties attached to positive tests. The survey test revealed 104 positives, a few percentage points above the 5% mark. Rather than destroying the tests or the list of positive players, the MLBPA union wanted to fight some of the positive tests as false positives in hope of getting the percentage of positive tests below 5% (thus avoiding mandatory testing for its players). This was all happening while the federal government was investigating Barry Bonds and the BALCO case. When the federal investigators working on the BALCO case learned of the survey steroid test, they asked the MLBPA union for the test results of the 10 baseball players that were associated with BALCO. The union refused to turn over the tests for the "BALCO ten." The federal investigators, not pleased with the refusal, returned with a subpoena for all the tests. So the confidential test and list of positive baseball players, while still sealed, was now in the hands of more people. Other names from the list, including Sammy Sosa, Manny Ramirez (who also was suspended 50 games during the 2009 season for testing positive), and David Ortiz, have surfaced in the newspapers as well. In August 2009, a federal appeals court ruled that federal investigators acted inappropriately when they seized all of the names on the steroid list.[63]

ATHLETES AND GUNS

Professional athletes, most of us came from the streets. We feel like we know the streets and can pretty much protect ourselves. But now we're in a position where we're being targeted, and the stakes are just too high.

NBA player Ben Wallace[64]

Estimates vary but anywhere from 20% to 80% of Major League Baseball, NBA, and NFL players own guns. There are no reliable statistics as many states do not make available to the public the names of registered gun owners. It is also hard to determine given the number of illegal guns and the differences in (or lack of) registration requirements for guns used for hunting (like shotguns). Whatever the percentage, guns have become part of the athlete's world. This may simply reflect a broader trend across the country, as the percentage of people across the country who own guns is around 30% with nearly 40% indicating that there is a gun in their house. The percentage is even higher among men, with 47% indicating gun ownership, with nearly two-thirds indicating that they have a gun for crime protection.[65] Thus, it is not surprising given athletes' wealth that many feel compelled to own a gun for protection. So while most estimates place gun ownership among athletes over 50%, it may not simply be ownership but rather use or even misuse of guns that is at issue.

Gun related incidents are not confined to the professional ranks:

> University of Nevada point guard Armon Johnson and four other Wolf Pack athletes were involved in incidents that led to Ahyaro Phillips being arrested and dismissed from the basketball team for carrying a handgun on campus. Phillips was arrested for carrying a gun after he confronted two football players on campus following an earlier altercation with them at an off-campus party, Nevada athletic officials said.[66]

There have been a number of high-profile incidents involving professional athletes and guns. In 2008, New York Giants wide receiver Plaxico Burress shot himself in the leg with an unregistered handgun inside a New York City nightclub. In addition to Burress, football players Pacman Jones (previously discussed), Tank Williams, and Marshawn Lynch, along with NBA players Allen Iverson and Gilbert Arenas, have faced illegal gun charges. Most recently, on September 24, 2009, Cleveland Cavaliers guard Delonte West was stopped for speeding on his motorcycle in Maryland. Police found a loaded handgun in his waistband, another gun strapped to his leg, and a loaded shotgun in a guitar case on his back.[67]

One of the more noteworthy incidents involved Seattle Seahawks receiver Brian Blades. On July 5, 1995, Blades shot his cousin Charles Blades dead after an argument. He was charged with manslaughter in the death of his cousin. Blades maintained that the death was accidental.[68] According to police, the semiautomatic handgun went off in close range and hit the bottom of his cousin's chin. Brian Blades called 911, indicating that the gun had gone off accidentally. According to testimony, Brian Blades and his brother, Bennie, who plays safety for the Detroit Lions, went out the night of the incident with some friends. They were called back to Bennie Blades' house when they heard that Bennie's former girlfriend wanted to pick up the child that Bennie had fathered. During a dispute between Bennie and his former girlfriend, Brian got involved and Bennie shoved Brian. Brian got angry and went back to his townhouse to get his gun. Brian's cousin Charles Blades went after Brian to try and calm him down. Their friends also went back to Brian's townhouse and heard a struggle between Brian and his cousin. They heard Brian say, "Let loose the gun," and heard Charles say, "Put the gun down."[69] Then the gun went off, hitting Charles under the chin and killing him. Then another shot went off; a bullet was found in the office desk. Brian Blades then called 911. One of the friends, Wilbur Peterson, went inside to try and calm Brian down. Peterson called 911 as well. He said that during his call, Blades picked up the handgun and pulled the trigger, although it was not clear where the gun was pointed. The chamber was empty, police said, thus no shot was fired.[70]

On June 14, 1996, after a week-long trial, Blades was found guilty of manslaughter and faced up to nine and half years in prison.[71] However, even before the verdict had been returned, defense attorneys filed a motion contending that the prosecution had not proved that Blades had acted with culpable negligence in the death of his cousin. The next day in court, the trial judge reversed the jury verdict, agreeing with the defense attorneys' motion.[72] Blades played for the Seattle Seahawks until his retirement in 1998.

Another noteworthy gun incident involved the NBA's Stephen Jackson. Jackson (discussed in the following chapter for his involvement in the brawl that took place between players and fans during a game in Detroit) and three of his teammates, Jamaal Tinsley, Marquis Daniels, and Jimmie Hunter, left a strip club and were followed by a group of men. After some words were exchanged, one of the men hit Jackson with his car. Jackson took out his gun and fired five shots into the air. The car drove off and the police arrived. The police found a small amount of marijuana in the passenger-side door of Tinsley's car along with Tinsley's and Daniels' guns (all of the guns had the proper permits). Indiana Pacers coach Rick Carlisle said the players committed an "error in judgment" by staying out late during training camp.[73] Jackson, who was the only player charged with a crime, eventually pled guilty to a felony count of criminal recklessness for firing the gun. He was fined $5,000 and had to perform 100 hours of community service. He was suspended for the first seven games of the 2007–2008 basketball season.[74] Deon Willford, who hit Jackson with his car during the incident, was convicted of felony battery and sentenced to two years in prison, two years probation, and 100 hours of community service.[75]

The NBA and NFL have similar policies regarding players and guns, each noting that even if players are licensed to carry a gun, they cannot carry them into stadiums and arenas, practice facilities, or on team planes.[76] The NFL's official advice: "In some circumstances, such as for sport or protection, you may legally possess a firearm or other weapon. However, we strongly recommend that you not do so."[77] Shortly after Stephen Jackson's arrest, the commissioner of the NBA said he is against NBA players carrying guns in public: "I don't think it's necessary to walk the streets packing a gun. I think it's dangerous for our players."[78] Roger Goodell, who has taken a strong stance against criminal behavior among NFL players, has handed down penalties for gun-related incidents. Before Chicago Bears defensive tackle Tank Johnson was found guilty for illegal firearm possession (he had a previous arrest for illegal firearms), Goodell suspended Johnson from the league for half of the 2007 NFL season.[79]

Even with league policies in place, an increasing number of athletes continue to carry guns. While many athletes are some of the biggest and strongest people on the planet, many carry guns for protection. The players believe more and more that they are a target for criminals. With their astronomical salaries, glamorous lifestyles, and celebrity status, many athletes are living in fear for their safety. Their fears have been fueled by a rash of recent incidents involving athletes. For example, a few of the stories involving athletes since 2007:

- In 2007, Miami Heat forward Antoine Walker, along with a cousin, was accosted and robbed at gunpoint inside Walker's home in an exclusive section of Chicago. Walker was confronted in his garage, bound with duct tape, and robbed of thousands of dollars in cash and jewelry, as well as his Mercedes.
- A few weeks after Walker's robbery, New York Knicks center Eddy Curry, his wife, and an employee were similarly robbed and tied up at Curry's home in suburban Chicago. Police believe it was the same group who robbed Walker. The group fled Curry's house with $10,000 in cash and several pieces of jewelry.[80]
- Houston Rockets forward Carl Landry suffered a minor leg injury after a gunman opened fire on his vehicle just hours after the team had returned to Houston after a game against the Hornets.[81]
- Denver Broncos cornerback Darrent Williams was killed when a gunman sprayed the stretch Hummer in which he was riding in downtown Denver early on New Year's Day.
- Washington Redskins safety Sean Taylor was shot and killed inside his South Florida home by intruders.

- In 2008, Oakland Raiders wide receiver Javon Walker was beaten and robbed in Las Vegas.
- Jacksonville Jaguars offensive tackle Richard Collier was shot as he sat in a vehicle with a former teammate, resulting in his paralysis.

Although these examples might not necessarily constitute a crime wave, it may be understandable why more athletes are looking for protection.[82] The story of Sean Taylor was most troublesome for athletes as he was in his home when robbers entered his house. Taylor, who was in his bedroom with his girlfriend, picked up a machete that he kept next to his bed when he heard noises in the house. The machete did him no good as the attackers came through the bedroom door, and shooting him in the thigh and severing his femoral artery.[83] Taylor died the following morning at the hospital. This was not the first time that someone broke into his house; on November 17, an intruder slipped through a front window of his house and went through drawers and a safe but apparently did not steal anything. No one was home at the time.[84] Taylor's death received national attention and he was mourned across the NFL. He was the second NFL player to be shot dead during the year; Denver Broncos cornerback Darrent Williams was shot and killed in his rented limousine as he was leaving a New Year's Eve party.

Ironically, Taylor had been in trouble with firearms previously. In June 2005, Taylor was arrested and charged with felony assault and battery after he pointed a gun at three men outside a house and accused them of stealing two all-terrain vehicles from him. Taylor, accompanied by several people, assaulted one of the men and made death threats before driving off. Minutes later, a group of men drove by Taylor's parked SUV and shot it with bullets from an AK-47 and a pistol. Taylor's vehicle was empty at the time, and the gunmen were never identified or arrested. Prosecutors negotiated a plea deal with Taylor and agreed to drop the felony charges. He was sentenced to 18 months probation and pledged to donate time and money to various charities and schools in southern Florida.[85] Five men (aged 17 to 20 years old) were arrested for the break-in and murder of Taylor. Two of the men had connections to Taylor (one dated his sister and had been to a party at his house, while another one had cut the grass and been to a birthday party at the house) and stated that they did not expect Taylor to be home when they broke in (Taylor was not with the Redskins because of an injury).[86] In May 2008, one of the five arrested pled guilty to second-degree murder and was sentenced to 29 years. As part of the plea, he agreed to testify against the other defendants in their trials.[87]

Taylor's story only reinforced to many athletes the belief that they need a gun to protect themselves. While his story is a terrible tragedy, others think athletes can reduce their risk of victimization by being more careful about where they go and with whom they associate. Former Utah Jazz forward and Hall of Fame player Karl Malone, who is a member of the National Rifle Association (NRA) and strong supporter of the right to bear arms, does not believe players should be arming themselves for protection but rather should stop hanging out in places of risk. He said:

> Three A.M.? My goodness gracious, what were you doing out at 3 o'clock in the morning? Who were you with? Where were you at? Do you need a gun to protect you or do you need a babysitter to get you where you need to be all the time so that you don't get in any trouble?[88]

Although protection from crime, given their enormous wealth, may be the most cited reason for gun ownership, there are other factors as well. For example, many professional athletes come from crime-ridden areas and do not abandon their home or childhood friends. Many athletes, like Michael Vick, for example, maintain close ties with their friends from growing up and continue to hang out in their old neighborhoods.[89] This makes them targets not only because of their wealth but also jealousy, which is a powerful motivator. Many people in the community may be jealous of the attention that the star athlete receives, especially when this attention comes from women.[90]

This also points to a cultural reason for gun ownership. Many athletes are from rough inner city neighborhoods where, unfortunately, guns are a part of life. Chicago Bears linebacker Bryan Cox, who owns seven guns, said: "Where I'm from in East St. Louis, a gun was like a credit card; you didn't leave home without it." In contrast, many other athletes are from rural areas where hunting is common. Carolina Panthers tight end Wesley Walls said he grew up hunting in the woods of Mississippi and that shooting a gun was part of everyday life.[91] Additionally, guns have become part of the culture for athletes with some viewing them as a status symbol or simply "cool."

> Sports, especially football, are getting more violent. Players get bigger and stronger and more athletic. And they hit harder. Their daily routine is about aggressiveness and violence, and maybe they take that into their leisure time, too. So for some, even their relaxing time is rough-edged. But in some cases, there seems to be a street-cred thing, too. Some athletes find themselves with so much money, and the guns are a sort of bling.[92]

In *Taking Sports Seriously: Law and Sports in Contemporary American Culture*, Standen says that while athletes' fame and money make them targets for crime, "athletes are no more rich and famous than actors or musicians. Yet players appear to come up on the police blotter as both perpetrators and victims of gun-related incidents far more than most other celebrities."[93] Many actors and musicians may not feel pressure to maintain a "rough edge" so don't mind paying a bodyguard to be the one carrying a gun. Likewise, while athletes make a lot of money, many do not make nearly as much as some actors or musicians who can afford to pay for security.

HIGH PROFILE EXAMPLE: NEW JERSEY NETS' JAYSON WILLIAMS

Jayson Williams was one of the leading rebounders in the NBA before his career was cut short by leg and knee injuries in April 1999. He played for nine seasons, the last seven with the New Jersey Nets. After the injury, Williams became a studio announcer on NBC's NBA coverage and became a visible celebrity at many charity events. On February 15, 2002, Williams hired Costas Christofi to drive friends (along with some of the Globetrotters) from a charity sporting event featuring the Harlem Globetrotters in Bethlehem, Pennsylvania, to a restaurant in Hunterdon County, then to Williams' nearby 30,000 square-foot estate.[94]

After arriving at Williams' place, Christofi was invited inside to take a tour of the home. Christofi, who was a basketball fan, was excited to be permitted in the house. Williams, who had been drinking (a state police test of his blood, taken eight hours later, showed his blood alcohol level to be 0.12%, or 0.02 percentage points higher than the state's legal definition of intoxication in 2002), led the group on the tour which took them up to his bedroom. According to testimony at his trial, Williams appeared in his bedroom with a 12-gauge Browning Citori shotgun. Shortly after entering the bedroom, Christofi was hit in the torso by 12 buckshot pellets fired from the gun. According to a witness, Williams said: "Oh, my God. What just happened? My life is over."[95] Rather than call for an ambulance, Williams changed his clothes and then conspired with the other guests to make the death look like a suicide. He coached his guests on what they should tell the police while a friend wiped Williams' fingerprints from the gun and later buried his blood-splattered clothes off a highway.[96] Christofi bled to death before the police arrived about a half-hour later.

After initially sticking to Williams' story to the police, the story began to unravel with the coroner's report, police suspicions, and witnesses coming forward. On February 25, Williams was charged with reckless manslaughter and four counts related to the cover-up of the death (the grand jury added aggravated manslaughter to the charges after finding that Williams' actions had shown "extreme indifference to human life").[97] Before the start of the criminal trial, Williams settled a civil suit with Christofi's family for $2.75 million.[98]

After a 15-week trial in 2004, Williams was acquitted of aggravated manslaughter and two other serious charges in Christofi's death and a mistrial was declared on the reckless manslaughter charge. He was convicted of four other lesser charges that he had covered up his involvement in the shooting. The judge did not set a sentencing date because the prosecution was entitled to retry Williams on the deadlocked reckless manslaughter charge.[99] A few weeks later the prosecutors announced that Williams would be retried on the charge of reckless manslaughter. The retrial is still pending.

This was not the first gun-related incident for Williams. In 1994, he agreed to enter a first-time offenders program after he was charged with reckless endangerment and unlawful possession of a weapon for firing his Sig Sauer automatic pistol at a security van outside the Meadowlands arena, where the Nets played. Over the objections of the prosecutor at the time, the judge accepted Williams' application to have the charges dropped in exchange for agreeing to take out ads in the local newspaper denouncing the dangers of guns, and for giving talks to young people on the dangers of drugs and guns.[100]

Then in 2001, about six months before the Christofi shooting, Williams had been drinking in a restaurant with two friends, including Dwayne Schintzius, a former professional basketball player who was staying at Williams' estate at the time. After the three men returned to Williams' house, Schintzius bet Williams $100 that he could drag one of Williams' watchdogs (a Rottweiler) out of the home. Schintzius won the bet, by dragging the dog by its legs out of the house. When Williams left the area, Schintzius thought he went to get the $100. He came back with a shotgun and fired two rounds at the dog, nearly decapitating it. Williams then reloaded the weapon, pointed it at Schintzius and told him, using a profanity, to get the "dog off my porch or you're next."[101] The prosecutors in his 2004 manslaughter trial learned of the dog shooting in an anonymous letter mailed to them; the judge ruled that it was inadmissible at the trial.

While awaiting the retrial, Williams continues to make news. In April 2009, he was stunned with a Taser by New York police officers after he resisted attempts by the officers to take him to a hospital. The police were called to a hotel in Manhattan around 4 A.M. when a female friend reported Williams was acting suicidal. When officers arrived, the 6-foot-10, 325-pound Williams appeared drunk and agitated, the police said. Then on May 24, 2009, Williams was arrested for allegedly punching a man in the face at a bar in Raleigh, North Carolina. He was charged with simple assault. The charges were later dropped by the victim.[102] Additionally, his wife filed for divorce claiming he was abusive, adulterous, and had a drug problem.[103]

CONCLUSION

On July 28, 2009, New Orleans Saints running back Reggie Bush broke up with his girlfriend Kim Kardashian. ESPN's Sportscenter considered this breaking news and covered the story at the top of the show. In a world where professional athletes' break-ups are news, it is no wonder that any criminal transgression receives intense media coverage. Although the media may be guaranteed to cover the crimes of professional athletes, making the problem look worse than it really is, there is no denying that there are serious criminal incidents involving professional athletes

Carolina Panthers wide receiver Rae Carruth became the first active NFL player ever charged with first-degree murder.[104] In 1999, Carruth hired three men to murder Cherica Adams, a girlfriend of his, after she became pregnant. Carruth drove in a car in front of Adams; when Carruth stopped his vehicle, she stopped her car as well. A car pulled up alongside her and opened fire.[105] Adams survived the shooting, as did the baby who was removed from the mother by caesarian section. However, Adams died a week later from injuries related to the shooting. Carruth was acquitted of first-degree murder but was convicted of conspiracy to commit murder, shooting into an occupied vehicle, and attempting to kill an unborn child. He is serving a minimum prison sentence of 18 years, 11 months. (Van Brett Watkins, who fired the shots into Adams' car, pled guilty to second-degree murder, conspiracy to commit first-degree murder, attempting to kill an unborn child, and shooting into an occupied vehicle. He was sentenced to a minimum of 40 years, five months.)[106]

Professional athletes, because of the lack of accountability that starts at earlier and earlier ages, in many cases develop a sense of extreme entitlement and "above the law" attitude. This attitude, mixed with the aggressive nature of many sports, can lead to violent outbursts off the field, especially when they are told "no" either by their wife, another woman, or a police officer. The combination is even more dangerous when you add to the equation guns and/or steroids, both of which are used by more and more athletes. All of these risk factors would not necessarily lead to crime, but the chance is increased by many athletes who continue to associate with friends from their old neighborhoods. Many professional athletes come from rough backgrounds and have a hard time leaving behind the negative influences of their hometown.

While the media may play a role in the perception of "athletes out of control," there is no denying that professional sports leagues have an increasing problem regarding violent behavior. It is easy to point to the fact that in earlier generations, reporters would not cover stories of players' transgressions (for example, Babe Ruth or Mickey Mantle); thus, it just looks like today's players are behaving worse. This would not be telling the whole story. Professional athletes may simply be reflecting the larger society which is increasingly more violent or possibly are being held to a higher standard by the public who demands more of its highly paid heroes. Either way, crime is an issue that has become central to the coverage of professional sports.

Chapter 4

CRIME AT THE ARENA:
SPECTATOR VIOLENCE, RIOTS,
AND CRIMES DURING THE GAME

C hapters 1, 2, and 3 looked at crimes committed by athletes off the field. This chapter is concerned with crimes that occur at the arena by both spectators and players. There are fights between fans, fights between fans and players, violence between parents and coaches, and crimes committed by players during games. Spectator violence has traditionally been associated with European soccer hooligans and the violence that surrounds soccer matches across Europe. However, recently violence at sporting arenas across the United States has become commonplace.

There are also legal issues surrounding criminal conduct committed during a sporting event. Within certain sports there is behavior that would be considered criminal if it took place outside the context of the sport. When someone crosses the acceptable and agreed-upon line in a sport, should criminal charges be filed? This question will be examined by looking at past examples of "criminal" behavior during sporting events.

Additionally, viewing sports has an impact on behavior. There traditionally has been concern, especially with children, with the impact of viewing violence on television and future behavior. Many sports would fall under the category of violent television. Can watching a football game make people more likely to act violently? This chapter moves past the question of whether athletes are more likely to commit crimes and asks the question: do sports cause criminal behavior in those who watch it at the arena or at home?

TYPES OF SPECTATOR VIOLENCE

There are numerous types of spectator violence that happen at sporting events across the country. Young's article provides a great starting point by categorizing five different types of spectator violence: missile throwing, field invasion, use of weapons and firearms, property destruction/vandalism, and fan fighting.[1] Missile throwing refers to the projection of objects onto the playing field or at fans or players. Fans have been known to throw all sorts of objects onto the field including cups, bottles, and batteries. The purpose is often to show displeasure with a referee's or umpire's call or are aimed at a particular player and team. The practice became so common that venues stopped serving glass bottles and typically remove the tops from plastic bottles of water or beer; this is to prevent a full bottle, even though plastic still could be very dangerous, being thrown at another player or fan. Some of the more well-known instances of missile throwing have involved giveaway nights at stadiums and arenas. In 1995 at Dodger Stadium, a free souvenir baseball promotion went wrong when, first during the seventh inning fans threw their baseballs at an opposing player after he made an error in the field. Then in the ninth inning after manager Tony Lassorda was ejected for arguing a third strike, hundreds of fans threw their balls onto the field prompting the umpires to call the game. The Dodgers were forced to forfeit the game, the first forfeit in the National League in 41 years. As a result, the Dodgers organization changed its policy on ball giveaways, now handing out free baseball certificates that can be redeemed at participating stores. On opening day in 1995 (after players returned from a strike in 1994), fans showed their displeasure all across the league:

> Fans in Detroit yesterday so endangered members of the Cleveland Indians by throwing objects onto the field that the Indians' manager considered pulling his team off the field . . . Hargrove and others at the stadium identified some of the objects that were thrown onto the field, primarily from the outfield bleachers, as a metal napkin dispenser, a hubcap, whisky bottles, cans, a battery, lighters and baseballs.
>
> On opening day in Pittsburgh last week, during an error-filled fifth inning, some fans tossed onto the field plastic tubes containing skull-and-crossbones flags they had received as a promotional giveaway. At the Mets' opener at Shea Stadium on Friday night, 10 fans ran onto the field at various times, some pausing to toss $1 bills at the players.[2]

Before the 1997 Major League Baseball season, a league bulletin was sent out to all the teams which told them it preferred that throwable objects not be given away prior to games.[3]

Fans will throw whatever they have available to them, which often leaves them throwing bottles, coins, and batteries. However, when it snows, fans have another option. On December 23, 1995, fans at Giants Stadium for the Giants game versus the San Diego Chargers began throwing snow and ice balls at the Chargers' sideline. Fifteen people were injured, most notably San Diego Chargers equipment manager Sid

Brooks, who was knocked unconscious by a snowball. Fifteen people were arrested and 175 ejected from the stadium. Giants season ticket holders who were ejected from the stadium had to forfeit their season tickets.[4]

Along with throwing items onto the field, another common form of spectator violence involves field invasion, in which fans run onto the field or court. Field invasions typically occur after an exciting win and normally at college sporting events. These types of invasion are usually a harmless celebration by exuberant college students. However, sometimes these incidents turn violent. In 1993, after the University of Wisconsin football team defeated the University of Michigan to clinch the Big Ten title and a trip to the Rose Bowl for the first time in three decades, thousands of fans poured out of the stadium trying to rush onto the field. They encountered a chain-link fence designed to keep them off the field. Some students made it onto the field but the rest were caught up in a mass of people being crushed against the fence and stands. More than 70 people needed to be hospitalized, and three were critically injured in the stampede.[5]

Field invasions are not always done for celebratory motivations. Sometimes the invasion involves an attack on a player or coach. In 2002, Kansas City Royals first base coach Tom Gamboa was attacked by a father and son who ran onto the field at Comiskey Park in Chicago. A folded-up pocketknife was found on the ground next to the two fans after the Royals players removed the fans from the coach.[6] The father was sentenced to 30 months probation after pleading guilty to two counts of aggravated battery; the son was sentenced to five years probation. After the attack on Gamboa and another similar on-field attack at a White Sox game, Illinois lawmakers stiffened penalties for unruly fans who enter the field at sporting events. Now fans will face possible prison time and a minimum fine of $1,000.[7]

One of the more dangerous instances of a fan attacking a player on the court involved tennis player Monica Seles. In April 1993, a deranged fan stabbed Seles, who was the number one ranked tennis player at the time, in the back during a match in Hamburg, Germany. The fan, 38-year-old Guenter Parche, ran onto the court and stabbed Seles between her shoulder blades. Seles was released from the hospital after a week, but did not return to tennis for more than two years. Parche, who was obsessed with Seles' rival Steffi Graff, was not sentenced to any jail time because he was found to be mentally unstable and was instead sentenced to two years probation and psychological treatment. Seles never played tennis in Germany again.

The Monica Seles incident involved the use of a weapon or firearm which is another form of spectator violence. The number of weapons or firearms at sporting events is unknown and there have not been extensive problems with them at games. However, there have been some dangerous incidents related to them. In 1999, a fan who was following Tiger Woods during a PGA event was removed after he became belligerent toward the golfer. When he was searched by security officers, they found a loaded semi-automatic handgun in his waist pack.[8] Most sporting arenas now have fans go through searches by security and metal detectors before entering the facility, which reduces the potential for weapons at the events. However, there have been numerous incidents of shootings at high school sporting events where security is much more lax. In November 2005, the National School Safety and Security Services released a report on the increasing amount of violence at high school football games.

> High school football violence since August has included one murder and nine people shot in three separate football games in one weekend in Richardson, Texas; the stabbing-death murder of a 15-year-old female student after a Montgomery County, Maryland, football game; an attempted murder shooting in a high school parking lot before an Anchorage, Alaska, football game; a male shot in the back while watching a high school football game in Los Angeles; two high school students shot outside an entrance to a Racine, Wisconsin, football game; and two individuals, including a police officer, stabbed during a fight in the stands at a Battle Creek, Michigan, football game.[9]

High school basketball games have also been the scene of quite a few shootings. In January 2009 *The Erie Times-News* reported that a girl was shot in the hip at an East High School boys' basketball game. Although no one was arrested, the "game was called off and the visiting team immediately left."[10] In another incident in the same month,

> The Major Case Squad of Greater St. Louis had no information to report Sunday on the arrests of two people in connection with the shooting death of an expelled 17-year-old Cahokia High School student during a girls' basketball game at the school Friday.[11]

The violence at high school basketball games has become so frequent that in 2009 the director of sports administration for Chicago Public Schools issued new guidelines for basketball games: "all varsity games—boys and girls—will begin at 4 P.M. No fans, other than those pre-approved by the host school's principal, from visiting teams will be allowed to attend the games, and in some instances, no fans will be permitted." Additionally, the plan requires students of the home school to present their IDs to watch games and parents of players on the home team might be required to sign in to watch the games; parents and fans of the visiting team's school would be permitted to attend, provided they are approved by the home school's principal.[12]

Typically, field invasions involve another form of spectator violence, property damage and vandalism. In college football, traditionally after a big win by the home team, fans run onto the field and in many instances try to tear down the goalposts. This tradition has become costly and dangerous on some campuses. Goal posts cost thousands of dollars to replace after being torn down and there have been numerous injuries from people either falling off the goal posts or having the goal post fall on them when it comes down. The following are examples of injuries sustained in goalpost incidents.

- Head trauma from a falling goal post caused the death of a student at the University of Minnesota, Morris over the weekend, according to an autopsy report released Monday. Rick Rose, 20, a junior from Benton City, Wash., died at a hospital after he and other students rushed onto the Morris football field to tear down a goal post after the school's team defeated Crown College on Saturday (2005).[13]
- On Oct. 22, 2003, when WVU defeated No. 3 Virginia Tech. Students rushed the turf at Mountaineer Field and tried to tear down the goal posts. A 40-minute battle with police ensued, during which pepper spray was used on the crowd. As many as 150 fires were set throughout town, Fetty said, many of them couches and chairs.[14]
- In Raleigh last Saturday [2002], fans stormed the field after N.C. State's 17-7 victory over Florida State in a wild celebration that ended in two fallen goal posts, three injuries and 21 arrests.[15]

The number and cost of these instances have led many schools to look into ways to eliminate the practice of tearing down goal posts. In 2005, Clemson and North Carolina State universities installed remote-controlled hydraulic goal posts that collapse before anyone gets a chance to tear them down. Other schools have installed similar collapsing goal posts that can be taken down in a matter of minutes, and some schools have been reduced to covering the goalposts in grease so students cannot climb them.[16] Injuries do not only occur to students trying to tear down the goal posts but also to the security officers whose job it is to keep the students under control.

The goal post system is the latest safety measure. . . . Documents from an athletic department task force before the 2003 season detailed injuries such as broken arms, knee injuries and repaired teeth as officers tried to keep people from tearing down the goal posts.[17]

The most frequent type of spectator violence involves fan fighting. Fights between fans are very common at sporting events, especially games between close rivals where fans of the opposing team are more likely to be present. On November 13, 1994, a game between the Los Angeles Rams and Los Angeles Raiders at Anaheim Stadium was the site of more than 26 fights. The fights resulted in 14 people arrested and 55 fans ejected from the stadium. A game between the same teams in the preseason resulted in more than 20 arrests.[18] Philadelphia Eagles fans are notoriously rough on the opposing team's fans. Fights at Veterans Stadium (the Eagles have played at Lincoln Financial Field since 2003 and some of the rowdy behavior has decreased with the increase in ticket prices) were becoming so common that the Eagles set up a court in the basement of the stadium.

> Fan misbehavior was at an all-time high at a Monday night game against the San Francisco 49ers in 1997. There were more than 60 fights, and one fan even shot a flare gun into some empty seats. That nationally televised episode prompted the city to set up "Eagles Court" in the bowels of the stadium to arrest, try and convict rowdy fans on the spot. "Anonymity and alcohol. You combine the two, and people start acting totally out of character," said Judge Seamus P. McCaffery, who founded and presides over Eagles Court.[19]

A sports fight led to the death of Matthew Beaudoin, a Boston Red Sox fan, after Ivonne Hernandez, a New York Yankees fan, ran her car into a crowd of people outside of a bar in New Hampshire after they began chanting "Yankees suck" after seeing a Yankee sticker on her car. Hernandez was charged with reckless second-degree murder, aggravated driving while intoxicated, and two counts of reckless conduct.[20]

Fights between fans are common at high school sporting events as well. Typically, the games that see the most violence are the local town rivalry games. In February 2005, in Malden, Massachusetts, two rival hockey teams had finished their game. As the teams exited, fans began taunting the losing team. The taunting turned into shoving between players and fans, which turned into an all-out brawl. The result of the brawl was that the next time the two teams played for the league championship the arena was empty, as no spectators, students, or family were allowed into the arena.[21]

Violence at sporting events is especially troublesome at the high school and lower levels when it involves the parents of the players. There have been numerous incidents involving parents attacking players, other parents, referees, and coaches, including the following:

- A soccer parent rushed onto a field and slugged a 15-year-old boy in the face during a freshman game in Eastlake (Ohio).
- A youth baseball coach in Florida broke the jaw of an umpire in a fight over a disputed call at third base.[22]
- In West Palm Beach, Florida, a Little Leaguer's dad pulled a gun on a coach during an argument about a batting cage. At first, the father went after the coach with an aluminum baseball bat, but then pulled a .40-caliber Glock pistol out of a gym bag.[23]
- The Texas parent, Jeffrey Doyle Robertson, had already been barred from attending games at the high school in Canton, located 60 miles east of Dallas, because of earlier confrontations with coaches and players. But on the morning of April 7, he entered the school's field house and, according to police officials, used a pistol to shoot the school's head football coach in the chest because of his son's limited playing time. Gary Joe Kinne was critically wounded. Police found Mr. Robertson in a wooded area two hours after the shooting and charged him with aggravated assault with a deadly weapon.[24]
- The mother of a boy who scored the winning run in a baseball game was knocked unconscious by angry parents from the losing team. After her 15-year-old son's run in the youth league game in Utah, two women allegedly poked Cindy Morrison with an umbrella, hit her with a baby stroller, and punched her in the face.[25]

One of the most famous incidents involving violence and parents took place at a youth ice hockey game on July 5, 2000, in Reading, Massachusetts. One player's father objected to the aggressive play of the opposing team, and began arguing about it with the team's coach, whose three sons played on the team.

> Mr. Junta argued with Mr. Costin about it, and later the two men scuffled just off the ice until Mr. Junta was told to leave the arena. But he soon came back, so enraged that he pushed aside the assistant rink manager, Nancy Blanchard, leaving a large bruise on her arm. . . .
>
> The two men soon encountered each other again, with Mr. Junta ending up atop Mr. Costin, punching him in the head and neck so hard that he severed an artery at the base of Mr. Costin's brain.[26]

Costin died from the attack. The "hockey dad" trial of Thomas Junta, which received widespread coverage and was broadcast on Court TV, put the national spotlight on parents' behavior at sporting events. Junta was convicted of involuntary manslaughter and sentenced to six to 10 years in prison.

Attacks on referees and umpires have become so common that some states have decided to add special legislation to protect them. For example Georgia passed a recent law, which mandates punishment for parents or fans who attack amateur sports officials, increasing fines for simple assault or battery of umpires and referees to a maximum $5,000, up from $1,000.[27] Stiffer penalties for those who attack sports officials are now the law in 14 states, and 14 others are considering similar legislation. Usually, these laws add referees to a special, protected class of public servants such as teachers, police officers, and jurors that intensifies the punishment for harming them.[28] In 2003 Texas passed a law that would make it a Class B misdemeanor to threaten or commit minor assault against a sports official during a sporting event, or in retaliation for something they did on the field. The maximum punishment for a Class B misdemeanor is 180 days in jail and a fine of up to $2,000. The law would apply to all sports officials, regardless of the level of competition.[29]

Another case, which took place in France, points to the level in which parents will go to help their children in sports. Christophe Fauviau drugged his teenage children's tennis rivals. He put Temesta, an anti-anxiety drug that can cause drowsiness, into the water bottles of six of his son's opponents and 21 of his daughter's between 2000 and 2003. In 2003, one of his son's opponents fell asleep at the wheel of his car after abandoning a match against his son and died in the crash. Fauviau was found guilty of causing an accidental death and was given an eight-year prison sentence in 2006.

This case was similar to the 1991 Wanda Holloway story in Texas. Holloway was convicted of trying to hire a hit man to murder the mother of her 13-year-old daughter's cheerleading rival. She hoped the murder of the mother would make the daughter unable to try out for the cheerleading squad because she would be grieving. Holloway was found guilty after her former brother-in-law recorded conversations where Holloway asked if it was possible to make the mother "go away." After being convicted and sentenced to 15 years in prison, she received a new trial when it was learned that a felon had served on the jury.[30] In 1992, a television movie based on the case (Willing to Kill: The Texas Cheerleader Story) aired on ABC.[31] Then in 1993, HBO made a dark comedy satire of the case and the media frenzy surrounding it called "The Positively True Adventures of the Alleged Texas Cheerleader-Murdering Mom."[32] In 1994, Holloway settled a civil suit with the mother she attempted to put a hit on. Finally in 1996, she was retried for the crime and found guilty. She was sentenced to 10 years and served six months.[33]

An odd type of crime that takes place at the field involves coaches being charged with a crime due to their training and practice methods. Jason Stinson, a Kentucky high school football coach, was charged with reckless homicide in the heat-exhaustion-related death of one of his sophomore players, Max Gilpin. Gilpin collapsed during practice on August 23, 2008, and died three days later. The player's body temperature reached 107 degrees and witnesses said Stinson had denied the student water on the hot August day.[34] Stinson was acquitted of the charges after two doctors testified that the excessive running did not cause Gilpin's heat stroke but rather a viral infection and his use of Adderall and creatine.[35] Charges against coaches are extremely rare. While there have been numerous deaths in the high school, college, and even professional ranks during practice, typically there are no criminal charges filed. In some instances, there have been civil complaints brought by family members against the school or team. For example, in 2005, Northwestern University settled a $16 million lawsuit brought by the family of Rashidi Wheeler who died during a football practice in 2001.[36]

Another violent form of spectator violence, which usually takes place outside of the arena or stadium, is rioting after a game. Typically after a big rivalry win in college sports or a championship win in professional sports, many fans and other people take to the streets to celebrate. Although most occasions occur with only minor incidents, sometimes the celebration can turn into a riot. The championship winning NBA cities have seen a number of violent riots after the decisive game. For example, on June 14, 1990, in Detroit, eight people died—four of them children—and 127 were injured in riots after the Detroit Pistons won their second consecutive NBA championship. Crowds smashed windows and overturned cars; one man died when a gun was fired into a crowd of revelers.[37]

After Detroit's back-to-back championships, Chicago saw its share of riots after the Bulls won a string of championships in the early 1990s. When police tried to move a crowd at State and Superior streets in Chicago after the Bulls won their third straight NBA championship, there were two shooting deaths and police made 682 arrests, mostly for disorderly conduct and scattered looting, as compared with 1,000 the previous year.[38]

Riots are also common on college campuses. There have been numerous incidents following championship wins and losses across the country on campus.

About 4,000 people spilled onto the main street in Durham after University of New Hampshire lost the championship game to Minnesota on Saturday night in Buffalo, N.Y. Some threw bottles and set off firecrackers, the mass of people blocked traffic and some tried to tip over cars, leading police to put on riot gear. It was almost two hours before the crowd began to disperse after police began spraying pepper gas in the street.[39]

Melnick, a sports sociologist and co-author of *Sports Fans: The Psychology and Social Impact of Spectators*, argues that:

> In sports psychology we call these things "celebratory riots." They are marked by a collective misbehavior when a large number of people are experiencing ecstasy and euphoria mixed in with large amounts of alcohol. These things tend to start off benign, with a lot of social milling. It doesn't take too much to get things going in a negative direction. It can start with a bonfire or a tipped-over car. . . . There is a thin line between ecstasy and antisocial behavior. It's like all the norms are suspended.

He also makes the point that the crowd is important for this type of behavior. It provides the anonymity and support for the destructive actions. He suggests placing security cameras in as many visible locations as possible: "When you know you can be identified, you are much less likely to do those things."[40]

HIGH PROFILE EXAMPLE: BASKETBRAWL

One of the most famous incidents of spectator violence involved the Detroit Pistons and Indiana Pacers basketball teams. The incident occurred in Detroit as the game was nearing its end. Indiana's Ron Artest had just committed a hard foul on Detroit's Ben Wallace. Wallace pushed Artest, who has a long history of on-court and off-court issues. Both teams converged and the refs were able to maintain order. As the referees were reviewing the tape and deciding on technical fouls, Artest was lounging on the broadcasters and scorers' table on the sidelines. As he was lying there, a fan threw a cup that hit Artest in the face. Artest immediately ran into the stands at the fan he believed threw the cup (he went after the wrong fan). As he began to attack the fan, other fans began to attack Artest. Other Pacers then entered the stands to protect Artest, which resulted in more punches between players and fans. Security was able to remove Artest and the other Pacers from the stands; however, the fans began to throw cups of beer and water at players and some fans went onto the court and confronted the players. When Artest was confronted by a fan, his teammate Stephen Jackson punched the fan across the chin. A chaotic scene took hold of the arena as fans were dumping beers on the players as they tried to exit the court, and mini skirmishes broke out across the arena. It was not until all of the players were removed from the court into the locker room that order was restored by security. The remaining time of the game was not played. The NBA suspended nine players for their role in the incident. Artest received the longest suspension in NBA history for an infraction not related to drugs or gambling. He was suspended for the remainder of the season, 86 total games (73 regular season and 13 post-season). Stephen Jackson received a 30-game suspension and Jermaine O'Neil was suspended for 15 games. Other players received lesser suspensions. On December 8, five Pacers and seven Pistons fans were criminally charged for their role in the brawl. Artest, Jackson, and O'Neil pled no contest to misdemeanor charges of assault and battery. They each received one year probation and community service. Bryant Jackson, the fan who threw a metal folding chair into a crowd of players and fans, was charged with felony assault. Jackson, who has prior criminal convictions, received two years probation. Fan John Green was convicted of assault and battery for punching Artest in the stands; he was sentenced to 30 days in jail and two years probation. He was also banned for life from any Pistons home games.

In response to the fight, the NBA imposed a new alcohol policy for all arenas. The policy (which does not seem too rigid) limited the size of alcohol cups to 24 ounces, limited an individual person from purchasing more than two drinks at a time and banned alcohol sales after the end of the third quarter. Additionally, in February 2005 the NBA passed a new code of conduct for its fans which outlined appropriate behavior at NBA games. The code states that fans have a right to enjoy the game "free from disruptive behavior, including foul or abusive language or obscene gestures." The policy also maintains that fans should not "engage in fighting, throwing objects or attempting to enter the court. . . . and guests will consume alcoholic beverages in a responsible manner." Fans who violate these rules "will be subject to ejection without refund and revocation of season tickets and may also be in violation of city ordinances resulting in possible arrest and prosecution." The policy, which doesn't add much new to existing rules at most arenas, is also supposed to serve as a "bill of rights" for fans concerned about the atmosphere at games.[41] The NBA needed to make attempts to improve its image after the Basketbrawl fiasco.

EXPLAINING SPECTATOR VIOLENCE: DIFFERENCES IN SPECTATOR VIOLENCE BETWEEN THE UNITED STATES AND EUROPE

Spectator violence, while not uncommon in the United States, is much more prevalent in Europe and South America, especially at soccer matches.

European hooligans have become synonymous with the problem of spectator violence. The scope of the problem surrounding European and South American soccer puts the North American situation into a clearer perspective. In 1964, a soccer match between Peru and Argentina resulted in more than 200 deaths and 5,000 injuries. Between June 1996 and October 1999, 48 soccer-related murders were reported in English newspapers (39 in Argentina, three in England, five in Italy, and one in the Netherlands).[42]

The lower levels of violence in the United States can be explained by numerous factors. First, there is less of an emphasis on gathering and attending games in large groups as is common in Europe, where large groups of friends gather at pubs before matches. There is also a different history involved with the rivalries in Europe. Where many teams in the United States may be relatively new to an area and teams can move from city to city, in Europe many of the teams represent cities and have been in existence for a much longer time. There is a much greater feeling of attachment and pride. Additionally, it is much easier for visiting fans to attend away games because of the geography of the countries. Although only a small number of away fans may attend a game in the United States, in Europe large groups may travel to away games and "invade" the visiting city or country. The higher ticket prices in the United States have resulted in a largely middle- to upper-class audience. In the United States, the spectators include children, women, young and old. There are many more young males who attend the soccer matches in England where there is a culture of violence that surrounds the games. In some countries, like Italy, there is also a connection between soccer teams, their fans, and political groups. The hooligans come to represent not only the soccer team but a political party with an agenda of its own.[43]

The stadium design is also important. In the United States, arenas carefully regulate seating. Everyone has an assigned seat, with the exception of a few stadiums that offer limited standing room tickets, which makes natural barriers between people and makes it hard for large crowds to congregate. It was not until the 1990s that seats became common place in England's soccer stadiums.[44]

Many believe that the problem of spectator violence is a result of too much alcohol consumed by fans. Stricter alcohol policies and increased security have become the norm across the professional sporting landscape. Fans are very passionate about their teams and when you add alcohol and the adrenaline of the game, people act more aggressively than they would in another environment.[45] For many people alcohol lowers their inhibitions, which in combination with a sporting event where people are already acting outside of social norms (such as face painting or screaming) may contribute to behaviors that people would not normally do (for example, fighting or destroying property).[46] The crowd environment makes people behave differently than they would by themselves. Many people will push the barrier of acceptable behavior when surrounded, and in many cases supported, by a crowd. For many people in our increasingly fragmented society, sports teams provide one of the few places that they feel part of a group. In this group environment with thousands of people dressed the same, chanting at a common opponent, people feel like they are a participant of the game. When this game is a part of a violent sport, we should not be surprised that violence sometimes erupts.

CRIMES ON THE FIELD BY ATHLETES

Another interesting issue of violence at the arena involves players committing crimes during the course of the game. This typically involves violence that crosses the acceptable line and crosses over to criminal behavior during the game. Laws in the United States (and Canada) do not distinguish between actions on the street and in the athletic arena. This is a very difficult area because behavior that would be deemed criminal if it occurred off the ice or field of play is sometimes an acceptable part of a sport. For example, fighting is a common sight during an NHL hockey game: the players receive a five-minute penalty but there are no criminal charges filed.

In Texas, an 18-year-old high school basketball player, Tony Limon, was sentenced to prison for elbowing an opposing player during a game and breaking his nose.[47] The incident took place in San Antonio in January 1999, in a game between South San Antonio and East Central high schools. Limon hit Brent Holmes, an East Central guard, late in the first half. Holmes' head snapped backward before he fell to the floor. Holmes suffered a concussion, a broken nose, and facial cuts. Limon stayed in the game but was suspended for the rest of the season after school officials reviewed a tape of the game. Then a month later, Holmes filed an assault charge against Limon. After reviewing a videotape of the incident, the District Attorney decided to charge Limon with aggravated assault. Limon pled no contest to the charges, expecting to receive probation, but the judge sentenced him to five years in prison. The severity of his sentence was due in part to a prior arrest; less than a month before the basketball incident, he was arrested for burglary at a shopping mall which resulted in him being placed on probation.[48] Other incidents also raise the question of what constitutes aggressive play versus criminal behavior.

- *1998:* Jason MacIntyre, who played for Phoenix in the West Coast Hockey League, was fined $500 and ordered to complete an anger management course, after he pleaded guilty to third-degree assault. MacIntyre slashed Tacoma's Thom Cullen in the face with his stick during an intermission. He was banned for life from the WCHL.
- *1999:* A Chicago teenager was charged with aggravated battery for a hit from behind during a high school hockey game that left Neal Goss, 15, paralyzed from the chest down.[49]

Some hockey players skate a fine line between what is legal and illegal on the ice. There remains an unwritten code where tough guys fight only other team's tough guys and fights draw five-minute penalties but are considered necessary in the game to enforce a sense of justice for dirty play and to protect their other "skill" players. Since 1969, 13 NHL players have been charged with crimes for on-ice incidents in the United States and Canada. In each case, the Canadian and U.S. prosecutors ruled that a hockey arena does not provide immunity from the laws of the land. Five of the 13 were convicted of assault, and one of them, former Minnesota North Star Dino Ciccarelli, was incarcerated (for a night) briefly in 1988. Of the nine criminal cases, eight were prosecuted in Canada:

- *Players:* Wayne Maki, St. Louis Blues; Ted Green, Boston Bruins
  When: September 21, 1969, Ottawa arena (preseason game)
  The facts: Maki fractured Green's skull in a vicious stick-swinging match during an exhibition game.
  The charges: Maki, assault causing bodily harm; Green, common assault
  The verdicts: Both players acquitted
- *Player:* Dave Forbes, Boston Bruins
  When: January 4, 1975, Met Center, Bloomington, Minnesota
  The facts: Forbes butt-ended Minnesota's Henry Boucha in the eye, permanently damaging the North Stars forward's vision.
  The charge: Aggravated assault
  The verdict: Hung jury in Hennepin County
- *Player:* Dan Maloney, Detroit Red Wings
  When: November 5, 1975, Maple Leaf Gardens, Toronto
  The facts: Maloney attacked Toronto's Brian Glennie from behind.
  The charge: Assault causing bodily harm
  The verdict: Maloney acquitted
- *Players:* Joe Watson, Mel Bridgman, Bob Kelly, Don Saleski, Philadelphia Flyers

When: April 15, 1976, Maple Leaf Gardens, Toronto

The facts: During a first-round playoff game, a fight between Bridgman and Toronto's Borje Salming spilled into the seats, where players, fans, and police clashed in a brawl that injured a female usher.

The charges: Bridgman and Kelly, assault causing bodily harm; Watson and Saleski, assaulting a police officer and possession of a dangerous weapon (sticks)

The verdicts: Kelly and Watson pled guilty and were fined a total of $950

- *Player:* Dave Williams, Toronto Maple Leafs

  When: October 20, 1976, Maple Leaf Gardens, Toronto

  The facts: Williams slashed Pittsburgh's Dennis Owchar in the face.

  The charges: Assault causing bodily harm and possession of a dangerous weapon

  The verdict: Williams acquitted

- *Player:* Jimmy Mann, Winnipeg Jets

  When: January 13, 1982, Winnipeg Arena, Winnipeg

  The facts: Mann sucker punched Pittsburgh's Paul Gardner from behind, breaking his jaw.

  The charge: Assault causing bodily harm

  The verdict: Mann pled guilty and was fined $500

- *Player:* Dino Ciccarelli, Minnesota North Stars

  When: January 6, 1988, Maple Leaf Gardens, Toronto

  The facts: Ciccarelli whacked Toronto's Luke Richardson over the head with his stick.

  The charge: Assault

  The verdict: Ciccarelli convicted, served one day in a Toronto jail and was fined $1,000

- *Player:* Marty McSorley, Boston Bruins

  When: February 20, 2000, General Motors Place, Vancouver

  The facts: McSorley clubbed Vancouver's Donald Brashear in the head.

  The charges: Assault with a dangerous weapon

  The verdict: McSorley convicted, sentenced to 18 months probation[50]

- *Player:* Todd Bertuzzi, Vancouver Canucks (detailed discussion follows)

  When: March 8, 2004, General Motors Place, Vancouver

  The facts: Bertuzzi punched the Colorado Avalanche's Steve Moore in the back of the head, breaking his neck.

The charge: Assault causing bodily harm
The verdict: Pled guilty, one year probation

HIGH PROFILE EXAMPLE: TODD BERTUZZI

The most recent incident of a hockey player being charged for on-ice violence involved the Vancouver Canucks' Todd Bertuzzi and the Colorado Avalanche's Steve Moore. On February 16, 2004, Moore hit Markus Naslund (the Canuck's captain) on what some considered a dirty hit or at least a penalty. No penalty was called and Naslund suffered a concussion and a bone chip in his elbow, which caused him to miss three games. The Canucks' coach and general manager criticized the play on Naslund. Several Canuck players issued warnings to Moore the next time that the two teams played. Three weeks later, on March 8, 2004, during the third period of an 8−2 Colorado lead, Bertuzzi, after trying to start a fight with Moore, came up behind him and punched him in the side of the head. The punch caused Moore to fall to the ground with Bertuzzi on top of him, driving his head to the ice. Moore was motionless on the ice and had to be removed on a stretcher; he had a broken neck and concussion. Bertuzzi was suspended indefinitely by the NHL (he served a 17-month suspension before returning). He was also charged with assault causing bodily harm. He pled guilty and was given a conditional discharge and one year probation.[51] The Vancouver Canucks were also fined by the league ($250,000) because of the culture and atmosphere that they created before the incident. Moore has filed a civil suit against Bertuzzi and the Canucks for lost income and punitive damages. In 2006, Bertuzzi offered $350,000 to settle out of court; Moore turned down the offer. To date, Moore has not appeared in another professional hockey game.

VIOLENCE AT HOME—SPORTS' LONG DISTANCE EFFECT

Can watching sports trigger violence away from the arena as well? Some studies have examined whether viewing violent sports can lead to violent behavior at home. One of the more well-known examples of this idea is seen in stories stating that Super Bowl Sunday has more incidents of domestic violence than any other day of the year. There was a public service commercial before the 1993 Super Bowl reminding people that domestic violence is a crime. Although this notion has not been corroborated with any scientific study, the popularity of the argument suggests that people do not find the idea all that far-fetched. There have been countless studies that examine the effects of exposure to violent media on children's behavior. Some sports, particularly boxing, hockey, Ultimate Fighting Championship, and football can definitely be classified as a form of violent media.

The basic idea behind media violence leading to aggression is based on imitation. The process can be seen most simply by examining children who, after watching something on television, will imitate the characters' actions. This can be seen clearly with children and professional wrestling. The most well-known case involved Lionel Tate in Florida. Tate, who was 12 at the time of the incident in 1999, slammed, punched, and kicked his younger cousin, Tiffany Eunick (six years old) until she died. Tate, who was 170 pounds (Eunick was 48 pounds), said he was imitating moves he saw watching professional wrestling. During the trial, defense attorneys argued that Tate did not mean to kill Eunick because he thought he could body-slam people and they would walk away unhurt, just like the wrestlers on television. Tate was found guilty and sentenced to life in prison without parole.[52] In 2003, the appeals court threw out Tate's conviction saying his mental competency should have been evaluated before his trial. Rather than a new trial, Tate accepted a plea deal sentencing him to the three years he had already served and probation requiring him, with few exceptions, to stay within feet of his front door, not carry any weapons and be honest with law enforcement.[53] Tate was rearrested in May 2005, accused of holding up a Domino's deliveryman at gunpoint for four pizzas worth $33.60. In February 2008, Tate was sentenced to 10 years in prison for the robbery, which will run concurrently with the 30 years he is serving for violating his murder probation by taking part in the robbery.[54]

The same year of the Lionel Tate incident, a seven-year-old Texas boy, after watching wrestling, ran across the room and struck his three-year-old brother in the neck with his forearm—a "clothesline" move he had seen watching wrestling. The three-year-old fell back and fatally struck his head; the boy died of brain injuries. When the seven-year-old boy was asked to demonstrate what he'd done, he backed up 10 feet and ran toward a police detective who was holding a toddler-sized doll. The boy forcefully stiff-armed the doll in the neck, knocking it backward. No charges were filed against the boy.[55] In another incident in Washington state, a 12-year-old boy repeatedly slammed his 19-month-old cousin to the ground in a wrestling move known as the "jackknife power bomb" (the wrestler lifts his opponent above his head and throws him down). The 19-month-old died from the attack. The 12-year-old was convicted of second-degree murder.[56]

There have been many studies that examined the link between violence on television and subsequent aggression. The previous incidents confirm the Rip Van Winkle Study that was started in the 1960s. The study followed third grade students for 20 years to examine the impact of television on aggression. The researchers concluded that watching television at an early age was not simply correlated with later aggressiveness, it helped cause it. One of the most famous studies to examine television and aggression was Albert Bandura's "bobo doll" experiment.[57] In this experiment, one group of children was exposed to a video containing aggressive behavior directed toward the bobo doll, while the control group was exposed to a video with nonaggressive behavior. Following the video, the children were placed in a room with an assortment of toys. The children who were exposed to the aggressive video were more likely to act both physically and verbally aggressive toward the bobo doll while playing. The study suggests that children engage in a level of imitative play that was directly influenced by what they had watched on television. This line of reasoning can be applied to violent sports as well. It is not a far leap to imagine children viewing a football game or hockey game to subsequently tackle or body check another child. The question becomes, does this imitation that we see in children have any relevance to adults' behavior?

Research suggests that viewing violent media leads to increased aggressive thoughts and behaviors. The theory that viewing violence might have a cathartic effect on the viewers (blow off steam) has not been supported by the research.[58] The question that has not been as well developed is whether increased aggression correlates with increased criminal behavior. A weakness of many of the studies in this area is that they are conducted in laboratory or artificial environments. Some studies have found increased heart rate and blood pressure during and after watching violent media. Only a few studies have examined whether this effect holds for viewing violent sports. One study was able to detect mood changes among spectators who viewed wrestling and ice hockey aggression, while no increase in aggression was felt by spectators who watched a swimming competition.[59] Sports violence could have a particularly powerful affect on behavior because violence that is rewarded, exciting, real, justified, and not criticized has been found to be the most likely to elicit aggression.[60] Sports violence would meet all of these criteria.

A few studies have examined this connection. One study found that there was an increase in emergency room visits by women in the Washington, DC, area the day following a Washington Redskins football victory.[61] In another rather intriguing study, Phillips (1983) found that there was a 12.46% increase in the murder rate in the days following a heavyweight prize fight.[62] These studies, although they are by no means conclusive, do suggest that sports' effect on behavior can extend well beyond the playing field. A key component in the discussion of athletes and criminal behavior and fans' criminal behavior at sporting events is the violence of some sports. Research has found that often violence from sports spills over into the players' personal lives off the field. The same effect seems to hold for some fans at sporting events where the violence on the field (among other factors) spills over into the stands. So it is not that far-fetched that the violence can affect fans viewing at home as well.

CONCLUSION

It is not surprising that fan behavior has become increasingly aggressive across the country. Part of the problem is that television, specifically the ESPN culture, encourages fans to feel like they are an important part of the game. From the common discussion of how fan noise can make a difference in a football game (for example, fans being encouraged to be the twelfth man on the football team) to the increasing phenomenon of teams encouraging their fans to wear all the same color to the game (such as Penn State football fans being encouraged to wear all white to have a "white out" and increasingly popular in college and professional ranks have been the "blackouts") fans are encouraged to feel like they are a participant in the game and can affect the outcome. A 2008 Vanderbilt news release decreed that wearing black spread to those even far out of sight: "The team and the Vanderbilt student body ask that all fans, even those watching from home, participate in a 'blackout.' "[63] It should not be surprising that some fans cross the line and actually enter the field or get involved in altercations with those at the game.

The issue of spectator violence, while important on the professional and college level given the large number of spectators, has also been mostly limited due to the presence of trained security at the facilities. This is not true at many high school or lower-level sporting events where security can be sparse or non-existent. This, along with the fact that in many cases children are playing the sports, makes these incidents even more dangerous and damaging. The increased pressure that many parents place on their children at younger and younger ages heightens the stakes of Little League or Pop Warner football games to such a level that violence can erupt. Gone are the carefree days of kids simply playing a kid's game for fun; now parents live and die with every pitch of a 12-year-old's baseball game. This is not a healthy environment for the children to participate in and is a situation that can have deadly consequences.

As attending a professional sporting event becomes more and more expensive, the issue of spectator violence at the game should become less of an issue. One reason is that the fans who can afford the game—a mix of men, women, and children in many cases—are not necessarily the ones looking for violence when attending a game. The security at games has heightened to such a level that if violence does erupt it should be handled much more effectively. The design of new stadiums also limits the chance of mass violence with effectively breaking seating areas into many different self-contained sections. Increasing the number of alcohol policies is also making it more difficult to purchase many beers (not to mention the price, which also limits many people). Given this scenario, any time that there are tens of thousands of people in one place for a common purpose, with many drinking alcohol, it should not be surprising when incidents erupt. The added element to this equation is what effect does the sport play in contributing to the violence? The emotion of the fans, the cheers for the hits, and the presence of the other team's fans are all factors that add to the environment.

Once the fans leave the arena there is an added risk of violence in the form of riots. The question here is, how many of the people involved in these riots are fans that were at the game or even fans of the team at all? In many cases, the rioters might simply be people using the sporting event as an opportunity to create mayhem. This is particularly true on college campuses where the student body has become almost conditioned to the fact that they are supposed riot after their team wins. College students feel it is their right, in many cases, to "celebrate."

The effect of viewing sports on participants both at the game and watching at home is an important area for future research. There is a lot of attention today on the effects of playing violent video games on children's behavior. Part of the concern is that video games are becoming increasingly interactive. The same can be said of being a spectator at a sporting event. Additionally the fact that many people actually participate in the sports that they watch adds an extra dimension to the potential mimicking of violent sports. Violence has pervaded every aspect of sports, from violent incidents that take place with the athletes during the game to the fan fighting that occurs in the stands. The violence has also spilled out of the arena in the form of riots and even into those viewing at home. Sports need to be included in any discussion of the effect of violence on the participants as well as on the viewers.

Chapter 5

GAMBLING

G ambling involves the wagering of money or other items of value on uncertain events, dependent either wholly or in part on chance. There are many forms of gambling that exist across the country, some legal and some illegal. This chapter will examine different types of gambling with particular attention on the legal issues surrounding them. Sports gambling will be examined with specific examples of point shaving and game fixing. The legal questions dealing with online gambling will also be addressed. Additionally, I look at the connection between gambling and organized crime. The chapter will end with an examination of the connection between casinos and increased crime and problem or pathological gambling and criminal behavior.

Gambling has existed in varying forms since the beginning of human history. It has waxed and waned in popularity and moved from legal to illegal. There has never been a more popular time for gambling in the United States than now, with the expansion of casino gambling, state run lotteries, and online gambling across the country. There is more money spent on gambling in the United States than recorded music, theme parks, video games, spectator sports, and movie tickets combined. Only two states in the country, Utah and Hawaii, do not have any form of gambling.[1]

DIFFERENT TYPES OF GAMBLING

Gambling can take many forms. The most popular form of gambling involves state run lotteries. In a lottery, tickets are sold for a set amount and a share of the proceeds is returned to the winners, usually through a random draw. During colonial times, lotteries were used by states as a revenue generator for the American Revolution and construction projects. After the Civil War, lotteries were used to try to recover from the devastation of the war. However, after some corruption, in 1890 Congress passed legislation that made it illegal for lotteries to use the mail or to be carried across state lines and excluded newspapers carrying lottery advertisements from using the mail. The law eliminated lotteries across the country. This law is still in effect.[2]

New Hampshire was the first state to re-introduce lotteries during the 20th century. The first drawing was held in 1964 and was the first legal lottery in the 20th century. Players filled out forms for drawings held twice a year. After the popularity of the New Hampshire lottery, neighboring states began to run their own lotteries. As of 2008, state lotteries exist in 43 states.

The second most popular form of gambling, behind lotteries, involves casinos.[3] Casinos are establishments where players make bets against the casino (the house) in games of chance. The games can vary from card games like blackjack and poker to mechanical games like slot machines and roulette. All games have a house edge, which means the casino has better odds of winning than the player. In games where players play against other players like poker, the casino makes its money by taking a percentage of the winning "pot."

Nevada was the first state to legalize casinos in 1931. Las Vegas became the casino capital of the world with its resort-style hotels, shows, and gambling. Las Vegas had a monopoly on casinos until New Jersey allowed casinos to be built in Atlantic City in 1979. After New Jersey, other states legalized riverboat gambling. As of 2009, there are 19 states that allow commercial casinos. The greatest increase in casino gambling took place after the United States Congress passed the Indian Regulatory Act in 1988, which allowed Native American tribes to open up gambling facilities on their reservations. By the beginning of 2000, more than half of the states (29) had some form of Native American gambling. Approximately 40% of the 562 federally recognized Native American tribes operate some form of gaming establishments.

During 2007, a quarter of the U.S. adult population visited a casino, according to Harrah's Entertainment/TNS polling data. The 54.5 million Americans who visited casinos in 2007 made a total of 376 million casino trips, 5 million more than in 2006. The approximately 450 commercial casinos produced gross gaming revenues of $34.11 billion in 2007; Native American casinos made another $26.02 billion. State lotteries' revenue totaled $24.78 billion. Card rooms generated $1.28 billion, charitable games and bingo, $2.22 billion; legal bookmaking, $168.8 million; pari-mutuel wagering, $3.5 billion. The combined total for legalized gambling revenue was $92.27 billion in 2007.[4]

SPORTS GAMBLING

Although sports gambling has been legal in Las Vegas for decades, it has never been as popular as it is today. One reason was that the federal government from 1951 to 1974 levied a 10% excise tax on sports wagers and since the profit margin before the tax averaged 5% or less, the tax resulted in making sports wagering generally unprofitable for the casinos. This changed in 1974, when Congress cut the tax from 10% to 2%, which greatly increased the profit margin for casinos. By 1988, wagers on both professional and college sports totaled $1.3 billion. With these increased profits, other states looked to get into sports gambling. However, in 1992, Congress passed the Professional and Amateur Sports Protection Act; the law prohibits gambling on amateur sporting events in all states except Nevada.

Betting on college and professional sporting events typically involves a point spread. This means that you not only bet on who wins or loses the game but by how much they will win or lose. For example, if the point spread favors the Villanova University basketball team to beat the University of Connecticut by ten points, then if you bet on Villanova, but Villanova wins by only seven points, you lose. If you bet on the University of Connecticut, you win. Casino sports books set the spreads for college and professional sporting events and the spread is covered in newspapers' sports pages across the country. A small number of major newspapers decided not to print the betting lines for college games, among them *The New York Times*, *The Washington Post*, *The Christian Science Monitor*, and *The Sporting News*. Other types of bets can be made as well, from total points scored by the two teams (over/under) to who will score the first touchdown.

Overall, Nevada's legal sports wagering represents less than 1% of all sports betting nationwide. In 2008, $2.58 billion was legally wagered in Nevada's sports books; the National Gambling Impact Study Commission (NGISC) estimated that illegal wagers are as much as $380 billion annually. Approximately two-thirds of all sports bets in Nevada are placed on professional, non-college sporting events. The FBI estimates that more than $2.5 billion is illegally wagered annually on March Madness each year. Comparatively, sports book operators estimate $80 million to $90 million, less than 4% of the illegal take, is wagered on the college basketball tournament legally through Nevada's 1,801 sports books. More bets are placed on the Super Bowl than on any other sporting event of the year, including March Madness. The 2009 Super Bowl earned nearly $6.7 million for the Nevada sports books. Approximately $81.5 million was wagered on the Super Bowl in the state's sports books in 2009, according to the Nevada Gaming Control Board. Of the total amount bet on the Super Bowl, only about 1.5% is wagered legally; these bets are made by those over age 21 and physically present in the state of Nevada.[5]

POINT SHAVING AND GAME FIXING

Legally betting on sporting events in the United States has been limited to Nevada. One of the main reasons for this is the concern over games being manipulated to win bets. There have been many instances of "fixing" games or point shaving in sports like boxing, college basketball, and football. For this reason, most sports leagues have extremely strict penalties for players betting on sporting events or associating with known gamblers. Penalties against gambling are more severe than for drug use or other criminal behavior; for example in Major League Baseball a player found to have bet on the sport faces a one-year suspension. A player betting on his own team receives a lifetime ban.[6]

Research indicates that 72% of student-athletes (Division I football and men's and women's basketball student-athletes) have gambled in some way since entering college. This number is even higher among male student-athletes (football and basketball) with 80% gambling in some manner while attending college. Among all student-athletes, nearly 35% have gambled on sports while attending college. Among all male student-athletes, more than 45% have gambled on sports. Five percent of male student-athletes provided inside information for gambling purposes, bet on a game in which they participated, or accepted money for performing poorly in a game.[7] Additionally, NCAA-funded research in 1996 found that 25.5% of athletes responding to a survey admitted to gambling on sporting events. The research used a random sample of male Division I basketball and football players. Although relatively infrequent, almost 4% admitted to gambling on events in which they played, and three respondents said they received money from a gambler for not playing well in a game.[8]

Point shaving typically involves players taking money from gamblers in exchange for ensuring that their team doesn't win or lose by too much (not cover the point spread) so that the gambler wins his or her bet. Typically, point shaving scandals involve college players. This is due to the large amount of money that professional athletes make today while college athletes are not paid at all. In the early days of professional sports, the players were not paid exorbitant salaries and they could still be "bought" by bookies. Today, it would take millions of dollars to buy a professional athlete. However, with college athletes it takes a lot less money to "buy" a player who might never play professional athletics and sees this as their only chance to make some money off the sport. The penalty for conspiracy to commit sports bribery and for unlawful use of interstate facilities is imprisonment for not more than five years and/or a $250,000 fine.

Boxing has historically been plagued with accusations of fixed fights. In the 1950s, fights were fixed to set up betting opportunities for the mob.[9] More recently the FBI has investigated a number of fights where fighters took a dive to increase the rankings of the other fighter so they could get a title shot and big payday. To many people boxing and corruption go hand in hand. It is an image that has been difficult to shake even with many reforms in the boxing world. A 1999 report by the *Miami Herald*, found that more than 30 prizefights from 1987 to 1999 were fixed or tainted with fraud. The investigations revealed that some fighters negotiated payments to throw matches while others were not bribed but fell down simply to avoid injury and get an easy paycheck.[10]

From the beginning of professional baseball, corruption and gambling were part of the game's reputation. The earliest known example of game fixing took place in 1865 when three members of the New York Mutuals accepted $100 a piece to throw the September 28, game against the Brooklyn Eckfords. Two of the three players were expelled from the league. Then in 1877 three Louisville Grays players took money to throw games. After being discovered, the three were banned from the league for their misconduct.

While the Louisville Grays' game fixing is not as well-known today, the 1919 Chicago White Sox World Series scandal has been the topic of books and movies, most notably *Eight Men Out* by Eliot Asinof. Charles Comiskey, the owner of the White Sox, famously underpaid his players. In 1917, the White Sox won the World Series and their players, who earned less than half the salary of players on other teams, asked for a raise. Comiskey refused. The players had no recourse in those days because of the reserve clause, which was a provision in every major league contract that gave the team exclusive rights to retain a player and prevent him from offering his services to other teams. The players responded by finishing sixth in 1918; Comiskey responded by cutting several players' pay. An example of Comiskey's cheapness can be seen with Eddie Cicotte. In 1917, Cicotte had a clause in his contract that he would receive a $10,000 bonus if he won 30 games. After winning 29 games with two weeks left in the season, Comiskey had the manager bench Cicotte so he didn't reach 30 wins.[11]

The team bounced back in 1919 and made it to the World Series as a heavy favorite over the Cincinnati Reds. Chick Gandil, along with help from local gambler Sports Sullivan, came up with the idea of having the White Sox throw the series. The fix received backing from New York gambler Arthur Rothstein. Gandil was able to recruit other players on the team to go along with the fix. The seven other players alleged in the scheme included Eddie Cicotte, Oscar "Happy" Felsch, "Shoeless" Joe Jackson, Fred McMullin, Charles "Swede" Risberg, George "Buck" Weaver, and Claude "Lefty" Williams. The World Series, with the recent boom in attendance at games, was a best of nine series in 1919. Game one pitcher Cicotte, who was the only player to receive money before the start of the series ($10,000) hit the first batter of the game, a sign to

Rothstein back in New York that the fix was on. Cicotte lasted only into the fourth inning and the White Sox lost the game 9 to 1. Suspicions surrounded the Series from the beginning with rumors of the fix swirling around. Lefty Williams, who lost three games in the series (still a World Series record today), lost game two for the White Sox. After receiving very little money, the White Sox players decided to win game three with Gandil driving in two of the three runs in the game. Before game 4, Sullivan, the gambler, sent $20,000 to Gandil, who gave $5,000 each to Risberg, Felsch, Williams, and Jackson. The White Sox lost games four and five. When no money arrived before game six, the White Sox won games six and seven. The gamblers made sure that the series ended in game eight. They sent someone to threaten Lefty Williams and his family; Williams lost game eight and the Reds won the series.[12]

The fix remained a secret for almost a year before *The Philadelphia-North American* reported that the 1919 World Series had been fixed. A grand jury was convened in Cook County, Illinois, where Cicotte and Jackson both confessed to their involvement. In October 1920, indictments were handed down naming eight Chicago players and five gamblers in the fix. Prior to the trial, key evidence went missing from the Cook County Courthouse, including the signed confessions of Cicotte and Jackson, who subsequently recanted their confessions. The players, with a wave of public support and expensive attorneys behind them, were all acquitted of the charges.

This did not end their troubles; the day after their not guilty verdicts, newly appointed commissioner Kennesaw Mountain Landis suspended for life all eight Chicago White Sox involved in the plan.

> Regardless of the verdict of juries, no player who throws a ball game, no player who undertakes or promises to throw a ball game, no player who sits in confidence with a bunch of crooked ballplayers and gamblers, where the ways and means of throwing a game are discussed and does not promptly tell his club about it, will ever play professional baseball.[13]

Buck Weaver, who from all accounts was not in on the fix but knew about it and did not report it, repeatedly appealed his suspension. In the World Series, Weaver hit .324 with four doubles. "Shoeless" Joe Jackson also tried to get his suspension lifted but to no avail.[14]

Baseball continued to experience problems with gambling through the 1920s with an investigation of Ty Cobb, the game's biggest star. After retiring, pitcher Dutch Leonard produced letters in 1926 that implicated Ty Cobb, Tris Speaker, and Joe Wood in a gambling scandal. He alleged that the Detroit Tigers players had conspired to fix one of the final games of the 1919 season. American League President Ban Johnson turned the letters over to Kennesaw Mountain Landis, who met with Speaker, Wood, and Cobb. Following the meeting, Landis quickly cleared the players of any wrongdoing in hopes of restoring their reputations and public confidence.[15]

More recently, in 1989, Pete Rose would become the most famous baseball player to be involved with gambling. After rumors spread of Rose's gambling habit, the commissioner of baseball retained John Dowd, a lawyer, to investigate the allegations. Pete Rose's famous quote regarding the gambling accusations was "I'd be willing to bet you, if I were a betting man, that I have never bet on baseball." The Dowd report concluded that Rose bet on baseball in 1985, 1986, and 1987, and that he specifically bet on the team that he was managing: the Cincinnati Reds. The report notes that he always bet on the Reds to win (including 52 times in 1987 at a minimum of $10,000 a game). On August 24, 1989, Rose accepted a lifetime ban from baseball, without acknowledging that he bet on baseball. However, part of the agreement allowed for Rose to reapply for reinstatement after a year. The gambling revelations also lead to criminal charges. He pled guilty to felony counts of concealing income on his 1985 and 1987 tax returns for which he was sentenced to two concurrent five-month prison terms, along with having to seek counseling for gambling addiction. Rose reapplied for reinstatement in 1997; commissioner Bud Selig took no action on his appeal. After 15 years of denying that he bet on baseball, Rose finally acknowledged in his autobiography, published in January 2004, that he made baseball wagers while he managed the Cincinnati Reds. The most widely discussed aspect of Rose's case is while being the all-time hits leader in baseball (and holding many other records as well), he has been deemed ineligible for the Hall of Fame. In 1991, the Hall of Fame stated that any player who has been deemed ineligible from baseball is not eligible for the Hall of Fame.

College basketball has seen its share of scandals since the 1950s when the New York City college basketball landscape was rocked with the discovery of point shaving involving 32 players from seven different schools. In 1951 four New York City schools had players indicted including City College (which won the National Invitational and NCAA tournaments the previous year), Manhattan College, New York University, and Long Island University. Along with the New York schools, the sport's biggest team, the University of Kentucky, was also involved (the University of Toledo and Bradley University were the other two schools implicated). Kentucky's legendary coach Adolph Rupp once boasted regarding point shaving that "they couldn't reach my boys with a ten-foot pole."

Kentucky's basketball team was suspended for the 1952–1953 season. The scandal involved 86 fixed games between 1947 and 1950.[16]

Point shaving continued to plague college basketball in the 1960s when in 1961, 37 players from 22 schools confessed to point shaving. The ring leader of the operation, Jose Molinas, an all-American college and NBA player, was sentenced to 10 to 15 years in prison (he served five years). The most notable result of the 1961 scandal was the involvement of Connie Hawkins. Hawkins, considered one of the era's best players, once took a loan from Molinas that was paid back before the point shaving allegations were made public. Unfortunately for Hawkins, his association with Molinas cost him getting drafted in the 1964 or 1965 draft; after the 1966 draft Hawkins was banned from the league. After playing with the Harlem Globetrotters and in the American Basketball Association (ABA), Hawkins was reinstated by the NBA (which settled a $1.295 million anti-trust lawsuit with him), and he went on to a Hall of Fame career.[17]

Besides Hawkins, the next most noteworthy college player to be implicated in a point shaving scandal is John "Hot Rod" Williams at Tulane University. Williams was arrested on March 27, 1985, and charged with accepting at least $8,550 for shaving points in games against Southern Mississippi, Memphis State, and Virginia Tech. Williams was charged along with two other Tulane basketball players. His first trial in August 1985 resulted in a mistrial. Williams, who was drafted in the second round of the 1985 NBA draft by the Cleveland Cavaliers, had to wait a year to become eligible for the NBA while awaiting his second trial. His second trial, in June 1986, which included testimony from the other players involved in the scheme, resulted in an acquittal. After his acquittal, Williams entered the NBA where he played 13 years, mostly with the Cleveland Cavaliers.[18]

Other schools have seen similar point shaving scandals. Arizona State University's basketball team was at the center of a point shaving scandal during the 1993–1994 season. Stephen Smith, Arizona State's second all-time leading scorer, agreed to fix four games over the course of the season for $20,000 a game. Another player, Isaac Burton, was also part of the scheme and was paid $4,300 a game. Smith had a gambling debt of $10,000 to campus bookie Benny Silman when the two came up with the point shaving idea. Smith and Burton missed shots during those games so that Arizona State would not cover the betting line; Smith refused to purposely lose games. Silman enlisted the help of other bookmakers, who had connections with organized crime in Chicago and New Jersey, and investors to finance the scheme. The first game was against Oregon State University on January 28, 1994, in which Arizona State was favored by 15 points but won by only six. The interesting aspect of this game is that Smith scored his career high 39 points and hit 10 three-pointers. Speaking to ESPN's *Outside the Lines*, Smith said "The only illegal thing I did was accept the money. As far as with the ball, when I had my uniform on, I gave 110%." The next fixed game was against the University of Oregon on January 30, 1994; Arizona State, favored by eleven and a half points, won by only six points; Smith had a subpar game, scoring only 13 points. In the third game, on February 19, 1994, Arizona State lost against University of Southern California even though they were favored by nine points. By the fourth game, the scheme had grown too big with nearly $1 million bet on the March 5, game against the University of Washington (Las Vegas officials say that a game like this typically generates around $50,000 in bets). The opening line had Arizona State favored by 15 points, but by game time, with all the money being bet on Washington, the spread dropped to just three points, leading some Las Vegas casinos to grow suspicious and take the game off the board, refusing to accept any more bets on the game. Arizona State won by 18 points, leading all the gamblers to lose their money. Sports bookmakers in Las Vegas informed the FBI of unusually heavy betting on the fixed Arizona State games.[19] This led to an investigation and subsequent arrests. The players and Silman pled guilty to sports bribery. Five gamblers and two players went to prison. The longest sentence went to Silman who was sentenced to 46 months in prison for his role. Burton received two months in prison. Smith, who was playing for the NBA's Dallas Mavericks in 1997 when he pled guilty to the charges, served a year in prison from 1999 to 2000 and was never able to make another NBA team.

The University of Toledo holds the distinction for the first (known) team to have point shaving going on with both the basketball and football teams at the same time.[20] The fixing took place beginning in the 2004 football season and ending during the 2005–2006 basketball season. Indictments were handed down in May 2009 to a number of organized crime figures and players including football players Adam Ryan Cuomo, Harvey Lamont McDougle Jr., and Quinton James Broussard, along with basketball players Keith Junior Triplett, Anton Du'Ane Currie, and Keith Lashon Payne. When the indictments were read, United States Attorney Berg stated, "Today's charges shine a light into the dark corner of illegal sports book-making and reveal the unfortunate consequences that the influence of money from betting can have on the integrity of both athletes and athletic contests." One of the investigators in the case, Special Agent Arena stated,

> This case is an example of how organized crime can influence intercollegiate athletics. These charges are an important step in maintaining the integrity

of intercollegiate athletics and a message to the athletes who decide to participate in such activities. The FBI is committed to investigating organized crime matters as well as sports bribery allegations.[21]

It is not only players but also referees that can affect the score of the game. In July 2007, NBA referee Tim Donaghy was accused of betting on NBA games in which he officiated and passing information about who was refereeing specific games (not public information) to gamblers (two of whom were also convicted and sentenced to prison—Thomas Martino to 12 months and a day in prison and James Battista received 15 months).

In 2007, Tim Donaghy pled guilty to gambling on games he officiated and passing information along to bookies. He was sentenced to 15 months in prison. The NBA did an investigation of its referees and concluded that while as many as half of the referees violated the strict no gambling rules, Donaghy was the only referee involved in gambling on games.[22] However, the league has been forced to confront various allegations from Donaghy that raised questions about widespread game fixing through the league, not just from referees but from the league officials. Donaghy told federal investigators that NBA executives directed referees "to manipulate games" to "boost ticket sales and television ratings." He singled out Game 6 of the Western Conference finals in 2002, when the Los Angeles Lakers shot 27 free throws in the fourth quarter (18 more than the Sacramento Kings) and beat the Kings, 106 to 102, to force a seventh game in the series. The Lakers are a much more popular team nationally with stars Shaquille O'Neal and Kobe Bryant. The Lakers went on to win the series and the finals.[23] The game's officiating generated great controversy at the time. Ralph Nader wrote a letter to the NBA commissioner David Stern stating:

> At a time when the public's confidence is shaken by headlines reporting the breach of trust by corporate executives, it is important, during the public's relaxation time, for there to be maintained a sense of impartiality and professionalism in commercial sports performances. That sense was severely shaken in the now notorious officiating during Game 6 of the Western Conference Finals between the Los Angeles Lakers and the Sacramento Kings.[24]

Nader was not alone in his concern over the officiating. Michael Wilbon, a sports columnist, wrote in *The Washington Post*, "The Kings and Lakers didn't decide this series . . . three referees did."[25] David DuPree, a sports writer for *USA Today*, stated: "I've been covering the NBA for 30 years, and it's the poorest officiating in an important game I've ever seen."[26]

Point shaving and game fixing will continue to be a problem as the market for sports betting continues to expand with many turning to online gambling. Additionally, Delaware approved sports betting in May 2009. Delaware offered a sports lottery in 1977 for only one year, after revenues were below expectations. This one-year experiment with sports gambling allowed Delaware to be grandfathered in (along with Oregon, Nevada, and Montana) under the 1992 federal law that bans states from establishing sports gambling.[27]

HIGH PROFILE EXAMPLES: BOSTON COLLEGE AND NORTHWESTERN UNIVERSITY

Two notable schools, Boston College and Northwestern University have experienced scandals involving both their basketball and football teams. Boston College's basketball team became involved with organized crime figures during the 1978–1979 season. Three players worked with members of the Lucchese crime family to shave points on games throughout the season. The Lucchese crime family included Henry Hill who wrote the book *Wiseguys* based on his life, which was turned into the movie *Goodfellas*.

Hill, who was in prison in Pennsylvania, met Paul Mazzei, a small time drug dealer from Pittsburgh. Hill and Mazzei, who had both been involved with bookmaking, hatched a plan to fix Boston College basketball games when Mazzei suggested that he could get Rick Kuhn, a Pittsburgh native and forward on the Boston College team involved. Mazzei was able to convince Kuhn with promises of easy money while Hill would be able to use his organized crime connections to make the bets. Kuhn was able to convince Jim Sweeney, the starting point guard, to attend a meeting with Hill and Mazzei at a Boston hotel where details of the plan were discussed. The plan was also discussed with the team's leading scorer, Ernie Cobb. Cobb would subsequently deny ever shaving points, although he did accept money after one of the games. The plan was not without its ups and downs. The first planned game was against Providence College where Boston College was favored by seven points. The plan was for them to win by less than seven; however, they won by 19 points with Cobb scoring 25 points. The next fixed game went more according to plan. The December 16, 1978, game against Harvard University had Boston College favored by 12 points; Boston College won by only three. This up and down, win/lose ride for the gamblers continued throughout the season. Part of this can be explained by the fact that Kuhn, who saw limited playing time as a role player, was the only player who was fully committed to the scheme. There were nine more fixed games throughout the season.

The point shaving might not have ever been uncovered if not for Henry Hill's arrest on unrelated drug charges. Hill agreed to testify against his former organized crime associates in exchange for immunity and entrance into the Witness Protection Plan. While talking with prosecutors, Hill referenced the time he was up in Boston fixing some games. Ed McDonald, working for the United States Attorney office, had attended Boston College. He pushed the issue until Hill disclosed all the details to him. Hill also disclosed the details for a February 16, 1981, *Sports Illustrated* cover story. Hill's testimony led to charges against Jimmy Burke, Paul Mazzei, Roco Pearla, and Rick Kuhn in the first trial.

Rick Kuhn and Ernie Cobb, the star shooting guard, stood trial for their involvement in the scandal while Jim Sweeney, the team's point guard, testified against them. Kuhn was sentenced to 10 years in prison which was the most severe sentence ever handed down for point shaving (it was later reduced to four years). Cobb was found not guilty but his basketball career in the United States was over. He later played professional basketball in Israel.[28]

Then in 1996, Boston College suspended 13 football players for the final three games of the season after allegations surfaced of betting on professional and college sports, which is a violation of NCAA rules. Two of the 13 players bet on Boston College football games, which was bad enough but adding to that they bet on their school not to cover the spread against Syracuse University. The players lost their $450 wager when Boston College won by 28, covering the 13-point spread. The head football coach Dan Henning resigned less than three weeks after the betting scandal became national news.[29] The other players received various punishments from the school (seven of the players' eligibility was returned the following season, while six of the players remained ineligible to play and three of the six players had their scholarships revoked). There were no criminal charges filed against any player.[30]

Northwestern University's football team came under scrutiny in 1994 when running back Dennis Lundy, according to his testimony in federal court, purposely fumbled the ball on the one yard line in a game against the University of Iowa. Lundy had bet against his team and fumbled away the easy touchdown to ensure that Northwestern did not get close enough to Iowa, who was favored to win by six points. Northwestern went on to lose the game 49-13. After the game, an assistant coach overheard another player accuse Lundy of fumbling the ball on purpose and reported the incident to the head coach. After an investigation by the school, it was discovered that Lundy and basketball player Kenneth Dion Lee, starting point guard on the 1994–1995 team, had been betting on and trying to fix college games.

The plan was orchestrated by Kevin Pendergrast, a former place kicker for the University of Notre Dame's football team. Pendergrast had run up $20,000 in gambling debts. In an effort to recoup his losses, he was able to convince Lee to go along with the point shaving scheme. Lee had his own gambling problems, already having been suspended by Northwestern for gambling, and had accumulated a large amount of debt. Pendergrast promised to pay Lee thousands of dollars for his involvement.[31] Lee was able to recruit another basketball player, Dewey Williams, to participate as well. The idea behind the operation was different than other point shaving incidents, where players on teams favored to win the game try to keep the margin of victory down under the spread. Northwestern players tried to lose by a larger margin than the betting line. In the two basketball games against the University of Wisconsin and Penn State University in which they won their bets (lost by more than the spread), Lee was paid $4,000 for his role. The third game of the operation against the University of Michigan did not go well; Northwestern, which was a 25-and-a-half-point underdog, lost by only 17. Lee and Williams both performed below average in all three games. Lee, who averaged 12 points a game for the season, scored nine, two, and eight points, and shot a combined one for eight from three-point range.[32]

Lundy would be sentenced to a month in prison for lying to a federal grand jury investigating the case. Lee and Williams, who played center and forward for the team, were sentenced to a month in prison for their role in shaving points during the 1994–1995 Northwestern basketball season.[33] Pendergrast, who organized the scheme, received two months in prison after pleading guilty and cooperating with authorities.[34]

ONLINE GAMBLING

In 2008, online sports betting generated $5.49 billion in revenues. This is more than triple the $1.7 billion generated by online sports betting in 2001.[35] Although it is flourishing, the legality of online gambling continues to be debated. There are a few existing laws that are cited when arguing the legality of online gambling. The most notable is the Federal Interstate Wire Act of 1961, which makes it illegal for someone to engage in the business of gambling using wire communication. Two issues with the applicability of the Wire Act to online gambling are: the act was clearly designed to limit use of the telephone in running of an interstate gambling business, so it is unclear whether it would apply to the Internet and secondly the act targeted the person or company receiving the bets, not the individual placing the bet. Additionally, the act addresses sports wagering and does not address other casino-type gambling. The application of this law to Internet gambling has yet to be determined.

There have been attempts made to update the Wire Act, including the Internet Gambling Prohibition Act of 1997, which specifically referenced the Internet and included penalties for the individual bettor. The Act passed the Senate but did not pass the House.

There are two other federal laws that may apply to Internet gambling. The Travel Act prohibits interstate or foreign travel to distribute the proceeds of illegal activities, manage, or carry on unlawful activity. Illegal activities specifically reference gambling. This act would most clearly apply to residents trying to set up an offshore casino. Another federal act that could be applied is the Organized Crime Control Act of 1970, which deals with anyone who "conducts, finances, manages, supervises, directs or owns all or part of an illegal gambling business." The gambling is seen as a violation if it violates the state or political subdivision in which it is conducted. The statute could be applied to the owners of the gambling Web site, the Internet provider, and individual gambler. Additionally, in a broad sense, the Racketeer Influenced and Corrupt Organizations (RICO) statutes could apply if the gambling organization is deemed large enough to have an effect on interstate commerce.[36] For a federal law to apply to gambling, typically it must include some level of interstate or international commerce. Thus most gambling prohibitions are seen on the state level. This is why the most successful attempt so far by the federal government to limit online gambling was the U.S. Congress passing the Unlawful Internet Gambling Enforcement Act of 2006 which made it illegal for banks and credit card companies to send payments to Internet gambling sites. The act made it more difficult for gamblers to set up accounts with gambling Web sites.

The legality of online gambling remains unclear because of the many difficulties and complexities involved with the issue, including the difficulty of enforcing such a ban. Some states have taken the issue on by going after online gambling companies that advertise in their states.[37] For example, are gambling operators who are located in a foreign jurisdiction protected from state and federal laws of the United States? Jay Cohen became the first person to be convicted by a jury and sent to prison in the United States for taking bets online in 2001. Cohen, who was licensed and operated out of Antigua, was charged with conspiracy to violate the federal Wire Act (Cohen was also taking bets by telephone).

The Department of Justice continues to maintain that it is illegal to bet online. However, the few times that they have gone after gamblers for making bets, judges have thrown the charges out. Fewer than 25 people have ever been prosecuted in the United States for online gambling. Most were bookies who were also taking sports bets on the telephone.[38] Almost all federal prohibitions on gambling deal with the organizing or running of a gambling business, not simply placing bets. While the Department of Justice maintains its position, in 2000 Congress amended the Interstate Horseracing Act to expressly make remote wagers across state lines on horseracing legal, as long as the bet is legal in the state where the bettor is, where the bet is accepted, and where the race takes place.[39] Although this act seems to contradict the Department of Justice's reasoning regarding online betting, it continues to maintain that online gambling is illegal and threatens people or businesses with prosecution for engaging in it. The threats have worked in limited advertising of online gambling Web sites in magazines, on other Web sites, and television.[40] However no one has ever gone to prison for making a bet online.

In May 2009, a bill was introduced that would roll back the ban on online gambling. The bill, introduced by Congressman Barney Frank, is the Internet Gambling Regulation, Consumer Protection and Enforcement Act, which seeks to undo the Unlawful Internet Gambling Enforcement Act by strictly regulating and licensing online casino and poker betting in the United States. The bill has not yet been debated by Congress.

GAMBLING AND ORGANIZED CRIME

Gambling has historically had an outlaw image, from the early frontier days and the gun battles over poker in the Wild West. During the 20th century, the outlaw image continued as gambling became associated with organized crime. Bookmaking, casinos, and numbers were central to the income and power of organized crime.[41] The emphasis on gambling decreased during Prohibition as bootlegging became a major source of income and then again as illegal drugs became more popular in the 1960s. However, gambling has consistently been part of organized crime's activities.

In Nevada, organized crime was influential in the creation of the early casinos and especially the famed Las Vegas Strip. Although the first casino opened in the early 1930s the Strip did not see its first casino until 1941, with the opening of the El Rancho Vegas, which was quickly followed by the Last Frontier and Desert Inn. In 1946, seeing the endless opportunities for money, famed mobster Bugsy Siegel opened the Flamingo Casino, which was financed by organized-crime kingpin Meyer Lansky.[42] Through its early years Las Vegas had a difficult time keeping organized crime's influence out of the casinos. Even beyond the clear links to organized crime there were problems associated with the practice of hidden ownership, teamster financing, and employing members of organized crime or former convicts.[43] The concern with organized crime's influence on gambling led Congress to create the Kefauver commission (a Special Committee to Investigate Organized Crime in Interstate Commerce) in the 1950s. The committee had a national focus with special attention to Nevada's casinos. The commission led to stricter regulation of gaming licenses and the creation of the Gaming Control Board in 1955 and the Gaming Commission in 1963 to enforce state gaming regulations in Nevada.[44]

Additionally, there are many federal criminal laws that monitor organized crime and gambling. The Gaming Devices Act of 1951 prohibits interstate transportation of gaming devices. The RICO statutes and amendments made in 1985 to the Bank Secrecy Act, also known as the Currency and Foreign Transactions Reporting Act, require several cash-intensive businesses, and explicitly casinos, to report cash transactions in amounts greater than $10,000. In addition, the Money Laundering Control Act of 1986 and the Treasury Department's Financial Crimes Enforcement Network were enacted to "establish, oversee, and implement policies to prevent and detect money laundering."[45]

The Organized Crime Control Act of 1970 was used by the Department of Justice to focus almost exclusively on the gambling activities of organized crime. In the first five years of the legislation, gambling cases accounted for 72% of the wiretaps sought by authorities.[46] This focus on gambling diminished as there was little effect on the Mafia's power and the authorities began to be more concerned with illegal drugs.

Even with all these regulations, the connection and influence of organized crime on casinos did not go away. During the 1970s, a number of casinos were found by Nevada authorities and the U.S. Department of Justice to be infiltrated by organized crime families who controlled union pension funds that facilitated casino expansion.[47] However, the strong state and federal regulations have allowed for casinos to expand across the country, diminishing the connection with organized crime. Most casinos today are owned by large corporations (even many of the Native American casinos) whose finances are reviewed by financial analysts and the Securities and Exchange Commission as well as by federal and state law enforcement agencies.[48]

With increased access to legal gambling, many believed illegal gambling would decrease. However, illegal gambling in many ways benefits from legal gambling, especially sports betting. Bookies use the legal sports books for their line or point spread and it gives them a place to lay off some of their bets. The chairman of the Nevada State Gaming Control Board, Steve DuCharme, said in a 1999 interview, "A lot of money made through illegal gambling is laid off in Las Vegas. If a bookie has a lot of money on one side of a bet, they bet the other one in Las Vegas to try and even the bet."[49] Most people cannot get to Nevada to place a bet on a sporting event legally. These people will turn to illegal bookmakers and more recently to the Internet.

The days of mob-owned casinos have become part of the mystique of Las Vegas and are now something looked back on with sentiment. In 2008, Las Vegas announced it was building a museum showcasing the historical connection of the city to organized crime. The Las Vegas Museum of Law Enforcement and Organized Crime, or as the locals call it, the Mob Museum, "will tell the story of the city's rise from a desert watering hole to glittering magnet for dreamers by focusing on what may have been the key: organized crime."[50]

Because of this history, the concern about organized crime is usually raised whenever a state discusses legalizing gambling. This concern is not completely unfounded as organized crime still maintains a hold on the illegal gambling industry.

- *June 4, 2009.* Two men, Raul Suner and Phillip John Bauco, were indicted for representing that they had the backing and approval of La Cosa Nostra and engaged in a campaign to take over certain illegal gambling operations in the Bridgeport area by using threats, violence, and intimidation to persuade bookmakers and gamblers to conduct their illegal gambling with the operation run by Suner and Bauco. The Indictment alleges that Suner was an associate of the Gambino Family of La Cosa Nostra and had authority to conduct and run illegal gambling operations in portions of Connecticut, including New Haven and Bridgeport. Bauco is alleged to have used his business, Auto Town Sales in Stratford, to hold meetings related to the criminal enterprise.[51]
- *August 27, 2008.* Two men with reputed ties to organized crime pled guilty on Tuesday to participating in an illegal gambling ring run out of a wholesale produce market at Hunts Point in the Bronx.[52]
- *February 8, 2006.* A former National Hockey League player, Rick Tocchet, who coached alongside Wayne Gretzky, faces charges of financing a multimillion-dollar sports gambling ring. The authorities said the ring had links to organized crime and clients including at least a half-dozen current or ex-players and Janet Jones, Wayne Gretzky's wife.[53]

GAMBLING AND CRIMINAL BEHAVIOR

The connection between gambling and criminal behavior has traditionally focused on organized crime. However, more recently the concern has dealt with crimes caused by casinos entering an area and by problem or pathological gamblers. Additionally, there is concern over whether the two issues are connected, such as the introduction of casinos in an area causing increased problem gamblers.

There are many areas to examine when looking at the impact of casinos on crime: street crime, domestic violence, child abuse, white-collar crime, and adolescent gambling. Much of the research done in the area has been partisan, with those against casinos and gambling finding increased crime rates, and gambling advocates finding no change while citing the many economic benefits that casinos bring to an area. There have been quite a few studies that examined the topic, however many of the early studies simply compared the number of reported crimes in an area before the presence of a casino to the number of crimes after the casino opened. The problem with that is it is natural for an area to see increased crime when the population increases in the area (as would happen when a casino opens). Much of the research does not separate the crime issue from the increased tourist population or compare casinos to other tourist attractions that bring visitors to an area. The question should be: do casinos increase crime in an area more than an amusement park or other similar tourist attractions? There is also the need to distinguish between crimes that happen on the casino grounds and those that occur in the community.

A number of studies examined Atlantic City before and after casinos were legalized in 1978. There was a drastic increase in crime from pre-casino years to post-casino years. However, Atlantic City has a resident population of 38,000 people but in 1983 alone 27 million tourists visited the city.[54] Subsequent studies that took the tourist population into effect showed little or no change in the crime rate of Atlantic City post-casinos. This is not to suggest that crime and the economy have been helped by the casinos either.

Studies have been mixed in regard to crime and casinos:

- A study of Biloxi, Mississippi, compared pre-casino and two-year post-casino crime rates and found no increase in crime.
- A study of counties with Indian casinos versus those counties without Indian casinos in Wisconsin found that that counties with casinos had higher than expected crime rates.

These contradictory studies are consistent with the research on this topic. Several studies have taken a more national approach, examining multiple states with similar results. A study of six new casino communities' crime rates compared with non-casino communities found some casinos with increased crime rates, some with no change, and others with decreased crime.[55] This is similar to the National Gambling Impact Study Commission (NGISC), which was charged in 1996 by Congress to investigate the impact of all forms of gambling on society. Their final report submitted in 1999 suggested that gambling offers both positive impacts and negative impacts on communities. The NGIC study found some casino communities experience many benefits from the addition of casinos while other communities suffer from the addition of casinos. The NGIC final report states:

> Communities that embrace gambling, and the areas that surround them, experience both gambling's positive and negative impacts. The key question is how do gambling's benefits measure against its cost? Even after the NGISC's 2 years of extensive research, the question cannot be definitively answered.[56]

The NGISC Report concluded in regard to crime that "taken as a whole, the literature shows that communities with casinos are just as safe as communities that do not have casinos."[57]

There is also concern over the crimes committed by compulsive gamblers to support their gambling habits. There are 10 symptoms of pathological gambling defined by the *Diagnostic and Statistical Manual of Mental Disorders, Fourth Edition* (DSM-IV). According to DSM-IV, pathological gambling needs to be defined as separate from any other manic episode. It is only diagnosed when the gambling occurred independent of other impulsive, mood, or thought disorders. In order to be diagnosed, an individual must have persistent and recurrent maladaptive gambling behavior as indicated by five (or more) of the following:

1. Is preoccupied with gambling (e.g., preoccupied with reliving past gambling experiences, handicapping, or planning the next venture, or thinking of ways to get money with which to gamble).
2. Needs to gamble with increasing amounts of money to achieve the desired excitement.
3. Has repeated unsuccessful efforts to control, cut back, or stop gambling.
4. Is restless or irritable when attempting to cut down or stop gambling.
5. Gambles as a way of escaping from problems or of relieving a dysphoric mood (e.g., feelings of helplessness, guilt, anxiety, depression).

6. After losing money gambling, often returns another day to get even ("chasing" one's losses).
7. Lies to family members, therapist, or others to conceal the extent of involvement with gambling.
8. Has committed illegal acts such as forgery, fraud, theft, or embezzlement to finance gambling.
9. Has jeopardized or lost a significant relationship, job, or educational or career opportunity because of gambling.
10. Relies on others to provide money to relieve a desperate financial situation caused by gambling.[58]

Compulsive or pathological gamblers have been found to have higher arrest and imprisonment rates than non-pathological gamblers. According to a National Opinion Research Center (NORC) study, a third of problem gamblers had been arrested compared to 10 percent of low-risk gamblers and 4 percent of non-gamblers.[59] A study of Gamblers Anonymous members found 57% admitted to stealing to finance their gambling. The study revealed that they stole on average $135,000 per individual.[60] Many problem or pathological gamblers engage in white-collar crimes like embezzlement, forgery, or fraud as a means to support their gambling habit; however, there is no conclusive evidence that these behaviors increase with the advent of a casino in the area. An added problem with examining the effects of problem gambling on the crime rate is that the crimes that are typically attributed to compulsive gamblers (bad checks, embezzlement, check forgery, and fraud) are often underreported.

In addition to white-collar crime, some studies have shown that between one quarter and one half of spouses of compulsive gamblers have been abused. The NORC study of ten casino communities showed that in six of the communities, domestic violence increased with the introduction of casinos.[61] Some anecdotal evidence in the NGISC Report and in the media suggests that child abuse and neglect are also related to casinos and problem gambling. There have been a number of high profile incidents where parents have left their children in the casino lobby or in the car while they go into the casino to gamble.

- A San Jose woman was arrested in Placer County and her five-year-old child is in protective custody after the woman left her in an unlocked car for five hours while gambling inside a casino.[62]
- In a case that demonstrated the destructiveness of gambling's grip, a Jefferson Parish judge handed down a 40-year sentence to a nanny who left a three-year-old boy to swelter to death in a locked van while she played video poker in a Bridge City restaurant.[63]

- Virginia Williams went gambling and left 11 of her children alone in their home for 12 hours. The house caught fire, and all 11 children—ranging from 10 months to 11 years old—were killed in one of the deadliest fires ever in the St. Louis area.[64]

Most states that introduce gambling require that some of the gambling revenues be put into treatment and call centers for problem gamblers. For example in 1992, when the Oregon Lottery received approval to operate video poker, the approval included a measure directing that 3% of gross revenues from video poker be returned to the counties' mental health departments to establish treatment programs for problem gamblers. The concern may be well-founded in Oregon; since video poker was introduced, the number of Gamblers Anonymous meetings around the state grew from three to more than 30. Additionally, approximately 1,000 individuals have entered the state-subsidized treatment programs since January 1995. The majority of these problem gamblers (81%) have gambled primarily on video poker and they have an average gambling debt of $16,000 which is more than half the average annual income of this group.[65]

With the continued expansion of gambling in all forms across the country and many states' continued dependence on gambling revenues to support their budgets, the number of problems associated with gambling will continue to grow.

HIGH PROFILE EXAMPLE: MICHAEL JORDAN

Michael Jordan, the NBA's biggest star during the 1990s, was followed throughout his career by gambling controversies. In December 1992, it was reported that a $57,000 check Jordan wrote to James (Slim) Bouler, an amateur golfer and convicted drug dealer, was confiscated by federal agents investigating Bouler for money laundering and drug charges. Then on March 19, 1993, checks totaling $108,000 were discovered by a North Carolina attorney, Michael Gheen, who said that Jordan had repaid golf and poker debts to his deceased client, Eddie Dow, a North Carolina businessman, and three others.[66]

In April 1993, the NBA announced the results of its investigation of Jordan's high-stakes gambling. After meeting with Jordan, NBA commissioner David Stern said that the league had found no cause for disciplining him. This was following an investigation into recent reports linking him to high-stakes wagering on golf matches and poker games in Hilton Head, S.C., where Jordan has a vacation home. Saying there was "no evidence that Michael has ever gambled on NBA games," Stern reported that

Jordan understood "the gravity of the situation" and would be more careful about his associations.[67]

On October 1992, Jordan testified in federal court in the trial of Bouler. Jordan testified that he paid Bouler, who was facing money laundering and drug charges, $57,000 to cover gambling losses from a weekend of golf and poker at a South Carolina resort. When asked during the trial about the $57,000, Jordan said it was: "For what I lost on gambling and golf and later in poker when he loaned me some money. I didn't have any money."[68]

Jordan's gambling continued to be the subject of speculation during the 1993 playoff series between Jordan's Chicago Bulls and the New York Knicks. The press learned that Jordan spent the night before game two of the series playing blackjack in Atlantic City, New Jersey. Reports included descriptions that Jordan lost thousands of dollars and was out late.[69] Regarding his Atlantic City visit Jordan said:

> I didn't have anything else to do in New York. I didn't want to go to a restaurant. I didn't want to go golfing, because I didn't have my golf clubs. If I had my golf clubs, I probably would have gone; then you would have criticized me for doing that. But I was just trying to relax away from the game of basketball, get my mind away from the game, and just do whatever felt comfortable to me to relax. That's it.

The Bulls lost game two of the series.

Shortly after the 1993 playoffs were over, Richard Esquinas, a San Diego businessman, released his book, *Michael and Me: Our Gambling Addiction. . . . My Cry for Help*, in which he claimed Jordan had lost $1.25 million in golf bets to him. Jordan confirmed that he had paid Esquinas $300,000 to cover gambling losses. The NBA then launched its second investigation into Jordan's gambling activities. The Lacey investigation, conducted by former federal judge Frederick Lacey, found that there was "absolutely no evidence Jordan violated league rules."[70]

A few days before the NBA finished its second investigation of Jordan, he surprisingly announced his retirement from the NBA at the age of 30. He claimed that he had lost his motivation for the game after winning three NBA titles in a row, and dealing with the murder of his father James Jordan in the off-season. After retirement, Jordan announced his plans to play baseball. He played for the Birmingham Barons, a minor league affiliate of the Chicago White Sox. The White Sox are owned by Jerry Reinsdorf, who also owns the Chicago Bulls and continued (for some reason) to pay Jordan's $3.9 million salary as he hit .202 for the minor league baseball team. In March 1995, Jordan announced that he would return to the NBA.

Jordan's return to the NBA, which included a second run of three straight titles for the Bulls, included speculation about what role the NBA's gambling investigation played in his "early" retirement. A few statements made by Jordan have only fueled the speculation. As detailed in the book *Sport Scandals*, when Jordan was asked during his retirement press conference whether or not he would return to the NBA, he said: "If David Stern (NBA commissioner) lets me back in the league, I may come back." Jordan continued that his retirement from the NBA "doesn't mean I'm not going to play basketball somewhere else" and he stressed that he was leaving "the NBA." Then after Jordan's second retirement in 1999 he thanked the commissioner for giving him the "opportunity" to play basketball.[71] This led to questions of why the commissioner would have to "let" Jordan back in the league and why he would thank the commissioner for the "opportunity" to play basketball.

Jordan returned again to play two forgettable seasons for the Washington Wizards before moving into a part ownership role for the Charlotte Bobcats. In 2005, after his final retirement, Jordan spoke with Ed Bradley on *60 Minutes* regarding his gambling.

> "Yeah, I've gotten myself into situations where I would not walk away and I've pushed the envelope. Is that compulsive? Yeah, it depends on how you look at it. If you're willing to jeopardize your livelihood and your family, then yeah," says Jordan.
> "And you're not willing to do that?" Bradley asks.
> "No," Jordan replies.

James Jordan, Michael's father, said that his son didn't have a gambling problem, but a competitive problem. People who know Jordan repeatedly say that he is the most competitive person they have ever met. As Jordan describes himself:

> I want to win. I want to go out on a limb and win. And sometimes that can take you past the stage that you know you probably should take a step back from. Sometimes I don't look at that line. I just step over that line. But once I step over it and I feel the lack of success, it's very embarrassing things. So you look at yourself in the mirror and say, "I was stupid. I was really stupid." But we all are. But you have to be able to look in that mirror and say that you're stupid.[72]

His behavior fits into many of the categories for problem gambling; for example, he is preoccupied with gambling, needs to gamble with increasing amounts of money to achieve excitement, has repeated unsuccessful efforts to cut back or stop gambling, gambles as a way to escape from problems, after losing money gambling keeps returning to get even, and has jeopardized career opportunities because of gambling. Six indicators are listed that fit Jordan's behavior during his NBA career, only five of these behaviors are needed to indicate a problem gambler.[73]

CONCLUSION

Gambling has become engrained in mainstream U.S. culture. What once was left to smoke-filled back alley card rooms and organized crime is now just another form of entertainment for many Americans. This can be seen most clearly in Las Vegas' transformation from a gamblers-only paradise to a family vacation destination. In addition, gambling has expanded out of casinos and bookies into state-run operations. Although sports gambling only comprises part of the gambling industry, the sports world is nonetheless affected by the continued growth and popularity of gambling. Even as gambling has, essentially, moved from an illegal to legal enterprise, there are still issues related to gambling and criminal behavior.

Betting and sports have always gone hand-in-hand. The expansion of sports gambling in Las Vegas, online gambling, March Madness office pools, and Super Bowl bets have made betting on sports more acceptable than ever. However, betting on sports can still impact the game. Instances of game fixing and point shaving tarnish the entire notion that sports gambling does not harm sports. The revelation of NBA referee Tim Donaghy's corruption reinforced many people's suspicions that NBA games are sometimes fixed (either by referees, players, or the league). Additionally, every year in the NFL, there is discussion about some meaningless play at the end of the game (for example, a team didn't run the ball into the end zone at the end of the game when it could have) that affected which team won with the point spread. Added to this is the fact that many people assume that there is corruption in sports like boxing and horse racing. Professional sports leagues need to be concerned if the betting world affects the integrity of their games.

Of even greater concern to society should be the continued expansion of gambling in all forms, most notably lotteries and casinos, by states across the country. Gambling historically has been tied to organized crime. Although those connections are not as strong as they once were, states still need to be aware of the possible influx of a criminal element when increasing gambling opportunities. More concerning than organized crime is the increased number of problem gamblers that inevitably results when states introduce greater access to gambling. Problem gamblers typically suffer from personal problems (for example, family breakup, stress, and alcohol abuse) as well as criminal problems. The desire to gamble leads to stealing from family members, places of work, or strangers. States need to take responsibility for the social problems that may result as they continue to expand gambling as a quick and easy way to increase their revenue. However, the issue of access to gambling within individual states may become irrelevant as online gambling becomes more and more the option of choice for gamblers.

Chapter 6

SPORTS AND CRIME REDUCTION

Basketball is my ticket out of the ghetto.

William Gates, *Hoop Dreams*

The "play movement" which started near the end of the 19th century and continued into the early part of the 1900s featured the first construction of playgrounds, parks, and gymnasiums for children. The movement featured the creation of parks and recreation departments by cities and involvement from the local boards of education. It was an attempt to keep kids off the physically and socially dangerous streets.[1] In his introduction to the 1917 book, *The Play Movement and Its Significance,* Curtis describes the rationale for the "play" movement which took hold in the late 1890s.

> But what nearly every parent and observer of children has seen is that there has been little for children to do in the cities, and that in this time of idleness the devil has found much for idle hands to do; that the children are an annoyance to their parents and the neighborhood and that they acquire many vicious habits during this unused time. The boys often learn to smoke and gamble and tell and hear many obscene and otherwise dangerous stories. There are many accidents to the children playing in the streets, and their parents are constantly worried about them. In the evenings the pool rooms and dance halls are crowded by young people in the early teens who are in a quest of a good time, and find no opportunities except those offered for gain where drinking and sex lure are the main enticements to the spending of money. The home seems to be disappearing, and crime, despite an increasingly effective police and probation system, is increasing everywhere. Through all of these means there has come a general though dim realization that if we would stem this tide, we must surround the children with a different environment.[2]

For many, sports have always been seen as a cure-all for many of the problems facing juveniles and adults.

This ideology grabbed hold of American society, particularly in the 1990s, when sports became a popular tool for crime prevention programs typically aimed at troubled and inner-city youth. Many programs in the 1990s directly targeted crime as one of the goals of the program. A National Parks and Recreation Report in 1994 highlighted 19 programs; eight of them listed crime prevention and public safety as their major focus.[3] Many of these referred to themselves as the "alternative" (suggesting that kids will either be on the streets or participating in sports).[4] In 1997 alone the National Recreation and Parks Association identified 621 new sports or recreation programs targeting at-risk youth.[5] This does not count all of the other activities started by YMCAs, Girls and Boys Clubs, Police Athletic Leagues, and other institutions across the country.[6] Sports programs have become a popular form of dealing with a variety of social problems for a few reasons. They are relatively inexpensive to start and sustain and they attract funding more easily than other types of activities (for example, art and music programs). The most important reason for the widespread support of these programs "has to do with long-held and deeply entrenched cultural beliefs about sports as a positive, progressive social force."[7] There is a belief that sports not only keep kids off the streets but also build character and discipline. Although this belief is popular there is little-to-no scientific evidence to support the notion that participation in sports programs has any effect on crime prevention.

Additionally, schools have long justified the money, time, and support for interscholastic athletic programs and physical education, not just as fostering healthy students, but also fostering school spirit, building self-confidence, and preventing delinquent behaviors.[8] Support for sporting programs has long been attached to broader social goals.

There is also the notion that sports can serve as a vehicle for escaping poverty and crime-ridden streets for many living in the inner cities. The idea that sports can be a way to reach the American dream and to avoid a life of crime has been an ideology that has permeated society for decades. An article in *The St. Petersburg Times* from 1969 demonstrates this:

> Basketball is more than a sport in the capital. It is a sociological phenomenon; it is a way of life for youth among the city's 560,000 Negroes. On indoor and outdoor courts, tiny lots, slum streets, wherever there's a board or pole with a basket, children play it from the time they're able to lift the ball. Elgin Baylor, a product of the Washington ghetto and now one of its heroes, said in 1969: "I think the success Dave Bing and I have had has been sort of inspiring to the young kids who don't have a chance to get out of the ghetto any other way."[9]

Additionally, the beginning of a 2008 article in *Sports Illustrated* reaffirms this philosophy:

> Once, if you wished to insulate yourself from the drugs and gangs or, like Fred (Lawson), turn your life around, your best chance was to dedicate yourself to a sport. In Oakland, NBA players Gary Payton and Drew Gooden, major league pitcher Dontrelle Willis, and, most recently, the Buffalo Bills' Marshawn Lynch, followed that course. Ken Carter at Richmond High was the inspiration for the film *Coach Carter*, which showed what teens motivated by hoops can achieve.[10]

The article goes on to show that the power of sports is being reduced in the inner city, not because of sports' less powerful role, but because of the increasingly violent and indiscriminate nature of crime in the inner cities, where star athletes used to be protected or given a pass from the crime that fills the streets.

While the preceding chapters have looked at many different ways that sports may contribute to various criminal behaviors, this is not the whole story. In many cases sports can act in a positive fashion by reducing crime. Many youth who participate in sports teams growing up are not driven toward criminal behavior; rather they walk away from the sports team a better person. The positive value of sports participation has been at the root of sports programs in prison, the use of sports as a rehabilitative tool for juveniles, and midnight basketball programs that operate in cities across the country. This chapter will examine the positive connections between sports and criminal behavior.

SPORTS IN PRISON

One of the most famous prison recreation supervisors was Leonard "Oakie" Brumm. He wrote about his experiences in the 1950s at Marquette Branch Prison in Michigan in the book *We Only Played Home Games*. Brumm started football teams, hockey teams, a Winter Carnival featuring ice-skating races, and even an 18-hole miniature golf course. The high point of his infusion of sports into prison came on February 2, 1954, when Gordie Howe and the Detroit Red Wings came to the prison to play a hockey game against an all-inmate team. The Red Wings dominated early play (leading 18-0 after the first period) and the teams were quickly mixed up. All the effort Brumm put into sports was not for the inmates' enjoyment but rather he says "we tranquilized them with sports."[11]

Sports play a large role in the lives of many inmates in prison. Many inmates have nothing but time on their hands and little to look forward to.

Sports are extremely popular in prison, with more than half of the nation's inmates participating. Some prisons have more active sports and recreation programs than others. In a series entitled *Sports in Prison* for *Newsday*, reporter Michael Dobie found that in Louisiana, about 25% of inmates play in intramural leagues and if you add pickup sports, holiday tournaments, and field days the figure rises to 90%. In Nebraska, nearly 60% of the inmates at the Omaha Correctional Center compete in the prison's Olympic-style Winter Games.[12] The most popular sports are typically weightlifting and basketball but other sports include softball, flag football, handball, and soccer.

The amount of time that an inmate can participate varies from inmate to inmate and prison to prison, but at minimum inmates receive one hour of recreation per day, five days a week. Participation in sports also varies based on the inmate's behavior; if the inmate receives disciplinary action, recreation time can be taken away. According to many correctional officers, this serves as a powerful incentive to keep inmates in line.

Budgets are modest and vary from state to state. New York's state prisons spend about $10 per inmate per year on equipment and supplies. Many prisons in other states run their sports programs entirely on profits from their inmate commissaries; no tax dollars are used.[13] After a boom in prison sporting programs in the 1970s and 1980s, spending on sports and recreation in prisons took a substantial hit in the 1990s as the public and politicians disapproved of the notion of coddling inmates. For example, in 1994, Florida's legislature banned the purchase of weight-lifting and other recreational equipment (including televisions). The rationale was that inmates are supposed to serving hard time, not playing games. However, in 2002, the legislature reversed its course by authorizing money for "wellness equipment." Senator Howard Futch who sponsored the bill said that he did so at the request of prison guards. Correctional officers told him that inmates needed sports equipment to improve their health and to keep them busy when they weren't working or in school. The officers said sports activities are an important part of prison security and that inmates who have unstructured time are potentially dangerous.[14] The federal government banned the purchase of new weight-lifting equipment at federal prisons in 1996 (some states followed their lead).

There is obvious controversy surrounding inmates participating in sports programs, especially weight lifting. Many shiver at the thought of inmates lifting weights and getting stronger before returning to society. Correctional workers, along with the general public, are split when it comes to weight lifting.

- Guards at the Oahu Community Correctional Center in Hawaii won't even let most of the inmates get near the shiny new

Universal weight machine in the yard. "The guards don't want the prisoners to be bigger than they are," says the facility's administrator Beryl Iramina.[15]

- "It would be much more dangerous, and I use that word deliberately," said Charles Fasano, who monitors Chicago's Cook County Jail and has visited about 100 prisons and jails nationwide as part of a nonprofit watchdog organization. Deny inmates sports, Fasano said, and "all that energy and frustration is going to be taken out on each other and it's going to involve the staff. It's going to be a nightmare."[16]

- A survey conducted in Florida in 1998 found that 51% of the general public disapproved of giving inmates access to weights while 49% approved. The staff of Florida's Department of Corrections approved of inmate weight lifting by the same 51 to 49 margin.[17]

Every discussion of sports programs in prison inevitably comes to the issue of whether convicted inmates should be spending their time playing sports, which doesn't equate with most people's idea of punishment. This is an especially pertinent point for the victims or victims' families when they hear about their offender spending time playing basketball or lifting weights.

A few inmates have actually taken their sports experiences in prison and turned them into successful athletic careers outside the prison walls. This has happened most often with boxing. Boxing in prison was very popular after World War II with nearly half of the states having organized boxing. New Jersey's program received extensive national acclaim in the 1970s, with professional fights taking place and being televised by NBC inside Rahway State Prison. Louisiana is the last state to have an organized boxing league. Most other states, including New Jersey, cancelled their programs in the 1990s due to budget cuts, concerns about medical liability, and criticism from the public.[18]

Sonny Liston, who won the heavyweight championship in 1962 by knocking out Floyd Patterson in the first round, learned how to box in prison. He lived on the streets through his teen years and was in and out of trouble with the law. In 1950, he was sentenced to two concurrent five-year sentences for robbery and larceny. While at the Missouri State Penitentiary in Jefferson City, he learned to box from a Catholic priest who ran the recreation program in the prison. In 1952, he was released on parole and after a short amateur career began boxing professionally. He went on to a 50−4 record.

Another boxer who began his career in prison was light heavyweight James "Great" Scott who was convicted of armed robbery and sentenced to Rahway Penitentiary in New Jersey (where another professional boxer named Dwight Qawi learned to box). It was at Rahway Penitentiary that Scott's professional career took off; he fought professional fights while still incarcerated at the prison. In 1978, NBC televised his fight against Eddie "The Flame" Gregory in which Scott won a 12-round decision. Scott was able to move up to the number two world ranking in his weight class from behind the prison walls.[19] The World Boxing Association, not wanting their champion to be a prisoner, stripped him of his ranking in 1979 before he received a title shot. He was released from prison shortly afterward and had a short professional career.[20] Rahway State Prison has since ended its boxing program.

Most recently, boxer Bernard "The Executioner" Hopkins made the transition from prison to the professional ranks. At the age of 17, Hopkins was sentenced to 18 years in prison for nine felonies. He served his time at Graterford State Prison in Pennsylvania where he learned to box. After serving five years, he was released and began boxing professionally. He became middleweight champion in 1995 and held the belt for 10 years.[21]

Boxing is not the only prison sport that has produced professional athletes. Ron Leflore, who became an All-Star outfielder for the Detroit Tigers in the 1970s, played baseball in the State Prison of Southern Michigan where he batted .569. Flore was serving five to 10 years for armed robbery when he was offered a tryout by Tiger's manager Billy Martin. He was able to leave the prison for a day to try out for the Tigers. He was assigned to their minor league team when he was paroled two weeks later. A year later he made the Tigers.[22] There was also Manuel "Jungle Jim" Rivera, who played major league baseball, mostly for the Chicago White Sox, for ten years after serving four years for attempted rape.[23]

Another sporting activity that has found a place in prison is the rodeo. The most famous prison rodeo, which started in 1965, takes place at the Louisiana State Penitentiary at Angola. The rodeo takes place every Sunday in October and one weekend in April in a 7,500-person stadium. All proceeds go to cover rodeo expenses and supplement the Louisiana State Penitentiary Inmate Welfare Fund which provides for inmate educational and recreational supplies. The most unique event at the rodeo, which features mostly traditional rodeo events, is convict poker. The event is described as:

> the ultimate poker game, and even winning has a price. Four inmate cowboys sit at a table in the middle of the arena playing a friendly game of poker. Suddenly, a wild bull is released with the sole purpose of unseating the poker players. The last man remaining seated is the winner.[24]

Only two other states have prison rodeos, Texas and Oklahoma. In the Oklahoma rodeo, which features inmates from across the state prison system, they have an event called the mad scramble in which a $100 bill is tied to the horn of a bull, and the inmates try to get it any way they can. Inmates routinely get trampled going after the cash.[25] Angola also has an inmate-built golf course on the prison grounds. Prison View, which opened in 2004, is open to the public and is off limits for the inmates to play.

Angola, which has the most extensive sports and recreation program in the country, offers intramural leagues in tackle football, basketball, volleyball, tennis, boxing, and slow- and fast-pitch softball. The champions of their prison league play teams from other prisons. Additionally, they have an Elderly Olympiad for inmates over 50. The warden, Burl Cain, thinks sports is one of the four things necessary to run a good prison (good food, medicine, and praying being the others).[26]

Good athletes are even recruited in prison, much like college athletics. An inmate at Carl Robinson Correctional Institution in Connecticut states: "Guys are familiar with the best in every facility, prior to him arriving they're waiting for him . . . They'll have a jump on it. They'll get word to the select players."[27] Wardens and prison administrators have even been known to recruit star athlete inmates to their prisons. Inmates will request transfers to different housing units within a prison to be on a different intramural team and in some cases request transfers to other prisons that have better sports programs.

Prison sporting programs have taken a hit over the years. In their heyday, prisons would run intramural programs and routinely played against other prisons. Now that is a rarity; however, sometimes outside teams still come into the prison to play the inmates. This happens with basketball, baseball, softball, tennis, and weight lifting. Many, but not all, of the teams that come to the prison are Christian ministry groups who are also looking to spread their message to the inmates. This happens with the baseball team at San Quentin prison, the nation's oldest prison baseball team. The coach of the San Quentin team, Kent Philpott, sees big benefits for the inmates playing on the team: "These guys learn to deal with losing, they learn to cooperate, build people up, and become team players." Inmates are extremely motivated for the opportunity to play on the team. In 2008, more than 50 tried out for the team but only 21 made it. Many of the inmates love baseball; others prefer sitting in the dugout to their cells. The captain of the 2008 squad, pitcher Chris Rich (who had a promising college career at St. John's University cut short by injuries), says the inmates realize that "it's a privilege to play," and he "is thankful for every game."[28]

Many states have done away with outside teams playing inmate teams for security reasons, cost, public perceptions, and fear of something happening between inmates and visitors. Additionally, the rise in hepatitis and AIDS among the prison population has also scared some non-inmate teams away from coming into the prison.[29] Sports are a big part of women's prison as well. At the York Correctional Institution in Niantic, Connecticut (Connecticut's only women's prison), volleyball tournaments are common along with running, basketball, and softball. The director of the prison's recreation program states:

> Competitive team sports help you work together and understand what it means to be part of a community . . . People on the outside hear recreation and think that, like oil and water, it doesn't mix with prison, they think it's about parties and fun, but it's also about teaching wellness and health.[30]

The stated goals of the National Correctional Recreation Association (NCRA), a nonprofit organization that serves the athletic programs for more than 200 prisons, is raising:

> . . . inmate morale by providing healthy activity which may help engender socially acceptable attitudes and conduct among the men, and to arouse the interest of the inmates in recreation to an extent that they will continue this type of activity following their release from prison.[31]

They look at the benefits of sports as more than releasing the inmate's frustrations and giving them something to occupy their time. The NCRA adopts the idealistic view that sports provide life lessons, promote cooperation, and encourage positive behavior. NCRA officials point to the fact that most inmates will eventually leave prison and that sports are a positive activity that they can take with them outside of prison to stay out of trouble. While this may be optimistic, prison officials will tell you that nothing else is working in reducing recidivism rates among inmates across the country. If sports can keep prisons safer while the inmate is in prison and may help them get better acclimated to society after release, it may be worth the limited amount of money that it takes to keep these programs operating.

Additionally, inmates who participate in sports are going to be in better physical shape while in prison which should reduce medical expenses, a growing burden on state budgets given the millions (and aging) of incarcerated inmates. In Louisiana, they have 36,000 inmates in state prisons whose annual medical bills reach $100 million. However, the potential savings in medical bills must also take into account injuries sustained while participating in sports, which is likely to happen with sports participation in or out of prison.[32] Broken bones and injuries are common at the prison rodeos. An inmate was killed during a 1963 prison rodeo at Utah State Prison after he was tossed from a bucking bronco and hit his head on a beam in the starting chute. [33]

The problem is what are we to do with the millions of inmates we have in the country. Locking them away for years with no productive outlets will not help society when they are eventually released from prison. If sports help make the prison easier to manage and makes it safer for inmates and correctional workers, that might be enough to allow it to continue.

Sports continue to play an important role for inmates after they are released from prison. The Odyssey House, a residential treatment center for drug addicts, began to use running marathons as a way to keep their patients clean and help them become productive members of society. The program director, Vito Tomaneelli, states:

> As they're training for the marathon, they're training for the world beyond Odyssey House. The lessons of long-distance running, from proper pacing to goal setting to delayed gratification are the same lessons the residents are learning in recovery.[34]

The Odyssey House program has received national attention and seems to tap into the notion that sports have much more to offer than physical activity. Research on addiction suggests that physical activity can play an important role, especially in alleviating depression which is an important risk factor for relapse.[35] The benefits of sports discussed for adult offenders may be even greater in number and more powerful for juvenile offenders.

JUVENILE OFFENDERS

There has been evidence that physical activity, along with sports, is an important part of not only a person's physical well-being but also their psychological well-being. Sports are a significant part of many juveniles' development from childhood play to adult responsibilities. Research has shown many benefits of recreational experiences: searching for identity, relating to others, improving talents, and filling time.[36] Although most discussions of sports within prison suggest that the main benefit is the cathartic effect (having the inmates tiring themselves out and blowing off steam), the effect for juvenile offenders may potentially be greater. In some cases sports may be used to strengthen treatment programs and teach life lessons for juveniles.[37] Many juvenile treatment programs offer sports programs with the goal of improving social skills, improving self-esteem, and improving levels of cooperation and trust.[38] Sports can be used as a behavioral exercise that demonstrates larger life lessons for the juvenile offender. Sports are also valuable because of their popularity with youth, which makes them a useful tool to amplify treatment and rehabilitative goals. There is a comprehensive program that links sports and recreation to counseling psychology known as the Life Development Intervention (LDI). It uses sports and life experiences as an opportunity to learn and change behavior. LDI focuses on the teaching of "life skills" that can be demonstrated through games and sports.[39]

Some juvenile detention centers have very active sports programs with some even competing in public or private school athletic leagues. Giddings State Home and School, which houses violent juvenile offenders in Texas, competes in football, basketball, and track against private and parochial schools. The juveniles must have served at least half of their sentence and maintained a good disciplinary record (not regarded as high risk) to participate on the school's sports teams. School officials note that their teams have never had an incident with another team. The players realize that any incident would jeopardize the whole program and their opportunity to play.[40] Metro Academy, in Colorado, is a maximum security facility for juvenile offenders, which offers high school classes. It also offers sports teams that compete against regular high school teams. The administration at Metro Academy believes that sports are as much a part of the juvenile's rehabilitation as their group counseling and their education. The trips outside Metro's fences for away games give the juveniles a taste of life outside the facility. The director of the juvenile facility, Caren Leaf, states:

> All the things we teach them, this is where they get the chance to practice it. Think about it: Impulse control, anger management. What better place to practice that than on a court? Someone charging at you, someone calling you a murderer, a rapist. What do you do?[41]

There is also the Rite of Passage, a national rehabilitation program for at-risk youths, in which athletics plays a big part of the curriculum. In addition to academic classes and meeting with counselors, students play on sports teams and can travel to play other Rite of Passage school teams.[42]

Research on juvenile offenders suggests that sports and physical activity can combine with other interventions to reduce crime by offering appropriate alternative activities. Sports alone will not have an effect; it must be connected with the broader community and combined with other treatments and activities. Case studies of sports-based interventions suggest that the key ingredients are not the competitive or physical aspects of sports, but the sense of belonging that comes from being part of a team, developing a positive self-image, and being supported by coaches and the community. On one level sports-based programs work in the short term by keeping young people out of trouble by participating in a positive activity. On another level, sports and physical activity can be used as strategies within a broader context involving, for example, development of values, social support, and positive role models.[43] Sports need to be combined with other activities and strategies to have any chance of having a meaningful impact on behavior.

HIGH PROFILE EXAMPLE: MICHAEL OHER

Michael Oher was essentially homeless for his entire childhood. His father was murdered and his mother was a drug addict. He had 13 siblings and was from the poorest part of Memphis. His siblings would eventually be scattered around Memphis in various foster homes after being removed from their mother. Michael repeated both the first and second grade, which he rarely attended (46 absences during first grade). He attended 11 schools in nine years (there is also an 18-month gap when Michael was 10 where he didn't attend school at all) and was homeless during much of that time.[44] Oher recalls: "As I look back on stuff, it's crazy how I got here. But it didn't seem tough at the time. I just lived day to day, did the best I could."[45]

His life took a turn after his freshman year in high school. He was living with a friend, Stephen Payne, and his father, Big Tony. Big Tony made a promise to Stephen's mother (who had died) that he would attend a "Christian" high school. Big Tony tried to get Oher, who slept on his floor most nights, into Briarcrest Academy. Oher's grades were not nearly good enough to get him into the school. At that time, Oher had an I.Q. of 80 (ninth percentile) and an aptitude test he took in eighth grade measured his "ability to learn" in the sixth percentile. However, they did not turn him away completely; they said that if he could get his grades up by home-schooling he could be admitted. That didn't work and Big Tony asked the school again what he could do to help Oher. The school, with its Christian mission, decided to help Oher and admitted him into the school, on the condition that he couldn't play sports his first year and had to concentrate on academics.[46]

After being admitted to Briarcrest, he came to the attention of the Tuohy family. Sean Tuohy, who played point guard for Ole Miss and was a successful businessman and radio commentator for the NBA's Memphis Grizzlies, was an unofficial consultant for Briarcrest's athletic program. Tuohy would often help out underprivileged students at Briarcrest by paying for their lunch accounts and in some cases tuition.

> Like every other parent and student at Briarcrest, Sean had been born again, but his interest in the poor jocks might have run even deeper than his religious belief. "What I learned playing basketball at Ole Miss, was what not to do: beat up a kid. It's easy to beat up a kid. The hard thing is to build him up."[47]

The Tuohys' involvement with Oher took a turn when Sean's wife, Leigh Anne, saw Oher walking in the cold on Thanksgiving Day in his shorts and t-shirt, the only outfit he ever wore, heading to the school gym simply because it had heat. Leigh Anne quickly took an interest in Oher, taking him shopping for new clothes and eventually letting him move into their house. The Tuohys also had a daughter that attended Briarcrest and an 8-year-old son. Oher has said about the Tuohys' taking him into their home:

> They've got big hearts. To take somebody from my neighborhood into your house? Nobody does that. I don't think I'd even do that. I'd help you out, but with a daughter and with all the violence and drugs where I come from . . . they didn't have to do that. I owe a lot to them.[48]

Leigh Anne also took over responsibility for his academics. Starting his junior year, he was eligible to play football and he quickly gained national attention and the spotlight of every college football team in the country.

He was the right size and speed to play the desired left tackle position. He weighed 344 lbs. and stood 6 feet 5 inches tall. Before even stepping onto the playing field, he was heralded as an All-American high school player and had scholarship offers lined up from all the big football programs, including Ole Miss. Football, along with the Tuohys, provided the impetus for his academics. His sophomore year grade point average was 0.9, he raised it his first year at the Tuohys to a 1.65. He started to earn passing marks and raised his grade point average to a 2.05 by the time he was ready for graduation. His grade point average was not enough to meet the minimums (2.65 GPA based on his standardized test scores) set forth by the NCAA to receive an athletic scholarship, but after taking some courses through Bringham Young University over the summer, he was able to raise his grade point average high enough to be accepted into

Ole Miss. At Ole Miss, he made first team freshman All-American.[49] In 2006, he was the subject of a book by Michael Lewis, *Blind Side: The Evolution of the Game*, which was made into a motion picture released in November 2009.

Newspaper coverage of Oher's story hit on the positive impact of sports on his life:

- An End Run Out of Poverty, Into an N.F.L. Trajectory (*The New York Times,* October 5, 2006)
- Homeless Teen to Football Star, the Story of a Left Tackle (*The Washington Post*, October 15, 2006)
- Saved by Football: Street Kid's Talent for the Game Brought Him More Than Fame (*Pittsburgh Post-Gazette*, November 26, 2006)

Oher played well enough that he could have jumped into the NFL by his junior year but he decided to return for his senior season. He was drafted in the first round of the 2009 NFL draft by the Baltimore Ravens (23rd overall). He signed a five-year contract for $13.795 million ($7.8M guaranteed).

Oher's story demonstrates the power of sports in this country. Not all of us can benefit from sports the way Michael Oher did, as he was born with a body that is ideal to play offensive lineman in the NFL. Sports provided his motivation to come out of his shell both socially and academically. Without the NFL prize (and Tuohy family support), Oher would not have been able to improve his academics enough to get into college. Although this may not be the best motivation for staying in school, it is something that has worked for numerous other NFL and NBA players. The dream of being a professional sports star for many troubled teens is enough to keep them out of trouble and put some effort into their academics.

MIDNIGHT BASKETBALL

Midnight basketball was first started in 1986 by G. Van Standifier in Glen Arden, Maryland. The idea was to keep young men (17 to 25 years old) off the street during peak crime hours. The program operated between 10 P.M. and 2 A.M. three nights a week and gave the men an alternative to the streets. While basketball was the draw, there were also mandatory educational, counseling, and employment seminars and workshops that the participants had to attend to play basketball. After the success of the Maryland program, other cities started their own midnight basketball leagues. Chicago started their Midnight Basketball league in the fall of 1989 with funding from the Chicago

Housing Authority and Department of Housing and Urban Development. The program started in two of the worst housing projects in the city. The program quickly gained media attention and began to expand nationally. The biggest moment for midnight basketball occurred in April 1990, when President George H.W. Bush named the Midnight Basketball League, Inc. and its founders as one of his "1,000 Points of Light" (it was named the 124th Daily Point of Light). Further support came when President Clinton included funding for the programs in his 1994 Federal Crime Bill.

A 1991 *Sports Illustrated* article detailed Dyonne Bowman, who was one of the stars of the Chicago Midnight Basketball League:

> When he was a kid, I used to hate basketball," says Bowman's stepmother, Bernadine Pointer. "He would never go to school. He was always playing that damn game. But this Midnight League is keeping him away from the gangs. It gives him a goal and exposes him to people with ambition. Dyonne wants to go to college now. He even paid the $15 out of his own pocket to take the GED (General Equivalency Diploma).

The Chicago program was sponsored by the Chicago Housing Authority, and private investors pay $2,000 apiece to be "team owners." The article notes that many of the players are gang members but during basketball hours there is a sanctuary from the violence of the streets. Players and fans at Midnight League games can't wear baseball caps that identify them as gang members, smoke, or fight. As a further deterrent, the city police are present at all games.[50] These types of stories were prevalent in the media during the early 1990s. However, people started to become weary of basketball as a cure-all for the problems of the inner cities, especially when federal money was being put toward the programs.

The organizers and supporters of the programs maintain that there is more to the programs than basketball. They argue that basketball was chosen simply because it was the most popular activity among the targeted population, a means to an end. Although basketball was receiving all the attention, organizers claim the program is about helping the individuals better themselves and in turn help the community by making it a safer place to live. The description and goals of the programs frequently mention reduced crime, gang behavior, illegal drug use and breaking the cycle of poverty.[51] Not surprisingly, during the original league in Maryland, the coaches were from the Maryland State Department of Corrections or the U.S. Marshall Service, with little knowledge of basketball.[52]

Although there have been claims regarding reduced crime by many of the organizers and supporters of the programs in cities across the country, there is no scientific research to support their notions. Anecdotal evidence is typically offered as proof of the program's success. For example, a 1996 article in *Sports Illustrated* about Midnight Basketball states:

> According to the Kansas City police department, violent offenses, non-aggravated assaults and offenses against property each declined by one third to two thirds among juveniles in 1994, the fifth year of Mayor's Night Hoops, which is open to boys and girls ages 10 to 21. Given that the cost of incarcerating a single juvenile offender runs to nearly $30,000 per year, the $100,000 annual cost of the program, in which 1,200 youngsters participate, would appear to more than justify itself.[53]

For one thing, crime in all areas of the country dropped significantly during the mid 1990s when most cities were beginning their programs.[54] Some research has found that early adopters of midnight basketball programs experienced sharper decreases in property crimes than cities that did not adopt midnight basketball early or not at all. This finding only holds during a period of popular support for the program in the community. It suggests that the larger community context of positive publicity and community trust are essential in making the programs effective. Additionally, many of the cities that adopted Midnight Basketball Leagues also adopted a wide range of other community-related programs targeting crime. So Midnight Basketball in combination with other social service programs and community support may play a role in lower crime rates.[55]

HIGH PROFILE EXAMPLE: BADGES FOR BASEBALL

In our family, sports was the way that we were taught about life.

Cal Ripken, Jr.[56]

The Badges for Baseball program was started in 2007 by Cal Ripken, Jr., the former Baltimore Orioles Hall of Fame shortstop, and his brother, former Major League Baseball player Billy Ripken. The program was started in Virginia and has since expanded to other states. More than 2,300 kids in Virginia participated the first year.[57] The program is an off-shoot from the Cal Ripken, Sr. Foundation, which was started by the Ripkens in Baltimore, Maryland, as a tribute to their dad (former manager of the Baltimore Orioles), and teaches life lessons through sports. The program has been described as a crime prevention initiative that encourages healthy out-of-school activities, while improving relationships between law enforcement personnel and at-risk youth. Law enforcement volunteers and Boys and Girls Clubs staff use baseball, "Quickball" (a version of baseball where players only receive one swing) and softball to deliver vital life lessons to the student participants in a fun, engaging way.

Supporters of Badges for Baseball are quick to point out that it is more than just baseball and games of "Quickball," it is a mentoring program that teaches the Healthy Choices, Healthy Children curriculum (which was developed by the Ripken foundation and the University of Pittsburgh to teach leadership, perseverance, work ethic, teamwork, choosing friends, and the like).[58] Badges for Baseball typically partners with established organizations like Boys and Girls Clubs. Cal Ripken, Jr., who has authored books on developing programs for youths, states that:

> We use baseball as a hook to get your attention, but you really want to transfer some of those life lessons and start to give support to the kids. Once the kids have support in their lives—a positive influence—then they can take it into the directions that would be positive and productive for the community.[59]

The benefits are many and varied for the youth participants, law enforcement, and entire community including increased participation in physical activity; learning the value of a healthy lifestyle; and learning important life lessons including setting life goals and learning how to achieve these goals. Children and their family members begin to see local law enforcement as agents of change and safety in the community, creating a sense of safety in their neighborhoods.[60] The program teaches principles such as sportsmanship, leadership, trustworthiness, health, and accountability through baseball. It emphasizes using simplicity, fun, lots of explanations, and flexibility when teaching.[61]

Much like the Midnight Basketball programs, the program is also a way to keep kids off the streets during out-of-school hours when they are most likely to commit crimes or become victims of crime. Badges for Baseball received a grant from the Department of Justice to get it started. The program's Web site states that:

> While this program is beneficial for youth from a variety of socio-economic backgrounds, the Badges for Baseball program primarily targets areas with high rates of juvenile crime and delinquency related issues. Unfortunately these high crime rates often correlate with strained relationships between law enforcement officers and young people living in these neighborhoods. This strain provides an opportunity to reach young people at an impressionable age and gives them opportunities to begin seeing the law enforcement officials as mentors, friends, and coaches rather than an enemy on their streets.[62]

An interesting aspect of the program is that it uses police officers as team coaches. The idea is that as the juveniles get excited about baseball, they will also see their local law enforcement officials in a new and different light as coaches, mentors, and positive role models in their lives. Additionally, law enforcement personnel get to see a new side to these young adults. They become friends and the bond between them enables the law enforcement mentors to better understand the challenges that these young people face each day.

Although there have been no studies testing the effectiveness of the program, the organizers are quick to point to anecdotal stories that attest to its success. An officer who participated in the program in 2008 attests: "I learned something about kids—they just want to be heard, feel respected, and just feel like someone cares about them."[63] Program administrators also point to a story of "one girl who saw a policeman show up at one of her games. She asked the officer who he was there to arrest. When she found out he only came to watch her play ball, she hugged him."[64] North Carolina Attorney General Roy Cooper, who believes in the crime-fighting ability of the program, suggests that kids who used to run from a police car began running toward them because they knew the police officer.[65] Even though these stories have not been supported by systematic research, it seems by all accounts that the program has been extremely successful, in part due to the Ripken name attached to it. Badges for Baseball has expanded outside from Virginia and Maryland to North Carolina, Massachusetts, Mississippi, Kentucky, and Rhode Island, among others.

CONCLUSION

Although the negative effects of sports have been explored in this book, that is not the whole story. For most participants and fans alike, sports are an important and positive aspect of their life. Sports can play a positive role with both children and adults in teaching discipline, building character, and promoting a healthy lifestyle. These benefits have led law enforcement, correctional officials, and the community to see sports programs as a way to fight crime. Sports programs in prison, juvenile detention centers, and the community have been cited consistently as not only "sports" programs but crime reduction programs. Many believe that sports have the power to bring people together and transform individuals' lives.

In prison, sports are a controversial topic. Many in the public are disgusted by the image of convicted prisoners playing basketball and lifting weights. However, many of those who work in prisons will argue that sports provide many benefits that are essential to running successful prisons. Besides the very basic fact that prisoners who play a sport are going to get their energy out in an acceptable way, sports is one of the most desired activities by inmates in prison. This makes sports an important motivational tool in keeping inmates from misbehaving. If an inmate has disciplinary problems, he would lose his sports privileges. Additionally, if we maintain any notion that prison is still supposed to serve some rehabilitative function, or at least recognize that many of these inmates will be walking the streets again sometime, the fact that sports is a healthy activity that promotes teamwork, cooperation, and fun would be beneficial for the inmate. Sports help keep inmates healthier physically (and also psychologically) which is important given the fact that the public is responsible for paying the health care costs of inmates.

In juvenile facilities, the benefits of sports move beyond simply tiring the inmates out. Sports are also used as a tool to teach life lessons. There is much more of a focus on the positive aspects of sports participation with juveniles, who have a greater chance of turning their lives around. Learning to play by the rules, respecting authority figures, getting along with teammates, and dealing with adversity or loss are just some of the lessons that sports can help teach in juvenile facilities. Sports alone will not teach these lessons, but sports with proper mentoring and support can be the beginning of change in the juveniles' lives.

Programs like Midnight Basketball and Badges for Baseball continue to demonstrate the power of sports to reach juveniles and adults alike. As organizers of these programs state, sports may just be the hook to get people involved, but sports can also be a forum where change can happen. In many cases, sports reach across generational, economic, and racial lines. There is a simplicity to sports that allows it to be used to teach many different lessons. It is this power that continues to attract millions of children, and their parents, to sports every day. With the proper environment, coaching, and support, sports can be a powerful tool in fighting anti-social behavior like crime and building people of stronger character.

Chapter 7

CONCLUSION

Fortunately for me as I was writing this book and unfortunately for the sports world, the week of June 14, 2009, has become an all too typical week. On Sunday, June 14, after the Los Angeles Lakers won the 2009 NBA championship, people filled the streets surrounding the Staples Center (the Lakers' home arena) even though the game was in Orlando.

> What began as a lively but peaceful celebration took on a different tone for those remaining a few hours after the game. Some in the crowd vandalized a shoe store, buses and police cars, set small fires and threw rocks and bottles at police. Police say 18 people were arrested for disturbing the peace, arson and other infractions.[1]

Then on June 17, *The New York Times* released a story that baseball player Sammy Sosa, who is sixth on the career home run list, had tested positive for performance-enhancing drugs in 2003. Although this was not a surprise to many who followed baseball, it was another black spot on baseball's recent past. The same day, Cleveland Browns wide receiver Donte Stallworth began serving a 30-day jail sentence for killing a pedestrian while driving drunk in Florida. Stallworth also reached a confidential financial settlement with the family of Mario Reyes, a 59-year-old construction worker who was struck and killed March 14.[2] The plea agreement also includes two years of house arrest. On June 19, NFL Commissioner Roger Goodell suspended Stallworth from the league indefinitely. Then on June 20, former NFL quarterback Ryan Leaf, the number two pick in the 1998 NFL draft, surrendered to Texas authorities to face burglary and drug-related charges. Leaf faces one count of burglary and eight drug-related counts associated with the painkiller Hydrocodone. He was arrested in Washington state after entering the United States from Canada. He posted bond there and flew to Texas before surrendering.[3]

ARE ATHLETES MORE LIKELY TO COMMIT CRIME?

The short answer is yes. When comparing male athletes (high school, college, and professional) to the general population, it should not be surprising that athletes, because of their gender and age, would be at a higher risk to be involved with crime. There is no more historical certainty than males commit more crimes than females. Add to that the fact that young males are more likely to commit crime than older males. The majority of athletes described in the book fall into the age group most likely to be involved in crime (16- to 25-year-olds). As people begin to age, their chances of being a professional athlete decreases, as does the possibility of being involved in criminal behavior. Additionally, elite athletes who are able to play into their late twenties and thirties (when crime rates decline for most males) are unique because the dynamics of being an athlete create a less than ordinary maturation process.[4]

However, there is more to the question than simply age and gender. If comparing male high school athletes to non-athletes (same age and gender), are the athletes more likely to commit crimes than their non-athlete peers? That is the more important question to address. The difficulty in answering that question lies in defining what athletes we are talking about. A high school athlete could mean a student who plays golf, or it could mean a student who plays football, basketball, and baseball. It could describe a student who participates in many different school activities (French club, school paper, student government) and also plays a sport and it could also describe a student who does nothing besides focus on athletics. It would be impossible to make any general statements about these diverse student athletes. When examining the research on high school athletes, it is important not to simply compare those who play sports versus those who do not, but rather to compare those who identify themselves as "jocks" versus those who do not. Those who accept the label or identity "jock" seem to be more likely to be involved with delinquent behavior. Accepting this jock identity leads to behaviors like hazing other athletes, increased alcohol use, and drunk driving. Additionally, the culture of the team is important to understanding the effects of athletic participation. Some teams, because of the coach and community, foster a positive mentality around being part of the team. However, in some towns or schools, the culture of the team could be the very thing that leads to destructive behavior. Excessive focus on a group mentality, especially in aggressive sports, can lead to a denigration of those who are not a member of the team. The team's focus on violence and aggression on the field could spill over into violence off the field and the team could form its own subculture of violence. Misogynistic and homophobic attitudes, which in some form are common in many locker rooms, could become prominent in the team's behavior. Aggression on the playing field, sexist language, attitudes used in the locker room, and an inordinate need to prove one's masculinity can combine in complex ways to predispose some male athletes toward off-the-field hostility. A community that puts their athletes on too high a pedestal might create athletes who think they are better than other students, deserve special treatment, and should not be held to the same expectations.

When athletes make it to the college ranks, the sense of entitlement and lack of accountability that began in high school often increases. This is especially true with some Division I football and basketball players who see playing in college only as a way to get to the professional ranks. Additionally, research has shown that college athletes enjoy their newfound freedom even more than their non-athletic peers by drinking alcohol and using drugs more often. Drugs and alcohol alone are important factors contributing to criminal behavior. Added to this situation, athletes' sense of entitlement leads them to more opportunities with women, which also increases the chance for sexual assaults. As the Crosset, Benedict, and McDonald study found,[5] Division I football and basketball players were responsible for a disproportionate number of the sexual assaults that occur on campus. Another problem that many college athletes face is that they may not fit in (racially and economically) with other members of the college community. This creates a strange situation for many athletes in that they are seen as special and celebrities on campus, yet many do not have the same financial status as the other students.

The few athletes who are able to make the jump into the professional ranks are faced with increased fame and wealth, something that would seem to help them escape any negative influences from their upbringing. However, this is not always the case. Many professional athletes' criminal problems are a direct result of their inability to separate themselves from their friends from the old neighborhood ("ghetto loyalty"). Whether it is Michael Vick or Adam "Pacman" Jones, the athlete cannot break the close ties with some of their old friends who may still have criminal tendencies. Additionally, many professional athletes have never really grown up (terminal adolescence) and did not experience normal social development. It is not just that they have never been told no or been held accountable, but that they have repeatedly been told that they are special and above the law. They have received preferential treatment for their entire lives, thus we should not be surprised that they have not developed proper self-control. Many are self-centered and have a feeling of invincibility that results in reckless behavior without any caring for how their behavior might affect other people. Inflated ego shaped by fan adulation, media attention, and their being catered to early on in their lives leads to arrogance and grandiose behavior.[6] These feeling can explain the rampant steroid use that has pervaded professional sports over the past decades and athletes' increasing use of guns.

HOW DO SPORTS AFFECT THOSE WATCHING THEM?

One of the more interesting aspects of the connection between sports and criminal behavior lies in its effect not just on athletes who are participating in the sport but on the fans who are watching it. Sports are highly emotional for those who participate in them but for many fans it is just as emotional. Our country's obsession with sports leads to fans who are more passionate about their favorite sports team than anything else in their life. In our increasingly fragmented society, sports continues to be one of the dominant areas in which people feel like they are part of a group and community. With sports teams and television coverage of sports making fans feel like they are part of the game (for example, the talk of fans being the twelfth man for their football team), it should not be surprising when some fans take their rooting to another level. The tradition of college students rushing the field after a big win is a prime example of sports fans' desire to get closer to the game and for them to feel like they are part of the team. With tens of thousands of fans at a game displaying this passion, fights can be expected, especially when you add alcohol to the mix. Alcohol, which has become part of the sports culture, contributes to the negative behavior that is witnessed at games across the country. The passion that comes with sporting events has lead to violent behavior at all levels. Spectator violence is not something that is unique to college and professional games but is also present at high school games, making it necessary for some rival high schools to play games with no spectators to decrease the chance of violent incidents. Violence occurs at sports events involving young children as well, with parents of little leaguers attacking umpires and parents of opposing players attacking kids on the opposing team. The emotion of sports for professional sports fans is one thing, but when the sporting event involves a son or daughter, the parents' feelings sometimes explode. The amount of pressure and attention that our country places on athletes begins at younger and younger ages. Thus it is not surprising that the negative behaviors, like spectator violence and steroid use, associated with higher levels have trickled down to younger and younger age levels.

Additionally, the relationship between fans' behavior and violence has extended beyond those present at the game. It has been found that sports violence can affect those watching at home. There has been much research on the effects of viewing violence on television (and also on playing violent video games). It has been consistently demonstrated with children that there is an imitation effect, with children imitating what they see on television. Thus, if children are viewing violence it not surprising that they behave violently afterward. There have been a number of tragic cases where after watching professional wrestling, young children have tried to recreate the wrestling moves on other children, sometimes with fatal results. Do these findings extend to adults? There is no doubt that the body responds differently (such as increased blood pressure and heart rate) watching a violent sport like football or hockey than watching swimming or golf. The question is: can this translate into aggressive behavior? Some studies seem to indicate that it does, but there has been too little research to draw any definitive conclusions. However, with continued focus by politicians on the effects of violence on television and video games on children, sports should be included in the discussion. Sports violence in many cases falls perfectly into the types of violence that have been found to affect people the most. The violence is real, in most cases praised and not punished. These are the exact criteria that lead to concerns about movie and television violence.

Sports fans engage in another sport-related activity that is, in most cases, criminal. Sports gambling is one of the most mainstream illegal activities in our society. It is another way that fans make themselves feel like they are part of the game. By wagering money on a game, fans become personally invested in the outcome in a way that moves beyond simply rooting for a favorite team. With the advent of Internet gambling, it is even easier and less risky (not having to deal with a bookie) to participate in sports gambling. Although still only legal in Nevada (Delaware has moved toward making it legal), sports gambling has become part of the fabric of our society. The office college basketball pool or Super Bowl bets are not looked on as anything illegal. Less than 1% of sports bets are made legally in Nevada and only 1.5% of Super Bowl bets, the biggest sports event of the year, are made in Nevada.[7] With all the passion and attention directed toward sports, it is not surprising that people bet not only to win money but also to heighten the experience of watching the game.

The interest in gambling on sports takes a serious turn when gamblers try to actually fix or affect the outcome of games by paying the athletes who participate in them. There have been numerous cases of point shaving and fixing games, most notably in college basketball. With the salaries that professional athletes make, they are somewhat immune from the risk of being bought by gamblers looking for them to throw a game or shave points. However college athletes, who are not paid and in many cases will not make it to the professional ranks to make money from their athletic ability, are typically the targets of gamblers. The athletes see this as an opportunity to make some money and can rationalize that they are simply affecting the point spread and not losing games on purpose. The people fixing the games are first and foremost looking to make money, but a secondary benefit is the power of feeling that they are controlling the game. It is the closest that a non-athlete can get to being part of the game.

Gambling also affects crime in other ways. The increasing spread of gambling across the country in the form of lotteries and casinos has led to an increased number of problem gamblers and state governments dependent on gambling revenues, which is a dangerous combination. Governments more and more are turning to gambling and loosening the restrictions on gambling because of the seemingly endless revenue that they can collect. However, greater availability of gambling has led to an increased number of problem gamblers who are more likely to engage in crime to support their gambling habits. The research is mixed as to whether the presence of a casino increases crime in the surrounding area; however, what is known is that gambling addicts are at greater risk of family and financial problems that often result in crimes like embezzlement, petty theft, and drug use. The effect of increased gambling needs to be examined more closely especially in light of the vast frontier of Internet gambling, which is becoming more and more a part of our culture. Federal and state governments need to come to a decision regarding Internet gambling. Either the government should legalize it and tax it or it should criminalize it and figure out how to enforce the law, rather than remaining in the limbo that exists today.

HOW CAN THE NEGATIVE INFLUENCES OF SPORTS BE TURNED AROUND?

Participation in sports has many positive aspects. It promotes a healthy lifestyle and gives kids a sense of discipline and a feeling of belonging. For those playing sports at school it enhances school spirit and keeps kids busy while participating in a positive activity. Many have seen these positives as making sports a prime activity to use in an effort to reduce crime. Programs like Midnight Basketball have played off of sports' positive attributes as a way to reach out to inner-city youths. Sports in prison is a valuable tool to keep inmates in line and tire them out rather than directing their energy to more dangerous activities. Additionally, many juvenile detention centers see sports programs as a key component to any form of rehabilitation. All of this points to the fact that sports can be a life-transforming positive activity. So why has there been so much negative and criminal behavior associated with sports recently?

The problems associated with spectator violence have been addressed aggressively in the professional and college ranks. Although much of the increased security was the result of terrorist attacks and not a response to fan violence, security is something that is taken quite seriously at events. At lower levels, the same ideas regarding creating a positive culture on sports teams should be addressed by parents and communities. Additionally, states have started to address the issue by increasing penalties for attacking umpires and referees and some towns have created codes of conduct for spectators at games.

The negative effects of gambling need to be addressed in this country. States continue to expand gambling opportunities as a way to help their revenue, but how long can they expect to see the positive benefits of increased revenue outweigh the negative effects of increased problem gambling and everything that comes with it? With this in mind, the issue of online gambling needs to be addressed both legally and socially. The uncertainty regarding the legality of online gambling is something that should be dealt with both federally and on the state level; the state of limbo that now exists needs to be fixed. With the debate over the legality of online gambling, the social implications also need to be examined. What will be the impact of unlimited access to gambling for every person with access to a computer? Additionally, how will this effect sports gambling and the opportunities for corruption within sports? While the law should address spectator violence and gambling, society as a whole needs to address the increasing linkage of athletes and criminal behavior.

Playing football, aside from the issue of the aggression on the field, doesn't necessarily lead to a sense of entitlement and being placed on a pedestal. It is because of the culture that has put so much emphasis on sports that athletes become celebrities starting at young ages. It is not something that is inherent in sports that leads to preferential treatment; it is our society's (school, college, and favorite professional team) desire to win that leads us to give athletes a pass when it comes to their behavior. There is nothing inherent in being able to hit a 90-mile-per-hour baseball that leads to a sense that one is above the law. Athletes are atop the social pyramid in high school, on the college campus, and in society as a whole. It is all of these influences that play a greater role in creating athletes who have a complete disregard for many of the norms or laws in society.

The problems that have been described related to athletes and fans have to do less with what takes place on the field (violence) than with the other peripheral things that come with sports in our culture. Thus it is not the participation in sports that is negative, it is all of the other aspects that our society ties into it. We value athletes above scientists, doctors, and teachers; we put them on a pedestal where they start to believe the rules do not apply to them. From Little League days, athletes are treated differently (for example, ESPN's coverage of the Little League World Series), so it should be no surprise that athletes sometimes believe they can behave differently as well.

To enhance the positive aspects of athletic participation, coaches, parents, and teachers can encourage student athletes to pursue interests other than sports as well, thus creating well-rounded children instead of "jocks." This has the added benefit of athletes not developing an "us" versus "them" (non-athletes) mentality. Additionally, coaches, who are responsible for the culture of their team, can encourage sportsmanship and discipline and discourage sexist and homophobic language and attitudes. Schools at all levels can hold athletes accountable and not treat student-athletes differently simply because they are stars on the playing field. Elite college and professional athletes need to recognize the perils that come with fame and fortune. The professional sports leagues conduct rookie seminars addressing these issues but the message needs to get across to professional athletes that they are accountable for their behavior and need to make better decisions in regard to where and with whom they hang out because they are a target. More attention needs to be directed toward guns and the issue of performance-enhancing drugs. Other sports leagues need to take their cue from the NFL, where Commissioner Roger Goodell has stepped up efforts to enforce a strict code of conduct for the players.

The suggestions offered are a way for the sports world to change the image of sports and athletes in the United States. While sports will continue to hold a special place in our society, crime is another subject that receives an enormous amount of attention in this country. Any story that merges sports and crime will bring heightened media attention and remain a fascination as it brings together two of our society's most passionate topics. Thus, to truly change the image of sports in the United States, an effort to avoid criminal behavior must be made by every participant in the sports world—athletes, coaches, and fans alike.

NOTES

INTRODUCTION

1. Wilson, J. and Herrnstein, R. *Crime and Human Nature.* New York: Simon and Schuster, 1985, p. 69.

2. Sheldon, W. (with collaboration of Hartl, E. and McDermott, E.). *Varieties of Delinquent Youth.* New York: Harper, 1949.

3. Hartl, E., Monnelli, E., and Eldeken, R. *Physique and Delinquent Behavior.* New York: Academic Press, 1982.

4. Glueck, S. and Glueck, E. *Physique and Delinquency.* New York: Harper-Collins, 1956.

5. Wilson, J. and Herrnstein, R. *Crime and Human Nature*, p. 89.

6. Federal Bureau of Investigation. *Crime in the United States, 2006.* Washington, DC: U.S. Department of Justice, 2007.

7. Wilson, J. and Herrnstein, R. *Crime and Human Nature.*

8. Olweus, D. "Testosterone, Aggression, Physical and Personality Dimensions in Normal Adolescent Males." *Psychosomatic Medicine* 42 (1980), pp. 253–269.

9. Udry, R. "Biosocial Models of Adolescent Problem Behaviors." *Social Biology* 37(1990): pp. 1–10.

10. Booth, A. and Osgood, D. "The Influence of Testosterone on Deviance in Adulthood: Assessing and Explaining the Relationship." *Criminology* 31:1(1993), p. 93.

11. "The Insanity of Steroid Abuse." *Newsweek,* May 23, 1988, p. 75.

12. Bernhardt, P. "Influences of Serotonin and Testosterone in Aggression and Dominance: Convergence with Social Psychology." *Current Directions in Psychological Science* 6:2 (1997), pp. 44–48.

CHAPTER 1

1. "5 Utah High School Football Players Arrested for Crime Spree." *The Salt Lake Tribune,* July 3, 2008.

2. Korte, T. "Horrific High School Football Hazing Case Shakes New Mexico Town." *USA Today,* September 24, 2008.

3. Perez, A. and Aymond, B. "Mixed News, Two Views on Prep Steroid Use." *USA Today*, July 24, 2008, p.1C.

4. National Federation of State High School Association 2007–2008 Study. Available at http://www.nfhs.org/

5. Miracle, Jr., A. and Rees, C. *Lessons of the Locker Room: The Myth of School Sports.* Amherst, NY: Prometheus Books 1994, p. 121.

6. Burton, J. and Marshall, L. "Protective Factors for Youth Considered at Risk of Criminal Behavior: Does Participation in Extracurricular Activities Help?" *Criminal Behavior and Mental Health* 15:1 (2005), pp. 46–64.

7. Hirschi, T. *Causes of Delinquency.* Berkeley: University of California Press, 1969.

8. Ibid.

9. Akers, R. and Cochoran, J. "Adolescent Marijuana Use: A Test of Three Theories of Delinquent Behavior." *Deviant Behavior* 6 (1985), p. 323.

10. Ferracuti, F. and Wolfgang, M. *The Subculture of Violence: Toward an Integrated Theory of Criminology.* Saddle River, NJ: Prentice Hall, 1967.

11. Hughes, R. and Coakley, J. "Positive Deviance among Athletes: The Implications of Overconformity to the Sport Ethic." *Sociology of Sport Journal* 8:4 (1991), p. 308.

12. Ibid., p. 311.

13. Ibid., p. 314.

14. Miracle, Jr., A. and Rees, C. *Lessons of the Locker Room*, p. 109.

15. Ibid., p. 17.

16. Hartmann, D. and Massoglia, M. "Reassessing the Relationship between High School Sports Participation and Deviance: Evidence of Enduring Bifurcated Effects." *Sociological Quarterly* 48:3 (2007), pp. 485–505.

17. Ibid., p. 486.

18. Rees, C., Howell, F. and Miracle, A. "Do High School Sports Build Character? A Quasi-experiment on a National Sample." *Social Science Journal* 27:3 (1990), pp. 303–315.

19. Gottfredson, M. and Hirschi, T. *A General Theory of Crime.* Stanford: Stanford University Press. 1990.

20. Burton, J. and Marshall, L. "Protective Factors for Youth Considered At Risk of Criminal Behavior," pp. 46–64.

21. Sanday, P. "Rape-prone versus Rape-free Campus Cultures." *Violence Against Women* 2 (1996), pp. 191–208.

22. Forbes, G., Adams-Curtis, L., Pakalka, A., and White, K. "Dating Aggression, Sexual Coercion, and Aggression-Supporting Attitudes among College Men as a Function of Participation in Aggressive High School Sports" *Violence Against Women* 12:5 (2006), pp. 441–445.

23. Watkins, R. "A Social Psychological Examination of the Relationship between Athletic Participation and Delinquent Behavior." *Dissertation Abstracts International* 60 (2000):4969.

24. Duncan, S., Duncan, T. Strycker, L., and Chaumeton, N. "Relations between Youth and Antisocial and Prosocial Activities." *Journal of Behavioral Medicine.* 25:5 (2002), pp. 425–438.

25. Eccles, J. and Barber, B. "Student Council, Volunteering, Basketball or Marching Band: What Kind of Extracurricular Activities Matter?" *Journal of Adolescent Research* 14 (1999), pp. 101–143.

26. Burton, J. and Marshall, L. "Protective Factors for Youth Considered at Risk of Criminal Behavior," pp. 46–64.

27. Miracle, Jr., A. and Rees, C. *Lessons of the Locker Room*, p. 90.

28. Miller, K., Mlenick, M., Farrell, M., Sabo, D., and Barnes, G. "Jocks, Gender, Binge Drinking, and Adolescent Violence." *Journal of Interpersonal Violence* 21:1 (2006), pp. 105–120.

29. Miracle, Jr., A. and Rees, C. *Lessons of the Locker Room*, p. 103.

30. "Judge's Ruling Divides 'Big Football Town.'" http://www.cnn.com August 19, 2006.

31. Miracle, Jr., A. and Rees, C. *Lessons of the Locker Room*, p. 73.

32. Hoover, N. and Pollard, N. "Initiation Rites and Athletics: A National Survey of NCAA Sports Teams. Alfred University Study (www.alfred.edu/sports_hazing), August 30, 1999.

33. www.Stophazing.org.

34. Nuwer, H. *High School Hazing: When Rites Become Wrongs.* New York: Scholastic, 2000.

35. Available at http:www.Stophazing.org.

36. Kirby, S. and Wintrup, G. "Running the Gauntlet: An Examination of Initiation/Hazing and Sexual Abuse in Sport." *The Journal of Sexual Aggression* 8:2 (2002), pp. 56–57.

37. Ibid., pp. 49–68.

38. Jacobs, A. "Violent Cast of School Hazing Mirrors Society, Experts Say." *The New York Times*, March 5, 2000, p. 1:35.

39. Available at http:www.stophazing.org/laws.html.

40. Nuwer, H. *High School Hazing.* Most of the details about Nick Haben were from Chapter 5, where Nuwer details the case in full.

41. "New Player Suffers Concussion" *Associated Press,* October 10, 2003.

42. Herszenhorn, D. "Hazing Is Team Tradition, a Defendant's Lawyer Says." *The New York Times*, February 2, 2000, p. B5.

43. Relative, S. "Sex Hazing Alleged at Wilson High School in New York: Hazing Not Just for College Fraternities Anymore." *Associated Content*, August 10, 2008.

44. Zeigler, C. "The Gay Side of Hazing." Available at http:www.outsports.com/campus, 2006.

45. "Northwestern: Men's Swimming, Mascots Also Hazed." *Associated Press*, May 18, 2006.

46. "Freshman Made to Sit in Own Vomit, Urine." *Associated Press*, September 12, 2005.

47. "Team Put on Three Years' Probation; Three Players Suspended." *Associated Press,* August 15, 2007.

48. Lapointe, J. "The Lost Season: A Special Report; a Hard Winter in Vermont." *The New York Times,* February 3, 2000.

49. Smith, S. "Hawks rookies victimized by practical joke." *The Atlanta Journal-Constitution,* February 11, 2008.

50. Jones, T. "Dinner: $24,000; Bonding: Priceless." *St. Petersburg Times,* January 23, 2006.

51. Lukas, P. "The Storied Tradition of MLB Rookie Hazing." Available at http:www.espn.com, September 27, 2007.

52. Kolker, R. "Out of Bounds." *The New York Magazine,* June 4, 2009.

53. Healey, P. "Three Athletes To Be Charged in Abuse Case, Police Say." *The New York Times,* October 2, 2003, p. B1.

54. Kolker, R. "Out of Bounds."

55. Wald, J. "Football Coaches Fired in Alleged Hazing Aftermath." Available at http:www.cnn.com, November 6, 2003.

56. Kolker, R. "Out of Bounds."

57. Ibid.

58. Ibid.

59. Ibid.

60. Healey, P. "Report Says Hazing Culture Led to Attacks on 3 Athletes." *The New York Times,* March 11, 2004, p. B1.

61. Ibid.

62. Healey, P. "Confinement for 2 Athletes In Sex Abuse of Teammates." *The New York Times,* January 15, 2004, p. B6.

63. Winzelberg, D. "Coaches Sue in Sex Assault Case." *The New York Times,* August 2, 2004, p. B4.

64. Longman, J. "At Mepham, Play Begins but the Pain Never Ends." *The New York Times,* September 29, 2004, p. D1.

Chapter 2

1. Glier, R. "F.S.U. to Bar as Many as 25 Players from Bowl." *The New York Times,* December 19, 2007.

2. Rosandich, T. "Collegiate Sport Programs: A Comparative Analysis." *Education* (2002), p. 476.

3. Doumas, D., Turrisi, R., Coll, K., and Haralson, K. "High-Risk Drinking in College Athletes and Nonathletes across the Academic Year." *Journal of College Counseling,* 10:2 (2007), pp. 163–174; Grossbard, J., Lee, C., Neighbors, C., Hendershot, C., and Larimer, M. "Alcohol and Risky Sex in Athletes and Nonathletes: What Roles Do Sex Motives Play?" *Journal of Studies on Alcohol & Drugs* 68:4 (2007), pp. 566–574.

4. Miller, K., Hoffman, J., Barnes, G., Farrell, M., Sabo, D., and Melnick, M. "Jocks, Gender, Race, and Adolescent Problem Drinking." *Journal of Drug Education* 33:4 (2003), pp. 445–462.

5. Applebome, P. "Off the Court, an Odd Lesson in Ethics." *The New York Times*, March 22, 2006, p. B1.

6. Moran, M. "Second Chance Not Lost on UConn's Williams" *USA Today*, March 8, 2006.

7. "Three CCSU Football Players Arrested." *The Associated Press State & Local Wire, State and Regional*, December 2, 2005.

8. Snyder, E. "Interpretations and Explanations of Deviance among College Athletes: A Case Study." *Sociology of Sport Journal* 11:3 (1994), pp. 231–248.

9. Teel, D. "Crime and College Athletes—Players Over the Edge or Overreported?" *Newport News Daily Press*, March 2, 1997.

10. Chandler, S., Johnson, D., and Carroll, P. "Abusive Behaviors of College Athletes." *College Student Journal* 33:4 (1999).

11. Rood, L. "College Athletes and Criminal Charges: Some Work to Keep Allegations Quiet." *The Des Moines Register*, August 31, 2008.

12. Holmstrom, D. "Do Aggressive Sports Produce Violent Men?" *Christian Science Monitor* 87 (October 16, 1995), p. 224.

13. Teitelbaum, S. *Sports Heroes Fallen Idols: How Star Athletes Pursue Self-Destructive Paths and Jeopardize Their Careers.* Lincoln: University of Nebraska Press. 2005, p.17.

14. Ibid.

15. Kirshenbaum, J. "An American Disgrace: A violent and unprecedented lawlessness has arisen among college athletes in all parts of the country." *Sports Illustrated*, February 27, 1989, p. 16.

16. New California Education Code, section (§) 67362, (AB 2165).

17. Weiss, S. "A Comparison of Maladaptive Behavior of Athletes and Non-athletes." *Journal of Psychology* 133:3 (1999), pp. 315–322.

18. "Study Shows 'Mythology' Exists about Student-Athlete Off-Field Actions." Available at http:www.Live.Psu.Edu/Story/26120, September 24, 2007.

19. Lavigne, P. "Has Penn State's On-field Progress Led to Off-field Problems?" www.espn.com, July 27, 2008.

20. McLane, J. "Looking Past the Distractions; Paterno Is Ready for a New Season Despite Some Unresolved Issues." *The Philadelphia Inquirer*, July 21, 2008, p. D1.

21. "Chisley Sentenced to Life." Available at http:www.wjactv.com, September 29, 2007.

22. "Dotson Seeks Permission to Appeal." *Associated Press Online*, January 4, 2006.

23. Yusko, R., Buckman, D., White, J., and Pandina, H. "Alcohol, Tobacco, Illicit Drugs, and Performance Enhancers: A Comparison of Use by College Student Athletes and Nonathletes." *Journal of American College Health* 57:3 (2008), pp. 281–290.

24. Page, R. and Roland, M. "Misperceptions of the Prevalence of Marijuana Use among College Students: Athletes and Non-Athletes." *Journal of Child & Adolescent Substance Abuse* 14:1(2004), pp. 61–75.

25. Yusko, R., Buckman, D., White, J., and Pandina, H. "Risk for Excessive Alcohol Use and Drinking-Related Problems in College Student Athletes." *Addictive Behaviors* 33:12 (2008), pp. 1546–1556.

26. Chandler, S., Johnson, D., and Carroll, P. "Abusive Behaviors of College Athletes."

27. Frinter, M. and Rubinson, L. "Acquaintance Rape: The Influence of Alcohol, Fraternity Membership, and Sports Team Membership." *Journal of Sex Education and Therapy* 19 (1993), pp. 272–284.

28. Benedict, J. *Public Heroes, Private Felons: Athletes and Crimes against Women.* Boston: Northeastern University Press, 1997, p. 215.

29. Chandler, S., Johnson, D., and Carroll, P. "Abusive Behaviors of College Athletes."

30. "NCAA News Release: NCAA Student-Athletes Graduating at Highest Rate Ever." Available at http:www.ncaa.org, October 14, 2008.

31. Freeman, M. "Clarett: Symbol of College Turmoil." *The New York Times*, August 24, 2003, p. 8:1.

32. Longman, J. "Maurice Clarett Scored the Winning Touchdown in the National Championship Game after the 2002 Season." *The New York Times*, August 13, 2006.

33. Litsky, F. "Chase Ends in a Scuffle and Trouble for Clarett." *The New York Times,* August 10, 2006.

34. Litsky, F. "Maurice Clarett Will Serve at Least Three and a Half Years in Prison. *The New York Times,* September 19, 2006.

35. Freeman, M. "Clarett: Symbol of College Turmoil," p. 8:1.

36. Ibid.

37. Vinella, S. "Big Enigma on Campus: Clarett's Fall from Superstar to Outcast." *Plain Dealer Reporter*, November 16, 2003.

38. Farrey, T. "Souls of the Departed Haunt Youngstown." Available at http:www.espn.com, November 12, 2004.

39. Miedzian, M. *Boys Will Be Boys: Breaking the Link between Masculinity and Violence.* Herndon, VA: Steiner Books, 2002.

40. Fischer, B., Cullen, F., and Turner, M. "The Sexual Victimization of College Women." *US Department of Justice Report*, Washington, DC: Government Printing Office December 2000.

41. Brown, J. and Pankratz, H. "Court Revives CU Rape Lawsuit." *Denver Post,* September 7, 2007.

42. O'Sullivan, C. "Acquaintance Gang Rape on Campus." In *Acquaintance Rape: The Hidden Crime*, Parrot, A. and Bechhofer, L. (Eds.). New York: John Wiley and Sons, 1991, p. 144.

43. Crosset, T., Benedict, J., and McDonald, M. "Male Student-Athletes Reported for Sexual Assault: A Survey of Campus Police Departments and Judicial Affairs Offices." *Journal of Sport and Social Issue* 19:2 (1995), pp. 126–140.

44. Humphreys, S. and Kahn, A. "Fraternities, Athletic Teams, and Rape." *Journal of Interpersonal Violence* 15:12 (2000), pp. 1313–1322.

45. Holmstrom, D. "Do Aggressive Sports Produce Violent Men?," p. 1.

46. Humphreys, S. and Kahn, A. "Fraternities, Athletic Teams, and Rape," p. 26.

47. Hildebrand, K., Johnson, D., and Bogle, K. "Comparison of Patterns of Alcohol Use between High School and College Athletes and Non-Athletes." *College Student Journal* 35:3 (2001), p. 358.

48. Chandler, S., Johnson, D., and Carroll, P. "Abusive Behaviors of College Athletes."

49. Holmstrom, D. "Do Aggressive Sports Produce Violent Men?," p. 1.

50. Fernas, R. "Athletes Part of a Violent Trend." *Los Angeles Times,* July 19, 2003.

51. Evans, T. and Thamel, P. "Oklahoma State Player Sentenced in Sex Assault." *The New York Times,* October 8, 2007, p. D2.

52. "Okla. State LB Collins Suspended for Season, But Will Keep Scholarship." Available at http:www.espn.com, October 10, 2007.

53. Haisten, B. "Gundy Dismisses Collins," *Tulsa World News*, November 13, 2007, p. B1.

54. Benedict, J. *Out of Bounds.* New York: HarperCollins, 2004, p. 218.

CHAPTER 3

1. Attner, P. "He listens and He Hears." *The Sporting News*, April 9, 2001.

2. Cranston, M. "Panthers' T. Bridges Arrested on Assault Charges." *The Associated Press,* December 8, 2008.

3. Benedict, J. and Yeager, D. *Pros and Cons: The Criminals Who Play in the NFL.* New York: Warner Books, 1998, p.100.

4. Freeman, M. "Stains from the Police Blotter Leave N.F.L. Embarrassed." *The New York Times*, January 9, 2000.

5. http://www.nba.com/news/cba_minimumsalary_050804.html.

6. http://asp.usatoday.com/sports/football/nfl/salaries/mediansalaries.aspx?year=2009.

7. Sutherland, E. "White-Collar Criminality." *American Sociological Review* 5:1 (1940), pp. 2–10.

8. Ibid.

9. Barak, G., Leighton, P., and Flavin, J. *Class, Race, Gender, and Crime: The Social Realities of Justice in America.* New York: Rowman & Littlefield Publishers, 2006, p. 104.

10. Simon, D. and Eitzen, D. *Elite Deviance.* New York: Allyn and Bacon, 1993.

11. Hirschi, T. and Gottfredson, M. "Causes of White-Collar Crime." *Criminology* 25:4 (2006), p. 949.

12. Gottfredson, M. and Hirschi, T. *A General Theory of Crime.* Stanford: Stanford University Press, 1990.

13. Grasmick, H. "Testing the Core Empirical Implications of Gottfredson and Hirschi's General Theory of Crime." *Journal of Research in Crime and Delinquency* 30 (1993), pp. 5–29.

14. Teitelbaum, S. *Sports Heroes Fallen Idols: How Star Athletes Pursue Self-Destructive Paths and Jeopardize Their Careers.* Lincoln: University of Nebraska Press, 2005, p. 19.

15. Ibid., p. 24.

16. Ibid., p. 26.

17. Dohrmann, G. "The Road to Bad Newz." *Sports Illustrated,* November 26, 2007, p. 72.

18. Ibid.

19. Jamieson, L. and Orr, T. *Sport and Violence: A Critical Examination of Sport.* London: Butterworth-Heinemann, 2009.

20. Baron, L. and Straus, M. "Four Theories of Rape: A Macrosociological Analysis." *Social Problems* 34 (1987), pp. 468–488.

21. Bloom, G. and Smith, M. "Hockey Violence: A Test of Cultural Spillover Theory." *Sociology of Sport Journal* 13 (1996), p. 67.

22. Ibid.

23. Robinson, L. "Professional Athletes—Held to a Higher Standard and Above the Law: A Comment on High-Profile Criminal Defendants and the Need for States to Establish High-Profile Courts." *Indiana Law Journal* 73:4.

24. Brown, C. and Battista, J. "Vick Goes To Court As Falcons Go To Camp." *The New York Times,* July 27, 2007.

25. Maske, M. "Falcons' Vick Indicted in Dogfighting Case: Star QB Alleged to Have Been Highly Involved." *The Washington Post,* July 18, 2007, p. E1.

26. Macur, J. "Vick Receives 23 Months and a Lecture." *The New York Times,* December 11, 2007, p. D1.

27. Rhoden, W. "After Reinstatement, Vick Has to Handle Teams and Public." *The New York Times,* July 28, 2009, p. B14.

28. Klein, J. "The Vick Rehabilitation Begins." *The New York Times,* August 15, 2009.

29. Thamel, P. "Virginia Tech's Vick Suspended for the Season." *The New York Times,* August 4, 2004, p. D7.

30. Schlabach, M. "Marcus Vick Arrested on Firearm Charges; Police Say Former Hokie QB Waved Gun at Teenagers." *The Washington Post,* January 10, 2006, p. E01.

31. "Marcus Vick Pleads Guilty to Driving Drunk." *The Washington Post,* October 21, 2008, p. E2.

32. Pennington, B. "Pro Football; N.F.L. Suspends 3 Players for Off-the-Field Violence." March 15, 2000.

33. Benedict, J. and Yaeger, D. *Pros and Cons,* p. xi.

34. Ibid., p. 10.

35. Blumstein, A. and Benedict, J. "Criminal Violence of the NFL Players Compared to the General Population." *Chance* 12: 3 (1999).

36. Ibid., p. 12.

37. Ibid., p. 15.

38. Johnson, W. "What's Happened to Our Heroes? Each Week Brings News of Athletes' Misdeeds. How Serious Is the Situation? Here Is the Result of an SI Inquiry." *Sports Illustrated*, August 15, 1983.

39. Benedict, J. *Out of Bounds: Inside the NBA's Culture of Rape, Violence and Crime.* New York: HarperCollins, 2004, p. 216.

40. Ibid., p. 156.

41. Dillon, D. "Game Over, Pacman." *The Sporting News,* April 16, 2007.

42. Myers, G. "Time to Pac It In. GMs Agree: Goodell Must Deal Harshly with Jones." *Daily News (New York),* April 1, 2007.

43. Wilner, B. "Goodell Gets Tough, Protects NFL Brand." Available at http:www.boston.com, April 10, 2007.

44. Myers, G. "Time to Pac It In. GMs Agree."

45. Goldberg, D. "Titans' Pacman Is Suspended for Season." *Associated Press Online,* April 10, 2007.

46. "Report: Cowboys Cut A. Jones for Alleged Role in 2007 Shooting." *The Washington Post,* January 9, 2009, p. E3.

47. Dillon, D. "Game Over, Pacman."

48. Reese, F. "Expect Commissioner to Punish Pacman." Available at http:www.espn.com, March 28, 2007.

49. "Pacman Jones Is Miles from Home." Available at http:www.dallasnews.com, June 8, 2008.

50. Garber, G. "Jones Gifted on Field, Troubled Off It." Available at http:www.espn.com, March 9, 2007.

51. Ibid.

52. Ibid.

53. "Research Report: Anabolic Steroid Abuse."

54. National Institute on Drug Abuse, U.S. Department of Health and Human Services. Infofact—Steroids. Available at http:www.drugabuse.gov, August 7, 2009.

55. Horn, S., Gregory, P., and Guskiewicz, K. "Self-Reported Anabolic-Androgenic Steroids Use and Musculoskeletal Injuries: Findings from The Center for the Study of Retired Athletes Health Survey of Retired NFL Players." *American Journal of Physical Medicine & Rehabilitation* 88:3 (2009), pp. 192−200.

56. "Bettman to Tell Congress Harsh Penalties Make NHL Steroid-Free." *Associated Press*, February 26, 2008.

57. Available at http:www.NCAA.org.

58. Scharrer, G. and Kahn, S. "Of 10,000 Tested, Two on Steroids" *The Houston Chronicle*, July 1, 2008.

59. Hambey, C. "High School Athletes Next for Steroids." Available at http:www.stateline.org, June 15, 2007.

60. National Institute on Drug Abuse. *Monitoring the Future: National Results on Adolescent Drug Use. Overview of Key Findings 2006.* Bethesda, MD: National Institute on Drug Abuse, 2006.

61. Williams, L. and Fainaru-Wada, M. "What Bonds Told BALCO Grand Jury." *The San Francisco Chronicle*, December 3, 2004.

62. White, K. and Stannard, M. "Agents Raid Supplement Lab." *The San Francisco Chronicle*, September 6, 2003.

63. Schmidt, M. "Court Rules U.S. Seized 2003 Tests Improperly." *The New York Times*, August 27, 2009.

64. Sprow, C. "NBA, NFL Go Anti-Gun: But Are They Protecting Their Athletes, or Protecting an Image?" Available at http:www.reason.com, January 8, 2008.

65. Carroll, J. "Gun Ownership and Use in America: Women More Likely Than Men to Use Guns for Protection." Available at http:www.gallup.com/poll/20098/gun-ownership-use-america.aspx, November 22, 2005.

66. Sonner, S. "Gun Charge Followed Fight with NV Football Players." *The Associated Press State & Local Wire*, April 23, 2009.

67. "For the Record: Arrested." *Sports Illustrated*, September 28, 2009, p. 22.

68. Nobles, C. Pro Football; Blades Charged in Death of Cousin." *The New York Times*, July 19, 1995, p. B13.

69. Ibid.

70. Ibid.

71. Nobles, C. "Pro Football; Blades Found Guilty." *The New York Times*, June 15, 1996, p. A26.

72. Nobles, C. "Pro Football; Blades's Manslaughter Conviction Gets Reversed." *The New York Times*, June 18, 1996, p. B15.

73. "Sports Briefing." *The New York Times,* October 7, 2006, p. D4.

74. "Sports Briefing." *The New York Times*, July 15, 2007 p. SP6.

75. "Jackson Expected to Plead Guilty to Recklessness Charge." *The Associated Press*, June 20, 2007.

76. Berko, A., Delsohn, S., and Rovegno, L. "Athletes and Guns 'Outside the Lines' Takes a Look at the Link between Athletes and Guns." Available at http:www.espn.com, December 15, 2006.

77. Lott, Jr., J. "Athletes and Guns." Available at http:www.foxnews.com, January 28, 2004.

78. Berko, A., Delsohn, S., and Rovegno, L. "Athletes and Guns."

79. "With the Recent Shooting Death of Sean Taylor, Professional Athletes Have Become Prey for Criminals." *Associated Press,* December 1, 2007.

80. Drehs, W. "The Professional Athlete as Target: 'Am I Next?' Athletes' High Profiles Make for Easy Crime Targets." Available at http:www.espn.com, Nov. 30, 2007.

81. Hogan, N. "Athletes Fear for Their Safety; But the Way They Deal with It Could Put Them in the Line of Fire." *Times-Picayune (New Orleans),* March 29, 2009, p. 1.

82. Drehs, W. "The Professional Athlete as Target."

83. Semple, K. and Aguayo, T. "Redskins' Taylor Is Seriously Wounded in a Gun Attack." *The New York Times,* November 27, 2007, p. D1.

84. Ibid.

85. Ibid.

86. Macur, J. "Four Arrested in Killing of Redskins' Taylor." *The New York Times,* December 1, 2007, p. D1.

87. LaCanfora, J. "Man Pleads Guilty in Taylor Slaying; Driver Sentenced to 29 Years in Prison, Will Testify Against Other Suspects." *The Washington Post,* May 16, 2008, p. E5.

88. Berko, A., Delsohn, S., and Rovegno, L. "Athletes and Guns."

89. Sprow, C. "NBA, NFL Go Anti-Gun: But Are They Protecting Their Athletes, or Protecting an Image?" Available at http:www.reason.com, January 8, 2008.

90. "With the Recent Shooting Death of Sean Taylor."

91. Freeman, M. "For Athletes with Guns, There Are Few Controls." *The New York Times,* August 11, 1997.

92. Couch, G. "No Denying Link between Athletes and Guns." *Chicago Sun Times,* November 18, 2005, p. 159.

93. Hogan, N. "Athletes Fear for Their Safety," p. 1.

94. Kelley, T. "Gun Owned by Ex-Athlete Killed Driver of Limousine." *The New York Times,* February 16, 2002, p. B4.

95. Pearce, J. "For Jayson Williams, the Trial Brings a Harsher Limelight." *The New York Times*, March 7, 2004, p. A14.

96. Peterson, I. "Ex-Nets Star Pleads Not Guilty in Shooting Death of Limousine Driver." *The New York Times*, June 8, 2002, p. B4.

97. Hanley, R. "Former Nets Star Faces New Homicide Charge." *The New York Times,* May 2, 2002, p. B2.

98. Pearce, J. "For Jayson Williams."

99. Hanley, R. "Williams Guilty of Cover-Up, but Not of Manslaughter." *The New York Times,* p. B1.

100. Peterson, I. and Baker, A. "After 11 Days, Former Nets Star Is Charged in Death of Chauffeur." *The New York Times*, February 26, 2002, p. A1.

101. Hanley, B. "Jury in Trial of Ex-Nets Star Won't Hear of Pet's Killing." *The New York Times*, February 5, 2004, p. B5.

102. "Assault Charge Dropped Against Jayson Williams." *The Associated Press State & Local Wire,* August 19, 2009.

103. "Former Net Williams Tasered by the Police." *The New York Times* (AP), April 28, 2009, p. B11.

104. Bamberger, M. "First-Degree Tragedy: Rae Carruth Was a Gifted but Unassuming Wide Receiver for the Panthers. Now He Stands Accused of Ordering the Murder of His Pregnant Girlfriend—A Horrific Crime That, Like Carruth Himself, Remains Grounded in Mystery." *Sports Illustrated*, December 27, 1999.

105. McKinley, J. "An Athlete Accused: A Special Report; Beneath the Smiles, A Tangled Relationship." *The New York Times*, December 21, 1999.

106. "Court News; Gunman Sentenced in Carruth Case." *The New York Times,* April 6, 2001.

CHAPTER 4

1. Young, K. "A Walk on the Wild Side: Exposing North American Sport Crowd Disorder." In *Fighting Fans: Football Hooliganism As a World Phenomenon,* Dunning, E., Murphy, P., and Waddington, I. (Eds.). Dublin: University College Dublin Press, 2002, pp. 201–217.

2. Chass, M. "Baseball; Unruly Fans Disrupt Tigers' Home Opener." *The New York Times,* May 3, 1995.

3. "MLB Notes: New Rule to Keep Fans from Having a Ball at the Stadium." *Sun Wire Reports,* April 8, 1997.

4. Hiestand, M. and Wood, S. "Fan Conduct High on NFL Priority List." *USA Today,* December 19, 2001.

5. "College Football; Wisconsin Victory Celebration Turns Dangerous." *The New York Times,* October 31, 1993.

6. "'I Was Stunned' Royals First Base Coach Assaulted by Father-Son Duo." Available at http:www.sportsillustrated.com, September 19, 2002.

7. "Gamboa Disappointed Ligue Sentenced to 30 Months Probation for Attack on Coach." Available at http:www.sportsillustrated.com, August 6, 2003.

8. Young, K. "A Walk on the Wild Side," p. 205.

9. "School Athletic Event Violence, Deaths, and Shootings Spike Since August: National School Safety and Security Services." *News Release Wire.* Available at http:www.schoolsecurity.org, November 24, 2005.

10. "Gunfire Ends Pa. High School Basketball Game." *The Associated Press State & Local Wire,* January 21, 2009.

11. Fitzgerald, M. "No New Info in Cahokia Case; 2 Arrested in Shooting Death of Student." *Belleville News-Democrat,* January 26, 2009.

12. Sakamoto, B. and Boghossian, C. "Chicago High Schools Battle Violence at Basketball Games: Afternoon Games and Smaller Crowds Are Part of a Formula to Ensure Safety in and around High Schools." *Chicago Tribune,* January 25, 2009.

13. Franklin, R. "Autopsy Finds Student Died from Head Trauma." *Star Tribune (Minneapolis, MN),* October 25, 2005, p. 5B.

14. Templeton, D. and Schackner, B. "WVU Hoping Fans Will Stay Cool; Officials Fear More Postgame Mayhem." *Pittsburgh Post-Gazette (Pennsylvania),* March 26, 2005, p. A1.

15. Hardin, E. "New Generation of Fools Should Be Kept Off the Field." *News & Record (Greensboro, NC),* November 30, 2002, p. C1.

16. Forinah, D. "Football Crowd Control: A National Issue." *The State Journal,* December 11, 2003.

17. Iacobelli, P. "Clemson Proceeding with Collapsible Goal Posts." *The Associated Press State & Local Wire,* July 19, 2004.

18. Hiestand, M. and Wood, S. "Fan Conduct High on NFL Priority List." *USA Today,* December 19, 2001.

19. "Veterans' Day NFC Title Game to Be Oft-maligned Stadium's NFL Swan Song." Available at http:www.sportsillustrated.com (AP), January 18, 2003.

20. Amore, D. "Tragic Side to Yanks-Sox." *The Hartford Courant*, May 5, 2008, p. A1.

21. O'Ryan, J. "Hockey Fans Banned from Rivalry Game." *The Boston Herald*, February 16, 2005, p. 2.

22. Warsinskey, T. "Out of Bounds; of Emotional and Physical Abuse in Their Wake." *Plain Dealer*, August 6, 2000, p. 1A.

23. Cowles, A. "Remember, Parents: It's Only a Game." *The Atlanta Journal and Constitution*, April 8, 1999, p. 1JI.

24. "Angry Parents Place Coaches in Tough Spots; Shooting of Texas Coach Highlights Concerns." *Education Week* 24:32 (April 20, 2005), p. 1.

25. "2 Angry Parents Attack Player's Mom." *Associated Press Online*, July 31, 2001.

26. Butterfield, F. "Father in Killing at Hockey Rink Is Given Sentence of 6 to 10 Years." *The New York Times*, January 26, 2002.

27. Cowles, A. "Remember, Parents."

28. Savoye, C., "Stiffer Penalties for Head-butting the Referee." *Christian Science Monitor*, March 20, 2001, p. 1.

29. Harmon, D. and Cantu, R. "New Bill Protects Sports Officials: Legislation Increases Penalties for Threats, Assaults on Officials." *Austin American-Statesman*, May 2, 2003, p. D1.

30. Keeton, L. "Cheerleader Mom' Hits Girl in Car Accident." *The Houston Chronicle*, November 2, 1992, p. A1.

31. Piller, R. "Holloway Settles with TV Network; 'Cheerleader Story' Set to Air Sunday." *The Houston Chronicle*, November 7, 1992, p. A34.

32. O'Connor, J. "TV Weekend; Travails of a Would-Be Cheerleader's Biggest Fan." *The New York Times*, April 9, 1993, p. B14.

33. Asin, S. "'Cheerleader Mom' Sentenced; 10-year Term Likely to Be Cut to 6 Months, Judge Says." *The Houston Chronicle*, September 10, 1996, p. A1.

34. "High School Football Coach Charged in Player's Death." Available at http:www.cnn.com, January 26, 2009.

35. "For the Record: Acquitted." *Sports Illustrated*, September 28, 2009, p. 20.

36. Pallasch, A. "Mother Still Fighting $16 Million Deal; Late NU Player's Mom Shouts at Judge, Offers to Go to Jail." *Chicago Sun-Times*, September 7, 2005, p. 23.

37. Edmonds, P. "No-Win Mix for Sports: Thrill of Victory, Agony of Violence." *USA Today*, June 22, 1993, p. A3.

38. "Bulls Fans Riot." *The Boston Globe*, June 22, 1993, p. A3.

39. Recht, M. "University Officials Searching for Answers." *The Associated Press State & Local Wire, State and Regional*, April 14, 2003.

40. O'Toole, T. "Police Seek Ways to Curb 'Celebratory Riots'" *USA Today*, April 9, 2002, p. C11.

41. "NBA Establishes Revised Arena Guidelines for All NBA Arenas." Available at http:www.nba.com/news/arena_guidelines_050217.html, February 17 2005.

42. Dunning, E., Murphy, P., and Waddington, I. *Fighting Fans: Football Hooliganism as a World Phenomenon.* Dublin: University College Dublin Press, 2002, p. 5.

43. Young, K. "A Walk on the Wild Side," pp. 201–217.

44. Roberts, J. and Benjamin, C. "Spectator Violence in Sports: A North American Perspective." *European Journal of Criminal Policy and Research* 8:2 (2000), pp. 163–179.

45. Handwerk, B. "Sports Riots: The Psychology of Fan Mayhem." *National Geographic News,* June 20, 2005.

46. Ibid.

47. Floyd, D. "Crimes in Athletics Need Prosecution." *Spokesman Review,* March 20, 2000, p. A12.

48. Milloya, R., "Basketball Player's Foul Draws a Jail Term." *The New York Times,* March 9, 2000, p. A12.

49. "On-Ice Violence." *The Patriot Ledger (Quincy, MA),* February 23, 2000, p. 24.

50. Ross, S., "Going, Going, Goon: McSorley Trial Could Have Violent Impact on Sports." *Daily News (New York),* September 24, 2000, p. 85.

51. "Bertuzzi Acted in 'Direct Disobedience': Crawford." *The Canadian Press,* August 19, 2008.

52. Spencer, T. "14-year-old Sentenced to Life in Wrestling Death." *The Independent,* March 10, 2001.

53. Wilson, C. "Florida Wrestling Death Teen Arrested Again." *Associated Press,* September 8, 2004.

54. Alanez, T. "Tate Gets 10 Years in Plea Deal for Robbery Case: Sentence for Role in Robbery to Run Concurrently with his 30-year Term." *South Florida Sun-Sentinel,* February 20, 2008.

55. Davis, J. "Domestic, Non-Washington, General News Item." *Cox News Service,* September 2, 1999.

56. Spencer, T. "Is Pro Wrestling to Blame for Girl's Death?" Available at http:www.southcoasttoday.com, April 16, 2000.

57. Bandura, A. *Social Learning through Imitation.* Lincoln: University of Nebraska Press, 1962.

58. Berkowitz, L. "Sports Competition and Aggression." In *An Analysis of Athletic Behavior,* Staub, W. (Ed.). Ithaca: Movement Publications, 1978.

59. Arms, R., Russell, G., and Sandilands, M. "Effects on the Hostility of Spectators of Viewing Aggressive Sports. *Social Psychology Quarterly* 42:3 (1979), pp. 275–279.

60. Comstock, G. "Types of Portrayals and Aggressive Behavior." *Journal of Communications* 26 (1977), pp. 189–198.

61. White, G., Katz, J., and Scarborough, K. "The Impact of Professional Football Games upon Violent Assaults on Women." *Violent Victimization* 7:2 (1992), pp. 157–171.

62. Phillips, D. "The Impact of Mass Media Violence on U.S. Homicides. *American Sociological Review* 48 (1983), pp. 560–568.

63. Branch, J. "When the Spotlight Is On, the Clothes Turn Black." *The New York Times*, October 4, 2008.

CHAPTER 5

1. "Fact Sheet: Gaming Revenue." Available at http:www.americangaming association.org.

2. Barker, T. and Britz, M. *Joker's Wild: Legalized Gambling in the Twenty-First Century*. Westport, CT: Praeger, 2000, p. 25.

3. "State of the States: The AGA Survey of Casino Entertainment, 2008." Available at http:www.americangamingassociation.org.

4. "Fact Sheet: Gaming Revenue." Available at http:www.americangaming association.org.

5. "Fact Sheets: Industry Issues." www.americangamingassociation.org.

6. Shpigel, B. "Mets Support Lo Duca as Gambling Stories Swirl." *The New York Times,* August 12, 2006.

7. Cross, M. and Vollano, A. The Extent and Nature of Gambling among College Student Athletes." Ann Arbor: University of Michigan Press, 1998 [Data for this research were collected from a paper and pencil survey that was mailed to 3000 National Collegiate Athletic Association (NCAA) Division I student athletes (1500 football, 750 men's basketball, 750 women's basketball) nationwide. The response rate for the study was 25.3% (n=758)].

8. Cullen, F. and Latessa, E. "The Extent and Sources of NCAA Rule Infractions: A National Self-Report Study of Student-Athletes." Kansas City, MO: National Collegiate Athletic Association, 1996.

9. Newfield, J. "The Shame of Boxing." *The Nation,* November 12, 2001.

10. Rodriquez, K. "Fixed Fights Down for the Count Fake Knockouts and Fraudulent Fights Tarnish Pro Boxing" *Miami Herald,* October 31, 1999, p. A1.

11. Asinof, E. *Eight Men Out: The Black Sox and the 1919 World Series*. New York: Henry Holt Company, 2000.

12. Ibid.

13. Linder, D. "The Black Sox Trial: An Account." Available at http:www. law.umkc.edu/faculty/projects/ftrials/blacksox/blacksox.html.

14. Ibid.

15. Holmes, D. *Ty Cobb: A Biography*. Westport, CT: Greenwood Press, 2004, p. 111.

16. Goldstein, J. "Explosion: 1951 Scandals Threaten College Hoops." Available at http:www.espn.com, November 19, 2003.

17. Finley, P., Finley, L., and Fountain, J. *Scandals in American History: Sport Scandals.* Westport, CT: Greenwood Press, 2008, p. 50.

18. Goldstein, J. "Recent Scandals: BC, Tulane, and Northwestern." Available at http:www.espn.com, November 19, 2003.

19. McCarthy, M. "Point Shaving Remains a Concern in College Athletics." *USA Today,* May 9, 2007.

20. Fish, M. "Six Ex-players Charged with Conspiracy." Available at http:www.espn.com, May 6, 2009.

21. "Eight Charged in 'Point Shaving' Scheme at the University of Toledo." *Department of Justice Press Release,* May 6, 2009.

22. Colston, C. "Probe: No Evidence of Other Referees' Misconduct." *USA Today,* October 3, 2008, p. C12.

23. Schmidt, M. "Former N.B.A. Referee Is Sentenced." *The New York Times,* July 30, 2008.

24. "Nader Urges Stern to Review Officiating." Available at http://www.USA-Today.com, June 6, 2002.

25. Wilbon, M. "Talk about Foul! Game 6 Was A Real Stinker." *The Washington Post,* June 2, 2002, p. D1.

26. Dupree, D. "NBA: David Dupree." Available at http:www.USAToday.com, May 31, 2002.

27. Perez, A. "Sports Betting Bill Becomes Law in Delaware; NFL Reacts." *USA Today,* May 24, 2009.

28. Porter, D. *Fixed: How Goodfellas Bought Boston College Basketball.* New York: Taylor Trade Publishing, 2002.

29. Finley, P., Finley, L., and Fountain, J. *Scandals in American History,* p. 60.

30. "8 Students Suspended for Bookmaking." *The Boston College Chronicle,* January 16, 2007.

31. Bartlett, D. and Steele, J. "Throwing the Game." *TIME,* September 17, 2000.

32. Belluck, P. "Ex-Northwestern Players Charged in Point-Shaving." *The New York Times,* March 27, 1998.

33. Finley, P., Finley, L., and Fountain, J. *Scandals in American History,* p. 58.

34. "Basketball: Jurisprudence—Northwestern; Sentences Issued in Gambling Case." *The New York Times,* November 25, 1998.

35. "Fact Sheets: Industry Issues." Available at http:www.americangaming association.org.

36. Rose, I. "Gambling and the Law: An Introduction to the Law of Internet Gambling." *UNLV Gaming Research & Review Journal* 10:1 (2006), p. 4.

37. Barker, T. and Britz, M. *Joker's Wild,* p. 106.

38. Rose, I. "Gambling and the Law," p. 1.

39. Ibid., p. 3.

40. Ibid. p. 5.

41. Reuter, P. & Rubinstein, J. "Illegal Gambling and Organized Crime." *Society* 20 (1983): p. 5.

42. Smith, R. "Legalized Gambling in Nevada Turns 75: Still Gaming After All These Years Legalization of Betting Put Nevada on the Map and Started the Strip." *Las-Vegas Review Journal,* March 19, 2006.

43. Eadington, W. *Indian Gaming and the Law.* Reno: Institute for the Study of Gambling and Commercial Gaming, University of Nevada, 1990, p. 147.

44. Barker, T. and Britz, M. *Joker's Wild,* p. 37.

45. "Gambling—Gambling and Organized Crime." Available at http://law. jrank.org/pages/1243/Gambling-Gambling-organized-crime.html.

46. Reuter, P. and Rubinstein, J. "Illegal Gambling and Organized Crime," p. 5.

47. "Gambling—Gambling and Organized Crime" Available at http://law.-jrank.org/pages/1243/Gambling-Gambling-organized-crime.html.

48. Ibid.

49. Bartlett, D. and Steele, J. "Throwing the Game." *TIME,* September 17, 2000.

50. Welch, W. "Vegas Bets on Its Ties to Mob Museum to Link Crime and Law." *USA Today,* December 16, 2008, p. A3.

51. Department of Justice Press Release, June 4, 2009.

52. Eligon, J. "2 Plead Guilty in Operation of Gambling Ring in Bronx." *The New York Times,* August 27, 2008, p. A3.

53. Lezin Jonesa, R. "N.H.L. Assistant Is Cited as Head of Betting Ring." *The New York Times,* February 8, 2006, p. A1.

54. Stitt, B., Nicholas, M., and Giacopassi, D. "Does the Presence of Casinos Increase Crime? An Examination of Casino and Control Communities." *Crime and Delinquency,* 49:2 (2003), pp. 253–284.

55. Ibid.

56. "National Gambling Impact Study Commission (1996–1999). Executive Summary." Available at http://govinfo.library.unt.edu/ngisc/index.html, pp. 28–29.

57. "National Gambling Impact Study Commission Report (note 70)." Available at http://govinfo.library.unt.edu/ngisc/index.html.

58. American Psychiatric Association. *Diagnostic and Statistical Manual of Mental Disorders, Fourth Edition* (Text Revision). Arlington, VA: American Psychiatric Publishing, 2000.

59. NORC Gambling Impact and Behavior Study. Available at http://www.norc.uchicago.edu/new/gambling.htm.

60. "National Gambling Impact Study Commission Report (note 64)." Available at http://govinfo.library.unt.edu/ngisc/index.html.

61. NORC Gambling Impact and Behavior Study. Available at http://www.norc.uchicago.edu/new/gambling.htm, p. 73.

62. Carroll, C. "Mother Arrested After Child Found in Car at Casino." *San Jose Mercury News,* March 10, 2005, p. B1.

63. Darby, J. "Nanny Gets 40 Years for Child's Death; Woman Left Boy in Van While Playing Video Poker." *Times-Picayune,* June 6, 1998, p. A1.

64. Hollinshed, D. "Gambling with Children's Lives Brings Double Dose of Blame." *St. Louis Post-Dispatch,* March 25, 2001, p. A1.

65. Volberg, R. "Gambling and Problem Gambling in Oregon." *Report to the Oregon Gambling Addiction Treatment Foundation,* August 26, 1997.

66. Brown, C. "N.B.A. Won't Discipline Bulls' Jordan." *The New York Times,* April 1, 1992, p. B12.

67. Ibid.

68. "Bulls' Jordan Says Check Covered Gambling Losses." *The New York Times,* October 23, 1992, p. B12.

69. Moran, M. "Jordan Drove the Fast Lane After Casino Visit." *The New York Times,* May 28, 1993, p. B9.

70. "N.B.A. Probe Clears Jordan (AP)." *The New York Times,* October 9, 1993, p. 35.

71. Finley, P., Finley, L., and Fountain, J. *Scandals in American History,* pp. 57–58.

72. Schorn, D. "Michael Jordan Still Flying High: Michael Jordan Talks to Ed Bradley about Gambling, Basketball, Business, and Privacy." Available at http:www.cbsnews.com, August 20, 2006.

73. American Psychiatric Association. *Diagnostic and Statistical Manual of Mental Disorders, Fourth Edition.*

CHAPTER 6

1. Curtis, H. *The Play Movement and Its Significance.* New York: MacMillan, 1917, p. 11.

2. Ibid., p. 8.

3. Hartmann, D. "Notes on Midnight Basketball and the Cultural Politics of Recreation, Race, and At-Risk Urban Youth." *Journal of Sport & Social Issues* 25:4 (2001), p. 340.

4. Ibid., p. 342.

5. Witt, P. and Crompton, J. "The At-Risk Youth Recreation Project." *Parks and Recreation* 32:1 (1997), pp. 54–61.

6. Hartmann, D. and Depro, B. "Rethinking Sports-Based Community Crime Prevention: A Preliminary Analysis of the Relationship between Midnight Basketball and Urban Crime Rates." *Journal of Sport & Social Issues* 30:2 (2006), p. 181.

7. Ibid.

8. Hartmann, D. "Notes on Midnight Basketball," p. 340.

9. Foley, T. "Basketball Provides Escape from Ghetto." *St. Petersburg Times,* March 11, 1969.

10. Dohrmann, G. "How Dreams Die: To Escape Gangs and Violence, Kids Often Turn To Sports. Many in Oakland No Longer See Them As the Way Out. *Sports Illustrated,* June 30, 2008.

11. Brumm, L. *We Only Played Home Games*. Oak Creek, WI: Brumm Enterprises LLC, 2001.

12. Dobie, M. "Sports in Prison: Frequently Asked Questions." *Newsday,* July 11, 2004.

13. Ibid.

14. "Prisons Set to Buy Sporting Goods (AP)." *St. Petersburg Times Online,* June 20, 2002.

15. Telander, R. "Sports behind the Walls for Convicts, Are Athletics a Form of Rehabilitation, an Outlet for Excess Energy, or Just a Way To Pass the Time?" *Sports Illustrated,* October 17, 1988.

16. Dobie, M. "Sports in Prison: Their Escape behind Bars." *Newsday,* July 11, 2004. 7/1.

17. Ibid.

18. Dobie, M. "Sports in Prison: Boxing Is Getting Punched Out." *Newsday,* August 8, 2004.

19. "Former Top Boxer Sentenced to Life on Murder Conviction." *The Associated Press,* March 20, 1981.

20. "The All-Prison Boxing Team." Available at http:www.eastsideboxing. com.

21. Donovan, J. "Still Waiting for Bernard Hopkins to Grow Old?" Available at http:www.thesweetscience.com, July 15, 2005.

22. Kaplan, J. "Man on a Tightrope: Ron LeFlore Came Out of Prison to Redeem Himself in Baseball." *Sports Illustrated,* May 12, 1975.

23. Telander, R. "Sports Behind the Walls for Convicts."

24. http://www.angolarodeo.com/events.htm

25. Telander, R. "Sports Behind the Walls for Convicts."

26. Dobie, M. "Sports in Prison: The Alcatraz of the South: Inside Angola, the Nation's Largest Maximum Security Prison." *Newsday,* July 18, 2004.

27. Dobie, M. "Sports in Prison: The Courting of a Hotshot Inmate." *Newsday,* July 11, 2004.

28. Kosa, F. "Prison Baseball Team Gives Inmates a Focus beyond Their Cells." *The Christian Science Monitor,* July 2, 2008.

29. Dobie, M. "Sports in Prison: Games Offer Escape Behind Bars." *Newsday,* July 11, 2004.

30. Fuchs, M. "Learning Team Spirit behind Bars." *The New York Times,* April 29, 2003.

31. Telander, R. "Sports behind the Walls for Convicts."

32. Dobie, M. "Sports in Prison: Frequently Asked Questions."

33. "Inmate, 23, Dies after Injury in Prison Rodeo." *The Desert News,* June 10, 1963.

34. Lorge Butler, S. "Rookie Marathoners Trade Addictions." *The New York Times,* November 3, 2005, p. D2.

35. Scott, P. "Bodies in Motion, Clean and Sober." *The New York Times,* October 12, 2006, p. G1.

36. Hultsman, W. "Benefits of and Deterrents to Recreation Participation: Perspectives of Early Adolescents." *Journal of Applied Recreation* 21:3 (1996), pp. 213–241.

37. Williams, D., Strean, W., and Bengoechea, E. "Understanding Recreation and Sports as a Rehabilitative Tool within Juvenile Justice Programs." *Juvenile and Family Court Journal Spring* 53:2 (2002), p. 32.

38. Ibid., p. 32.

39. Ibid., p. 34.

40. Bradley, J. "A Sporting Chance: The Violent Offenders at a State School in Giddings, Texas, Can Earn the Right to Play Football—But Not Everyone Is Happy When They Do." *Sports Illustrated,* December 15, 1997.

41. Dobie, M. "Sports in Prison: Different Worlds Find Common Ground." *Newsday,* July 14, 2004.

42. Dohrmann, G. "How Dreams Die."

43. Mason, G. and Wilson, P. *Sport, Recreation and Juvenile Crime: An Assessment of the Impact of Sport and Recreation upon Aboriginal and Non-aboriginal Youth Offenders.* Canberra, Australia: Australian Institute of Criminology, 1998, p. 8; Chaiken, M. *Kids, Cops and Communities.* Washington, DC: U.S. Department of Justice, National Institute of Justice, 1998.

44. Lewis, M. "The Ballad of Big Mike." *The New York Times Magazine,* September 24, 2006.

45. Bell, J. "Once Homeless, Never Hopeless; Oher's Spirit Didn't Break in Face of Family Difficulty." *USA Today*, April 24, 2009, p. 1C.

46. Lewis, M. "The Ballad of Big Mike."

47. Ibid.

48. Bell, J. "Once Homeless, Never Hopeless," p. 1C.

49. Lewis, M. "The Ballad of Big Mike."

50. Twyman Bessone, L. "Welcome to Night Court Chicago's Midnight Basketball League Provides Young Inner-City Males with a Brief Respite from Urban Violence." *Sports Illustrated,* December 2, 1991.

51. Hartmann, D. "Notes on Midnight Basketball," p. 345.

52. Ibid., p. 344.

53. Kennedy, K. and O'Brien, R. "'Round Midnight." *Sports Illustrated*, August 19, 1996, p. 32.

54. Hartmann, D. and Depro, B. "Rethinking Sports-Based Community Crime Prevention," p. 183.

55. Ibid., p. 180.

56. Jarobe, K. "Giving Back: Cal Ripken Sr. Foundation." *The Daily Record* (Baltimore, MD), July 26, 2007.

57. McAllister, R. "'Badges for Baseball' A Win-Win." *Richmond Times Dispatch*, August 21, 2007, p. B1.

58. Ibid.

59. Jarobe, K. "Giving Back: Cal Ripken Sr. Foundation." *The Daily Record* (Baltimore, MD), July 26, 2007.

60. http://www.ripkenfoundation.org/programs/badges

61. Jarobe, K. "Giving Back: Cal Ripken Sr. Foundation." *The Daily Record* (Baltimore, MD), July 26, 2007.

62. http://www.ripkenfoundation.org/programs/badges/.

63. Henderson, J. "Law Enforcers Battle Crime with Sport." *Rocky Mount Telegram*, September 10, 2009.

64. Ibid.

65. Ibid.

CHAPTER 7

1. "Police: 8 Officers Hurt in Laker Victory Melees." *Associated Press Online,* June 15, 2009.

2. "Browns' Stallworth in Jail (AP)." *The New York Times*, June 17, 2009, p. B13.

3. "Friday's Sports in Brief." *The Associated Press,* June 20, 2009.

4. Jamieson, L. and Orr, T. *Sport and Violence: A Critical Examination of Sport.* London: Butterworth-Heinemann, 2009.

5. Crosset, T., Benedict, J., and McDonald, M. "Male Student-Athletes Reported for Sexual Assault: A Survey of Campus Police Departments and Judicial Affairs Offices." *Journal of Sport and Social Issue* 19:2 (1995), pp. 126–140.

6. Teitelbaum, S. *Sports Heroes Fallen Idols: How Star Athletes Pursue Self-Destructive Paths and Jeopardize Their Careers.* Lincoln: University of Nebraska Press, 2005.

7. "Fact Sheets: Industry Issues." Available at http:www.americangaming association.org.

INDEX

ABOUT THE AUTHOR

CHRISTOPHER S. KUDLAC, PHD, is associate professor of criminal justice at Westfield State College, Westfield, Massachusetts. He is the author of Praeger's *Public Executions: The Death Penalty and the Media*.